From Angels to Werewolves

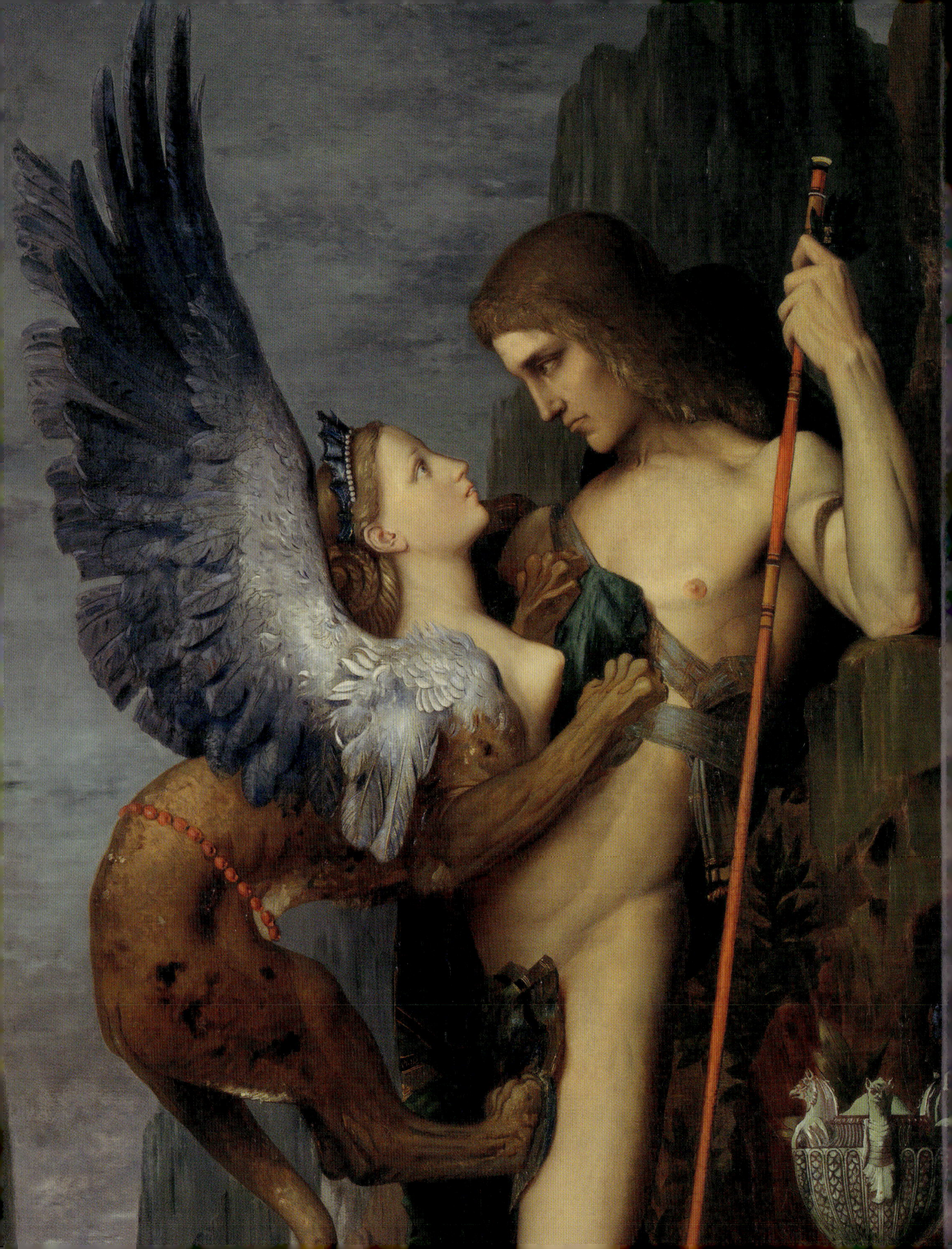

Philip F. Palmedo

FROM ANGELS TO WEREWOLVES

Animal-Human Hybrids in Myth and Art

Abbeville Press
New York London

FRONT COVER TOP: Giotto (c. 1266–1337). Detail of *The Dream of Joachim*, c. 1305. Fresco. Scrovegni Chapel, Padua.
FRONT COVER BOTTOM: George Andreas Wolfgang the Elder. *Jove Turns Lykaon into a Wolf*, 1665. Etching on laid paper, 5⅞ × 5¾ in. (15 × 14.6 cm). National Gallery of Art, Washington, DC.
BACK COVER LEFT: Statuette of Anubis, Egyptian, Ptolemaic period, 332–30 BC. See plate 1.1.
BACK COVER RIGHT: Relief of dancing Ganesha, North Bengal, 11th century AD. See plate 1.11.
PAGE 2: Gustave Moreau (1826–1898). Detail of *Oedipus and the Sphinx*, 1864. See plate 2.6.

Editor: David Fabricant
Designer: Misha Beletsky
Layout: Julia Sedykh
Photo research: Lauren Orthey
Indexer: Peter Rooney
Production manager: Louise Kurtz

 The text of this book was set in New Caledonia. Printed in China.

First edition
10 9 8 7 6 5 4 3 2 1

ISBN 978-0-7892-1446-1

Library of Congress Cataloging-in-Publication Data available upon request

For bulk and premium sales and for text adoption procedures, write to Customer Service Manager, Abbeville Press, 655 Third Avenue, New York, NY 10017, or call 1-800-ARTBOOK.

Visit Abbeville Press online at www.abbeville.com.

IMAGE CREDITS

Sources of images other than as noted in the captions are as follows. The publishers have endeavored to identify and credit all rightsholders, and ask that they be informed of any inadvertent omissions.

Front cover top: Cameraphoto Arte Venezia/Bridgeman Images. Back cover right, 1.4, 1.11: Jean-Pierre Dalbéra, CC-BY-2.0. 0.1: Dagmar Hollmann, CC-BY-SA-4.0. 0.2: Thilo Parg, CC-BY-SA-3.0. 1.2, 1.5, 2.2, 4.5: © The Trustees of the British Museum. 1.6: D. Tamino Boehm, CC-BY-SA-4.0. 1.8, 2.10: Walters Art Museum, Baltimore, CC-BY-SA-3.0. 1.9: The Yorck Project. 1.13: © 2023 Estate of Pablo Picasso/Artists Rights Society (ARS), New York; photo © Ashmolean Museum/Bridgeman Images. p. 24, 2.11, 2.14, 5.4: Photo © Raffaello Bencini/Bridgeman Images. 2.1: Courtesy of the Oriental Institute of the University of Chicago. 2.3: Tangopaso/A. Parrot. 2.4. Rijksmuseum, Amsterdam, CCo. 2.7: Shonagon, CCo. 2.8: Ailura, CC-BY-SA-3.0-AT. 2.9: Sodacan, CC-BY-SA-3.0. 2.12: Jnzl, PD. 2.13: HIP/Art Resource, NY. 2.15: Scala/Art Resource, NY. 2.16: Scala/Ministero per i Beni e le Attività Culturali/Art Resource, NY. 2.17, 4.10, 5.12, p. 116, 8.9: Bridgeman Images. 2.18: Staatliche Kunstsammlungen Dresden/Bridgeman Images. 2.19: Superstock/UIG/Bridgeman Images. 2.20, 6.8: Photo © Fine Art Images/Bridgeman Images. 2.21: © Israel Museum, Jerusalem/Gift of Fania and Gershom Scholem, Jerusalem; John Herring, Marlene and Paul Herring, Jo Carole and Ronald Lauder, New York/Bridgeman Images. 2.22: © Keith Haring Foundation. 2.23: Marion Curtis/Starpix/Shutterstock. p. 48, 3.6: Timothy A. Gonsalves, CC-BY-SA-4.0. 3.1: Daderot, CCo. 3.2: © Sotheby's/akg-images. 3.4, 4.12: Pictures from History/Bridgeman Images. 3.5: Brigham Young University, CC-BY-SA-4.0. 3.7: Oskar Seyffert, *A Dictionary of Classical Antiquities* (London: William Glaisher, 1895)/Cornell University Library/Internet Archive. 3.8: Jebulon/Materialscientist, CCo. 3.10: Wojciech Kocot, CC-BY-SA-4.0. 3.11: Jami Dwyer, CC-BY-SA-2.0. 4.1: New York Public Library. 4.2: Petar Milošević, CC-BY-SA-4.0. 4.4: © British Library Board, all rights reserved/Bridgeman Images. 4.6: Arjunem3/Steve McCluskey, CC-BY-SA-3.0. 4.7: Photo Dharma, CC-BY-2.0. 4.8, 6.4, 7.6: Library of Congress. 4.11: Photo courtesy of Sophie Bass. 4.13: user snotty, CC-PD-Mark. 4.14: © Edvard Eriksen Estate; photo by Avda-berlin, CC-BY-SA-3.0. 4.15: Livioandronico 2013, CC-BY-SA-4.0. 4.16: Sailko, CC-BY-3.0. 4.17: © Norman Rockwell Family Agency. 4.18: Starbucks Corporation, CC-BY-4.0. 5.1: Museum der Universität Tübingen, CC-BY-SA-4.0. 5.2, 5.7: British Library/Granger, all rights reserved. 5.3: Carole Raddato, CC-BY-SA-2.0. 5.5: Photo © Christie's Images/Bridgeman Images. 5.8: IssamBarhouni, CC-BY-SA-4.0. 5.9: Atomhawk/Wizarding World/Pottermore. 5.10: © 2023 Banco de México Diego Rivera Frida Kahlo Museums Trust, Mexico, DF/Artists Rights Society (ARS), New York. 6.1: © National Gallery, London/Art Resource, NY. 6.2: Architas, CC-BY-SA-4.0. 6.3: Jastrow, PD. 6.5: Skokloster Castle, CCo. 6.7: Sailko, CC-BY-SA-4.0. 6.11 left: Jessica Bolser, USFWS Midwest Region, CC-BY-2.0. 6.11 right: Tom Koerner, USFWS Mountain-Prairie Region, CC BY-2.0. p. 106, 7.1: © Archives Charmet/Bridgeman Images. 7.3: Library of Wrocław University of Science and Technology, PD. 7.7: George H. W. Bush Presidential Library and Museum, PD. 7.8: geico.com. 8.1: Museo de Altamira y D. Rodríguez, CC-BY-SA-3.0. 8.2, 8.3: Wellcome Library, London, CC BY 4.0. 8.4: © Iberfoto/Bridgeman Images. 8.5: Ratno Sardi. 8.6: Rock Art Research Institute, University of Witwatersrand. 8.7: Courtesy Pieter Jolly; figure 1 in Pieter Jolly, "Therianthropes in San Rock Art," *South African Archaeological Bulletin* 57, no. 176 (December 2002), pp. 85–103. 8.8: Google Books. 8.10: © 2023 Artists Rights Society (ARS), New York/SABAM, Brussels. 8.11: Biswarup Ganguly, CC-BY-3.0.

CONTENTS

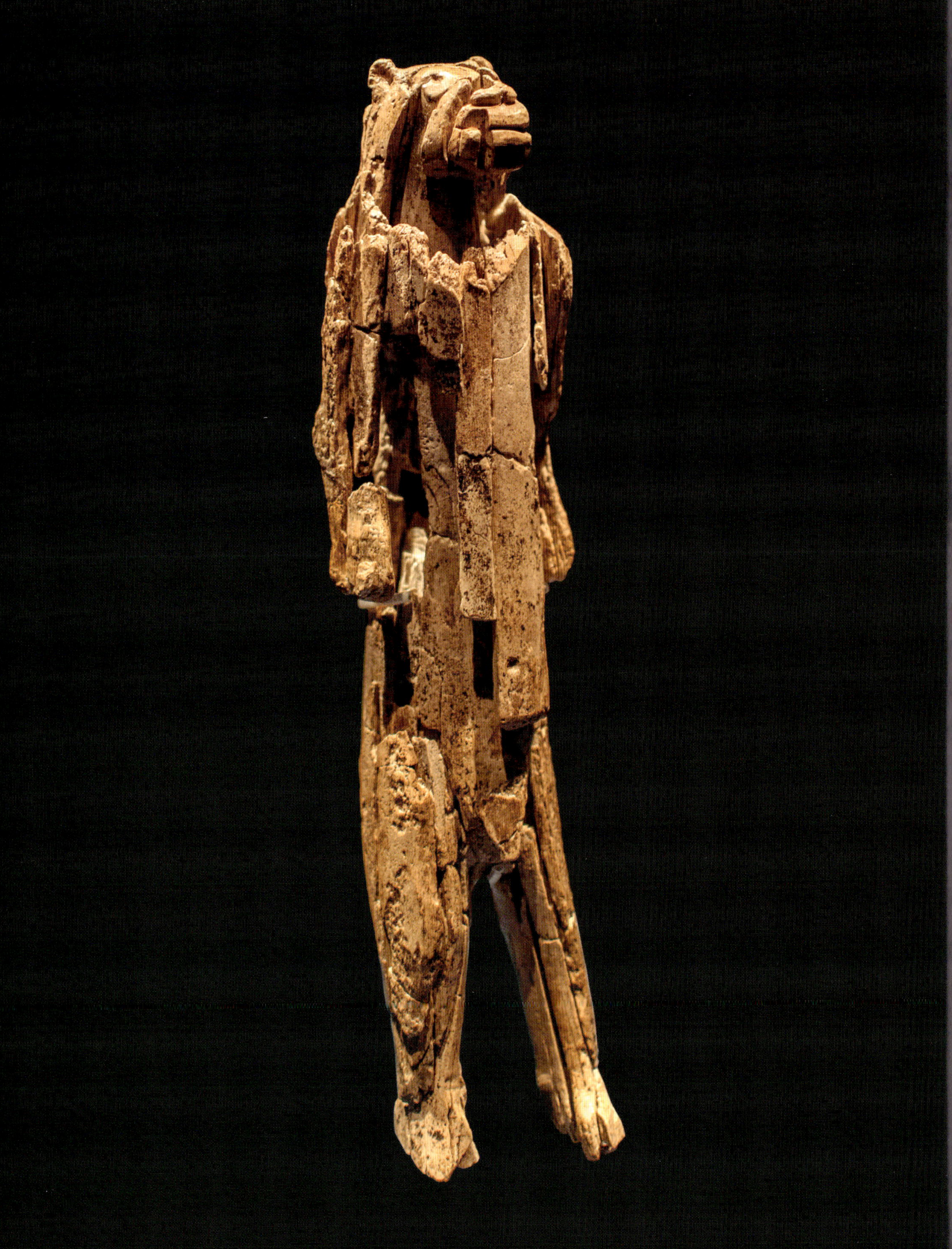

PREFACE

This book resulted from two crises, one tiny and personal, the other giant and international. The personal one arose when I was finishing my book on art and science, titled *Deep Affinities*. I had spent three years working on that book and enjoyed the process immensely. I was occupied, learning, and relishing the craft of writing. Near the end of the process, I looked forward to sending the manuscript off to the publisher. But as I neared that point, I realized I was not looking forward to not having the book to work on. Then I recalled an extraordinary imaginative sculpture, created some forty thousand years ago, that I had written about in *Deep Affinities*. The Löwenmensch, or Lion-Man, figurine, carved out of woolly mammoth ivory, represented a man with a lion's head (plates 0.1 and 0.2). It was the first, that we know of, of a genre of mythical beings that is nonobvious yet widespread: animal-human combinations.

0.1. Löwenmensch figurine, 40,000–35,000 BP. Mammoth ivory, 12¼ × 2¼ × 2⅜ in. (31.1 × 5.6 × 5.9 cm). Ulm Museum, Germany.

As I started to explore the subject, I found that these combinations, technically termed *therianthropes*, were even more abundant and widespread in cultures through space and time than I had imagined. Mythology is full of bizarre creatures: centaurs, with the upper body of a human and the lower body of a horse; the Minotaur, with the head and tail of a bull and the body of a man; angels; and mermaids. The list is long. Furthermore, these hybrid creatures appear in the earliest writings (and surely in the oral traditions that preceded them). They appear in cultures through the ages and everywhere in the world. Many of these winged or animal-headed creatures were not simply viewed as fictions. They were believed in deeply and some were worshipped as gods. These vastly widespread creatures were fundamental somehow to human nature. But how did they come about, and why?

I also came to realize that therianthropes have been rich subjects for artists since the very first paintings on cave walls. Indeed, it has been the particular genius of painters and sculptors that has created our visual sense of what angels and centaurs and mermaids look like. A book on therianthropes could not only be visually attractive, but could demonstrate the role of art in creating human belief.

Although myths have been studied by various disciplines since Plato, little attention has been given to animal-human combinations in particular. I had found an engaging and understudied subject to explore to solve my tiny crisis. But how could I find the time to explore animal-human hybrids in myth and art? That's when the giant crisis arrived. The awful Covid-19 pandemic forced me to stay at home with abundant time on my hands. And, some years before, some smart folks had invented the World Wide Web, and others had developed marvelous institutions such as Wikipedia. Others had managed to provide access to academic journals online. So, all the resources I needed were there in my computer. In that way the awful giant crisis solved the tiny one, and I was awarded the time and informational resources to work on this book.

It is difficult to communicate the richness of animal-human creatures in the mythologies of various cultures over time without overwhelming the reader. They evolve, multiply, have complex stories, play different roles at different times, and are viewed differently in different cultures. I came to realize that, if my book were to be readable, I could only discuss a fraction of the therianthropes that have been conjured up through the ages.[1] And only hint at the complex lives and roles of even those. We'll start with a selection of these creatures and then, in the final chapter, investigate the origins of therianthropes and their meanings to humankind.

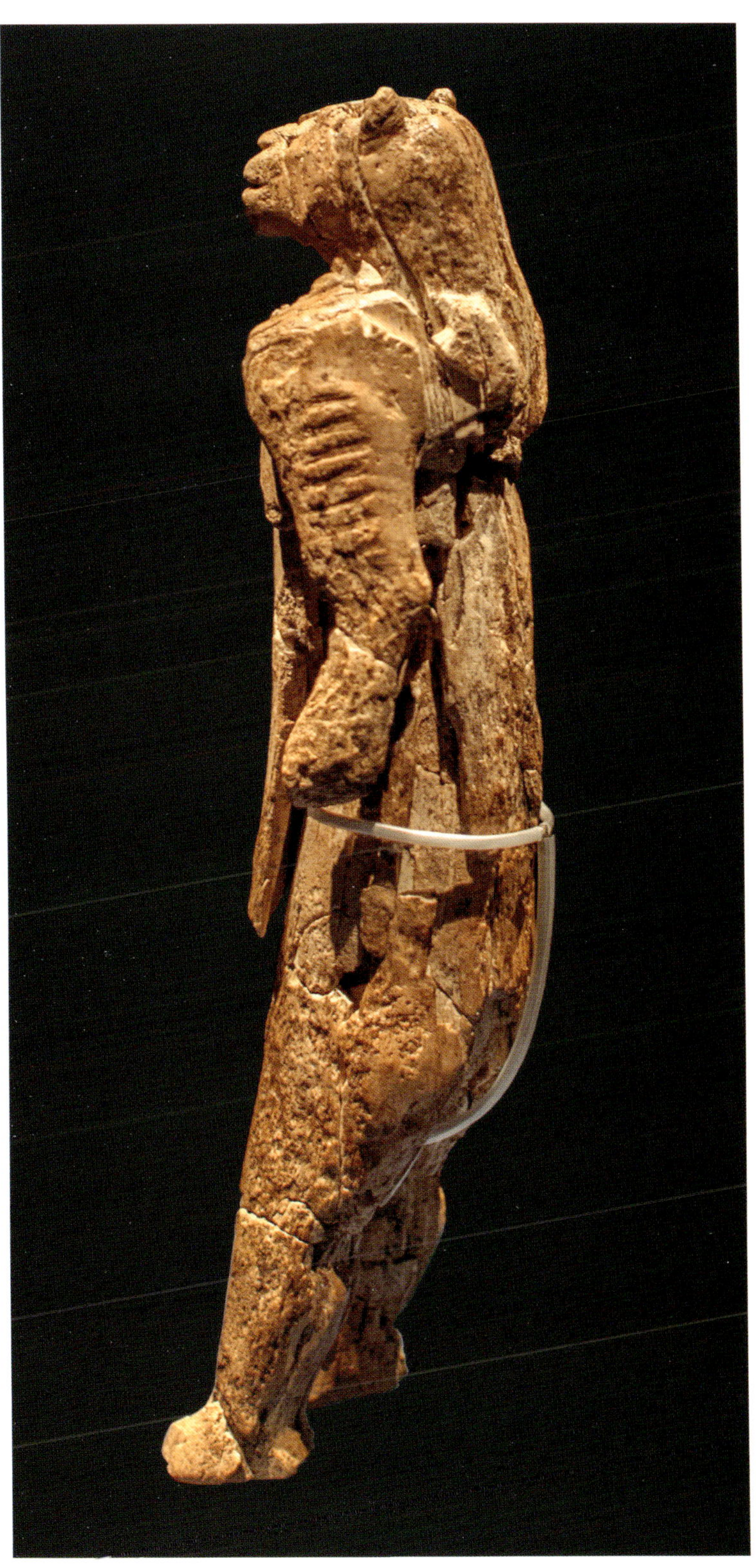

0.2. Side view of the Löwenmensch figurine.

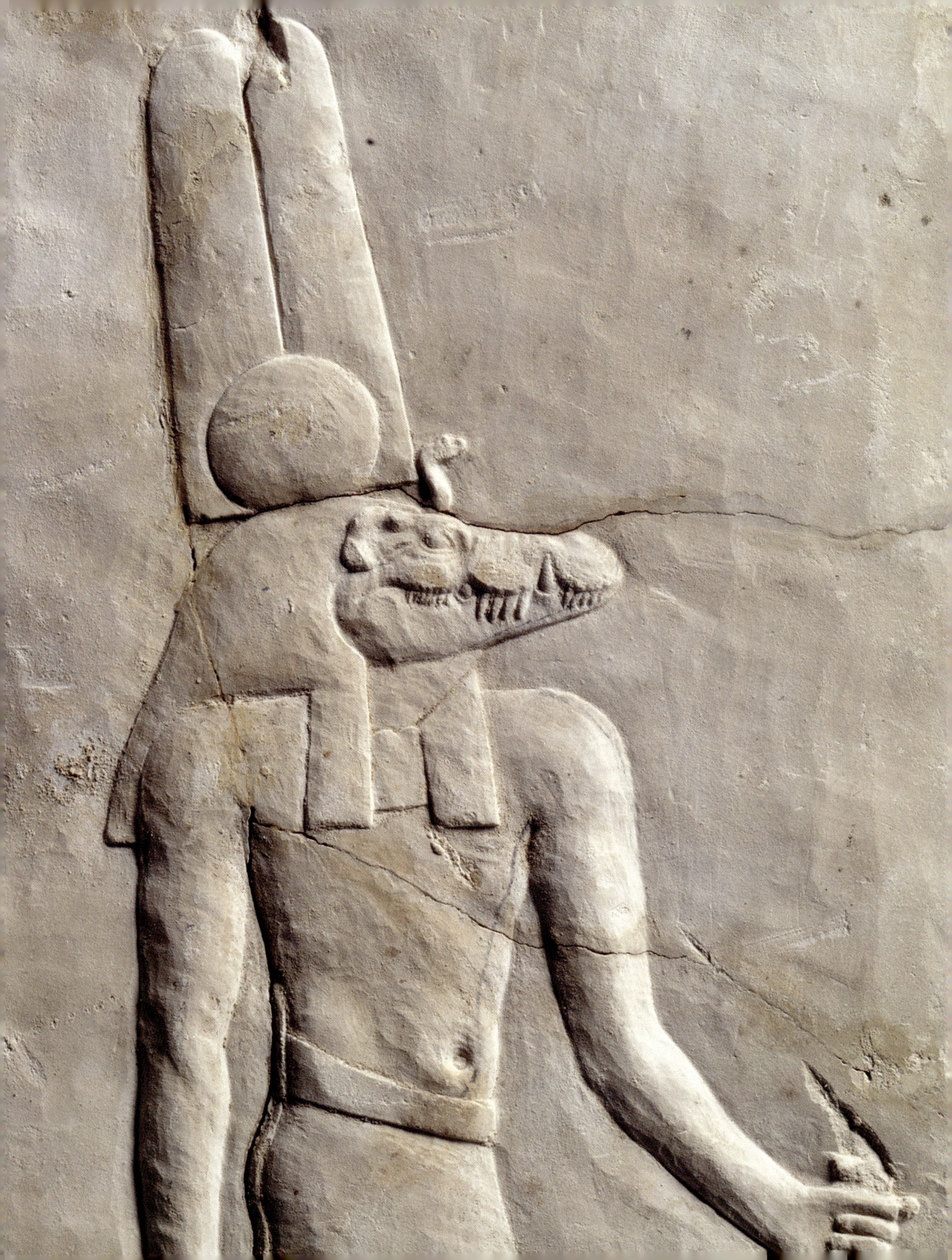

1
ANIMAL-HEADED HUMANS

Detail of an Egyptian plaque with a relief of Sobek. See plate 1.7.

Through history, therianthropes have combined human and animal features in all sorts of ways. Many of the earliest were humans with the heads of animals. (The technical term for that is *theriocephaly*.) They were probably the easiest combined creatures to imagine and enter into myths. But those early animal-headed humans were not just ordinary fantastical beings. In time, they became gods, and were devotedly worshipped. (Some even became the objects of human sacrifice, as we will see in chapter 3.)

Among the most prominent types of theriocephalic beings are dog-headed humans, a phenomenon given the technical term *cynocephaly*. Dog- or jackal-headed creatures are found in the legends of ancient Egypt, Greece, and China, and medieval Asia and Europe. The ancient Egyptians, drawing on the precedent of Mesopotamia, were particularly creative in this regard. An early example is the Egyptian god Anubis, who was portrayed, as early as 3000 BC, with the head of a jackal (plate 1.1).

Death must have been a source of mystery to the earliest humans and, understandably, myths grew around the phenomenon. Early deities often provided access to the afterlife, and Anubis played that role. Not everyone was allowed to enter the realm beyond, and Anubis weighed the hearts of aspirants to determine whether a soul would be admitted. It wasn't easy to pass the test. A scene from a manuscript of the Egyptian Book of the Dead shows Anubis weighing the scribe Hunefer's heart on the scale against the feather of truth (plate 1.2). The heart must weigh exactly the same as the feather, and the ibis-headed Thoth, scribe of the gods, is there to record the result. If Hunefer fails the test, his heart will be eaten by the waiting devourer of the dead, the goddess Ammit, whose body is composed of Egypt's most deadly creatures: the crocodile, lion, and hippopotamus.

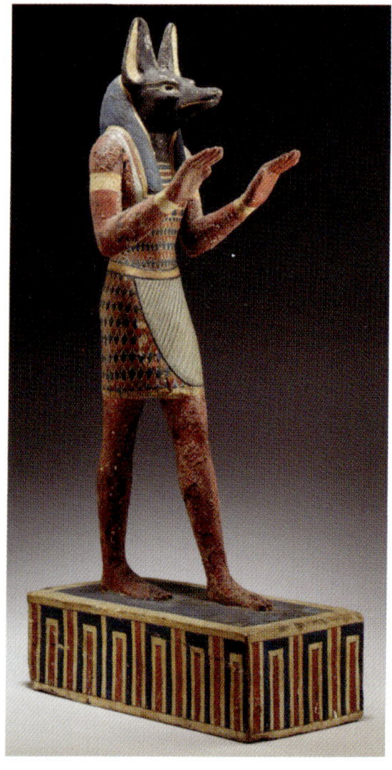

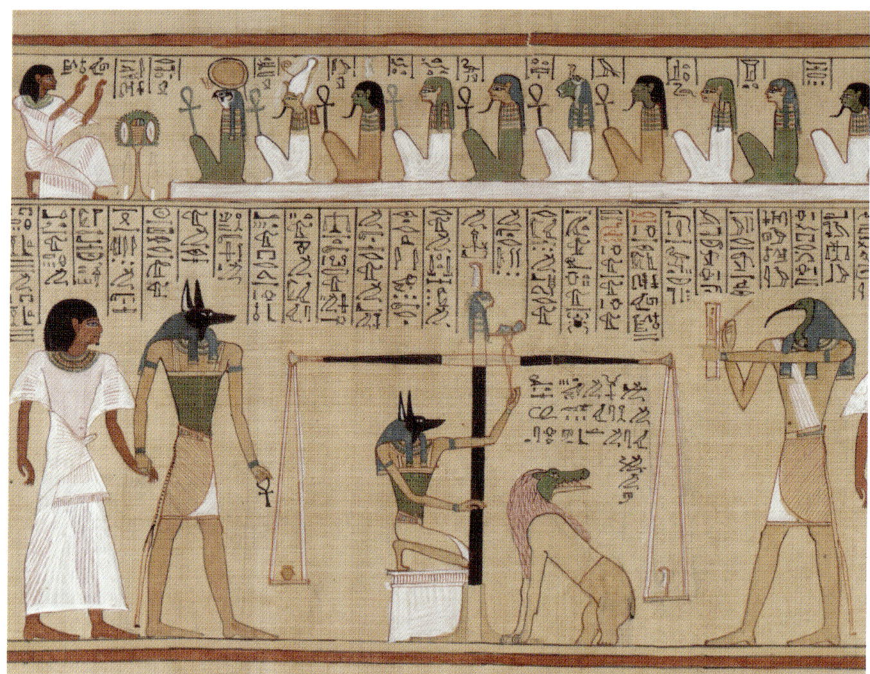

1.1. ABOVE LEFT: Statuette of Anubis. Egyptian, Ptolemaic period, 332–30 BC. Plastered and painted wood, 16⅝ × 4 × 8⅛ in. (42.3 × 10.1 × 20.7 cm). Metropolitan Museum of Art, New York.

1.2. ABOVE: Scene from the Book of the Dead of Hunefer, showing the weighing of the scribe Hunefer's heart. Egyptian, 19th dynasty, c. 1275 BC. Painted papyrus scroll, 16 in. (40 cm) high. British Museum, London.

Jackal- and wolf-headed creatures continued to appear in the pantheon of Egyptian deities. Wepwawet was a creature whose early role was as a scout for the pharaoh's army, and then as a guide for souls into the realm of the dead.

Early humans, well before the Egyptian civilization, had a deeply felt dependency on nature, and in particular on animals. They were a source of danger as well as a source of food. This created an incentive to imagine the control of animals, and their domestication. In Europe and parts of Asia, wolves represented the greatest danger. When the rare docile wolf or a lost wolf cub appeared, it would have been welcomed. The where and when of the domestication of wolves are matters of dispute. It could have been southern China, Mongolia, or Europe, and anywhere from 40,000 to 20,000 years ago (the period of cave art in Europe). Over time, wolves evolved into our human-friendly and much-appreciated dogs.

The positive attributes of dogs led to positive roles in myth. That was true with Anubis in Egypt, and it prevailed even into Christianity. A version of Saint Christopher with the head of a dog appeared in the Eastern Orthodox Church around the year 300 (plate 1.3). Given its origins in Africa, this Saint Christopher probably descended from Anubis. It wasn't until the eighteenth century that the dog-headed image of Saint Christopher was banned by the Orthodox Church.

Upper Paleolithic cave art shows that horses were carefully observed and admired, presumably for their speed, intelligence, and confident grace. Admiration and envy led to deification. Horse-headed deities had elevated roles in the ancient Egyptian canon and are recurring themes in Hindu mythology. The origin of the horse-headed Hindu deity Hayagriva has been traced back to 2000 BC (plate 1.4). An avatar of Vishnu, Hayagriva is worshipped as the god of knowledge and wisdom. He often has an extra

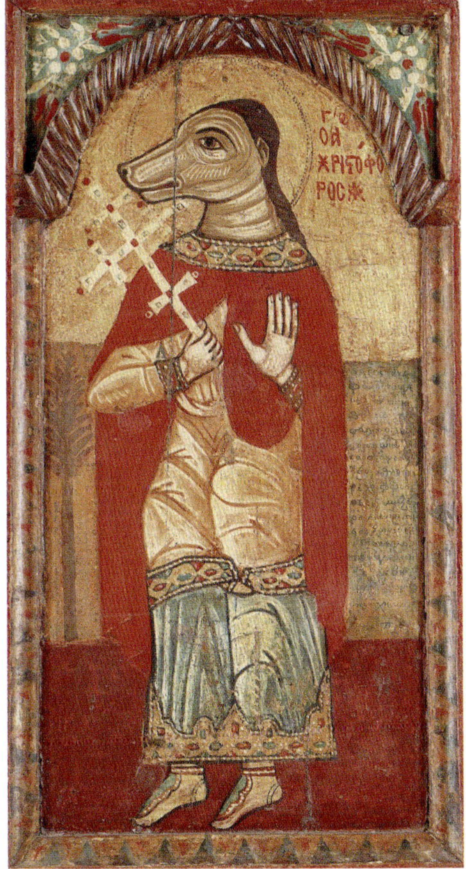

1.3. Icon of Saint Christopher with the head of a dog. Kemira, Cappadocia, 17th century. 26⅜ × 13¾ in. (67 × 35 cm). Byzantine and Christian Museum, Athens.

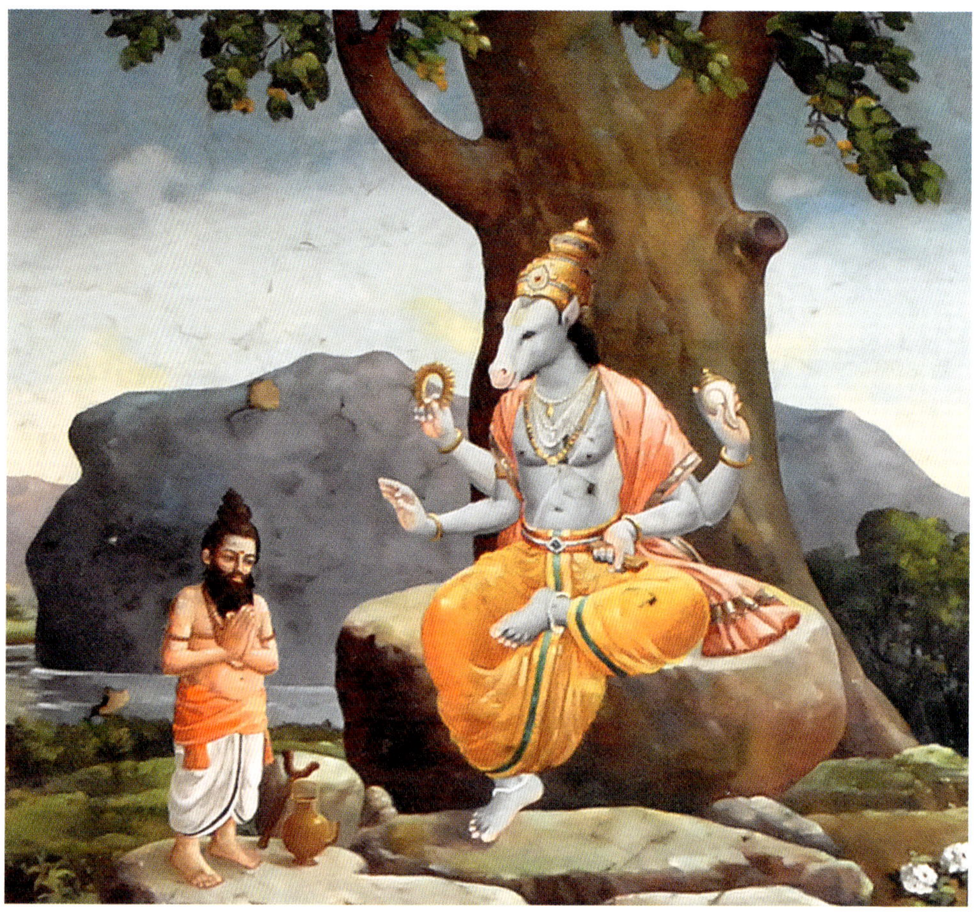

pair of hands to help hold his multiple gifts to humans. Hinduism spread to Southeast Asia around AD 200, and Hayagriva was not only welcomed but worshipped there, particularly in the Philippines.

Illogic isn't foreign to therianthropes. It's not obvious why, for example, the Hindu deity who is considered to be the greatest celestial musician has the head of a horse. But, at least in southern India, Tumburu is often portrayed that way (plate 1.5). Legend recounts that Tumburu performed difficult services for Shiva. As a reward, Shiva granted Tumburu's quirky multipart request to endow him with skill in playing music and singing; to allow him to forever reside with Shiva; and all of this with the head of a horse. In a nineteenth-century painting, Tumburu holds a *veena*, a lute-like resonant instrument. He efficiently personifies the people of southern India's love of horses and music—and their creative imagination.

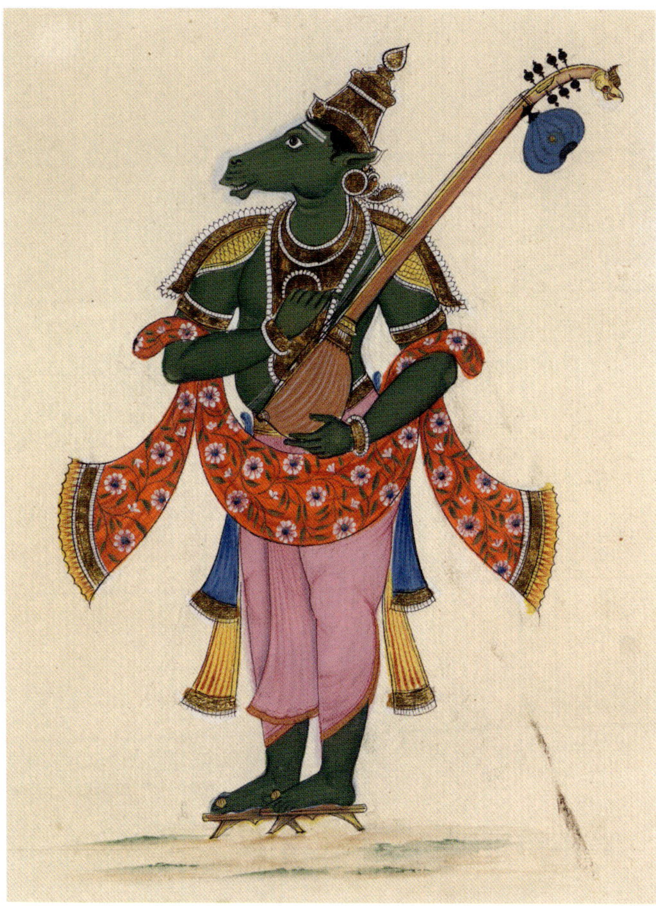

1.4. OPPOSITE: Painting of Hayagriva from the Thillai Nataraja Temple, Chidambaram, Tamil Nadu, India.

1.5. LEFT: The divine musician Tumburu. Southern India, c. 1820. Gouache on paper, 11 × 9 in. (28 × 22.8 cm). British Museum, London.

Although dogs and horses are prominent among animal-headed therianthropes, few animals were spared the honor—or indignity—of having their heads placed on human bodies. Early rock paintings in Africa, dating to at least 10,000 years ago, show men with the heads (and hands and feet) of insects (plate 1.6). Early deities had heads of ibis, snakes, falcons, frogs, and even beetles. Khepri, the Egyptian god of creation, the movement of the sun, and life and resurrection, was portrayed as a man with the head of a scarab or a dung beetle.

There was often fluidity in both the appearance and the character of therianthropic deities. The ancient Egyptian deity Sobek, who first appeared around 2500 BC, was at times represented as a crocodile, but most often as a human with a crocodile head (plate 1.7). At various times he was associated with fertility, with military power, and with the power to protect from the flooding of the Nile: a versatile creature indeed.

1.6. RIGHT: Ancient rock painting in Kondoa District, Tanzania, depicting human figures with possibly insectoid heads.

1.7. OPPOSITE LEFT: Plaque with a relief of Sobek. Egyptian, Late period–Ptolemaic period, 400–30 BC. Limestone with traces of paint, 10⅞ × 10 × 1⅛ in. (27.5 × 25.5 × 3 cm). Metropolitan Museum of Art, New York.

1.8. OPPOSITE RIGHT: Figurine of Taweret. Egyptian, early Ptolemaic period, late 4th–3rd century BC. Faience with glaze, 5⅝ × 1⅝ × 1⅝ in. (14.3 × 4.3 × 4.1 cm). Walters Art Museum, Baltimore.

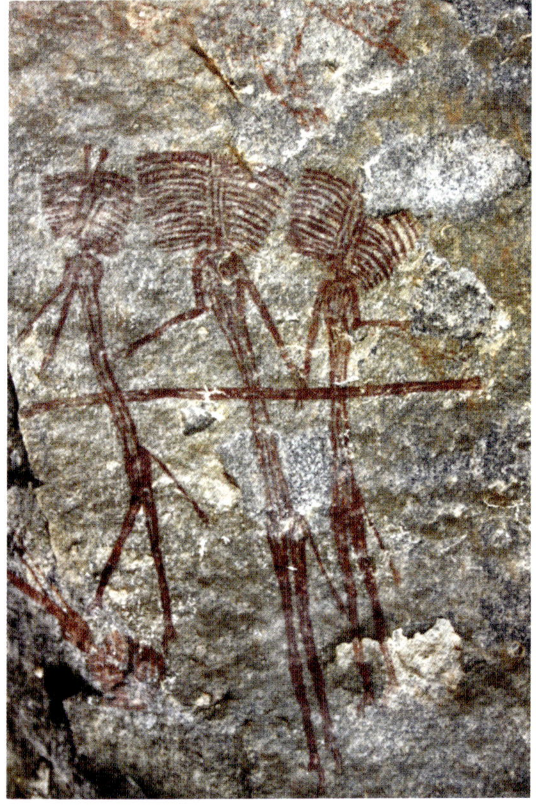

In Egypt, animal heads appeared on female as well as male deities. The goddess Taweret, who presided over fertility and childbirth, had the head of a hippopotamus (plate 1.8). Taweret also appeared in multiple forms, including as an upright hippopotamus with lion's paws. She was usually shown pregnant.

Not surprisingly, early humans aspired to fly, as evidenced by the number of early deities with wings. They also created deities with the heads of birds. In ancient Egypt, at a time when there were many gods, the most revered of all was Ra. The counterpart of the Greek god Zeus, Ra was considered to be the king of the gods, the creator of everything. Ra was the sun god and, just as life on earth depended on the sun, it also depended on Ra. Ra's head was that of a falcon, and in most depictions, there was a solar disk on top of his head, surrounded by a cobra (plate 1.9).

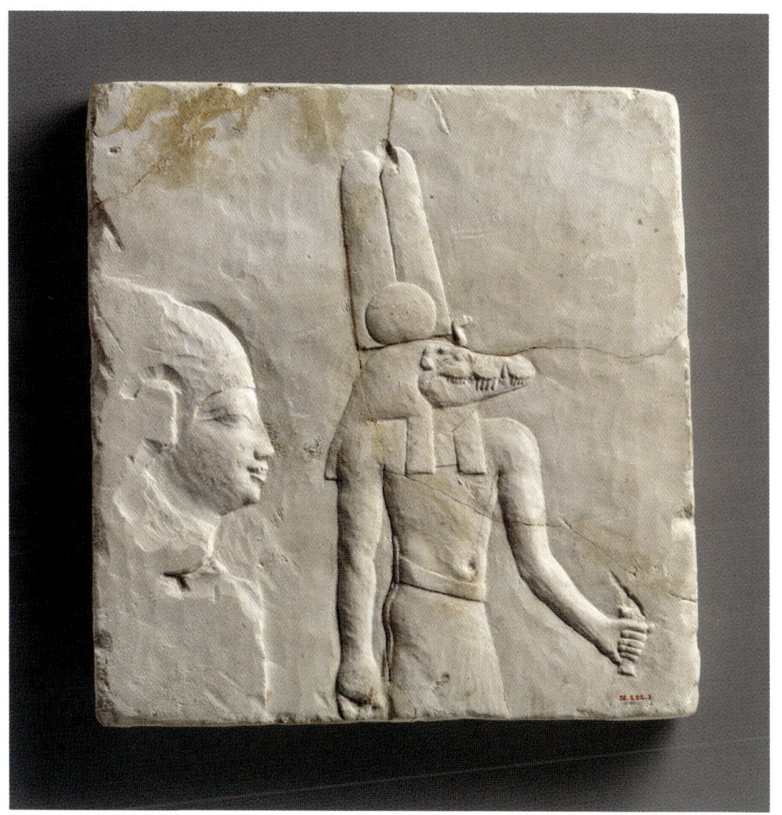

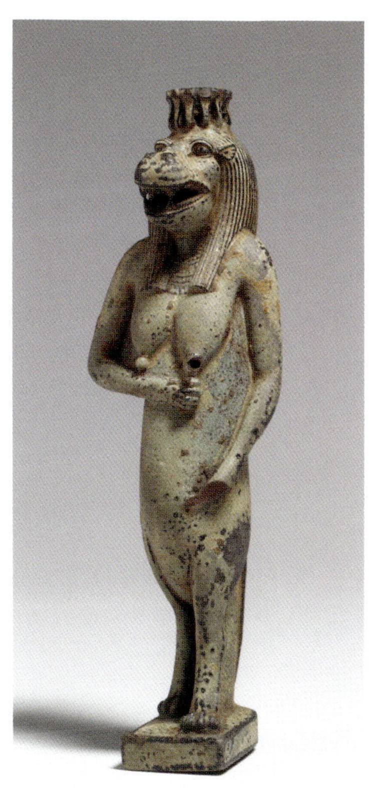

Some animal-headed mythological creatures had a way of evolving that mimicked real-world genetic evolution. Housecats descended from the African wildcat, a smaller relative of lions and tigers, and were first domesticated by 8000 BC in the Middle East. That process was mirrored in the evolution of the ancient Egyptian goddess Bastet. Worshipped as early as 3000 BC as a goddess of the sun, Bastet was first represented with the head of a lion and was a fierce warrior. But over time she was increasingly depicted with the head of a domestic cat on a slender female body (plate 1.10). Cats were highly regarded in ancient Egypt, for both practical and aesthetic reasons. They protected homes from mice, rats, and snakes. And to the Egyptians their god-like hauteur made them natural objects of reverence. They also had the reputation of being model mothers. As a cat deity, Bastet was the goddess of pregnancy and childbirth. Just as fitness was a determinant of biological evolution, appeal and relevance were keys to mythological evolution. Author Terry Pratchett once quipped, "In ancient times cats were worshipped as gods; they have not forgotten this."[1]

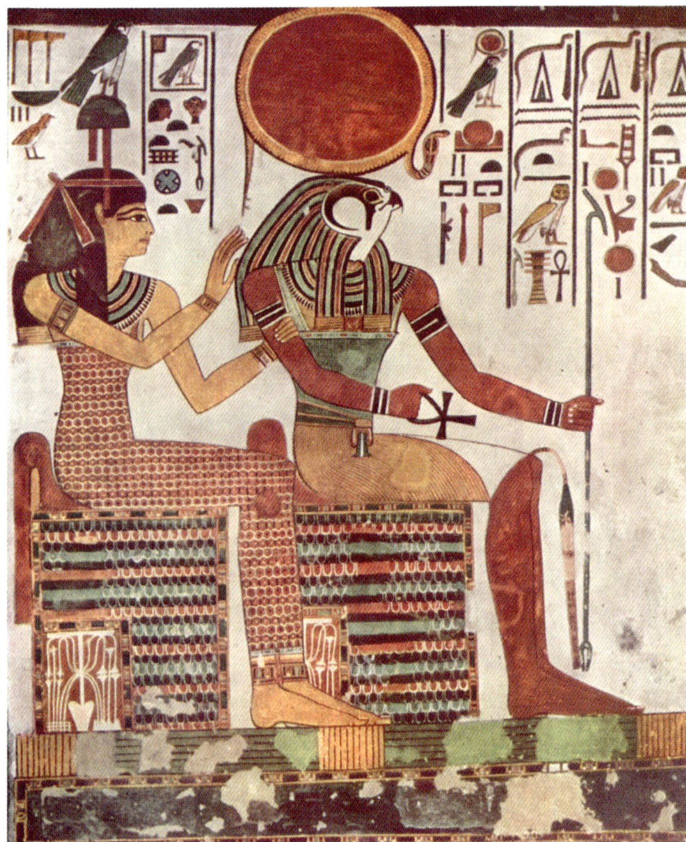

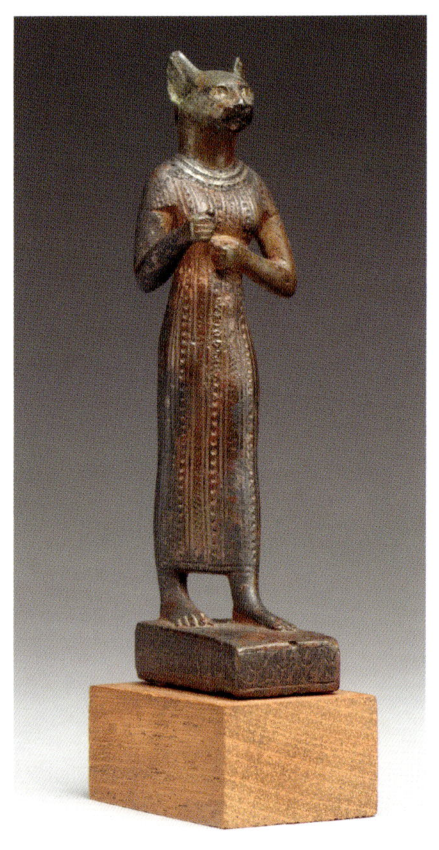

1.9. ABOVE LEFT: Painting of Ra with the goddess Imentet, from the tomb of Nefertari in the Valley of the Queens, Thebes, 13th century BC.

1.10. ABOVE RIGHT: Statuette of Bastet. Egyptian, Late period–Ptolemaic period, 664–30 BC. Leaded bronze with precious metal and black bronze inlays, 4⅛ × 1¼ × 1½ in. (10.5 × 3.2 × 3.9 cm). Metropolitan Museum of Art, New York.

Animal-headed gods are alive and well in modern religions. A prime example is Ganesha, a rotund man with four arms and the head of an elephant who is revered throughout the Hindu world and among Jains and Buddhists (plate 1.11). His drawn and sculpted image appears throughout India, Nepal, Sri Lanka, Thailand, Indonesia, and Bangladesh. Many animal-human gods are worshipped for their power to harm. But Ganesha is worshipped—and worshipped avidly and widely—because of his power to do good.

Positive therianthropes give credence to our hopes and desires. Ganesha represents reincarnation, a role deriving from his origin. In one account, he was the son of Parvati, who had rejected Lord Shiva's advances. In anger, Shiva cut off Ganesha's head and then, on second thought, replaced it with that of a passing elephant. As the Lord of Beginnings, Ganesha is invoked in prayer at the start of ceremonies or before taking new action. His statue often guards doorways. For believers, he brings wisdom and success

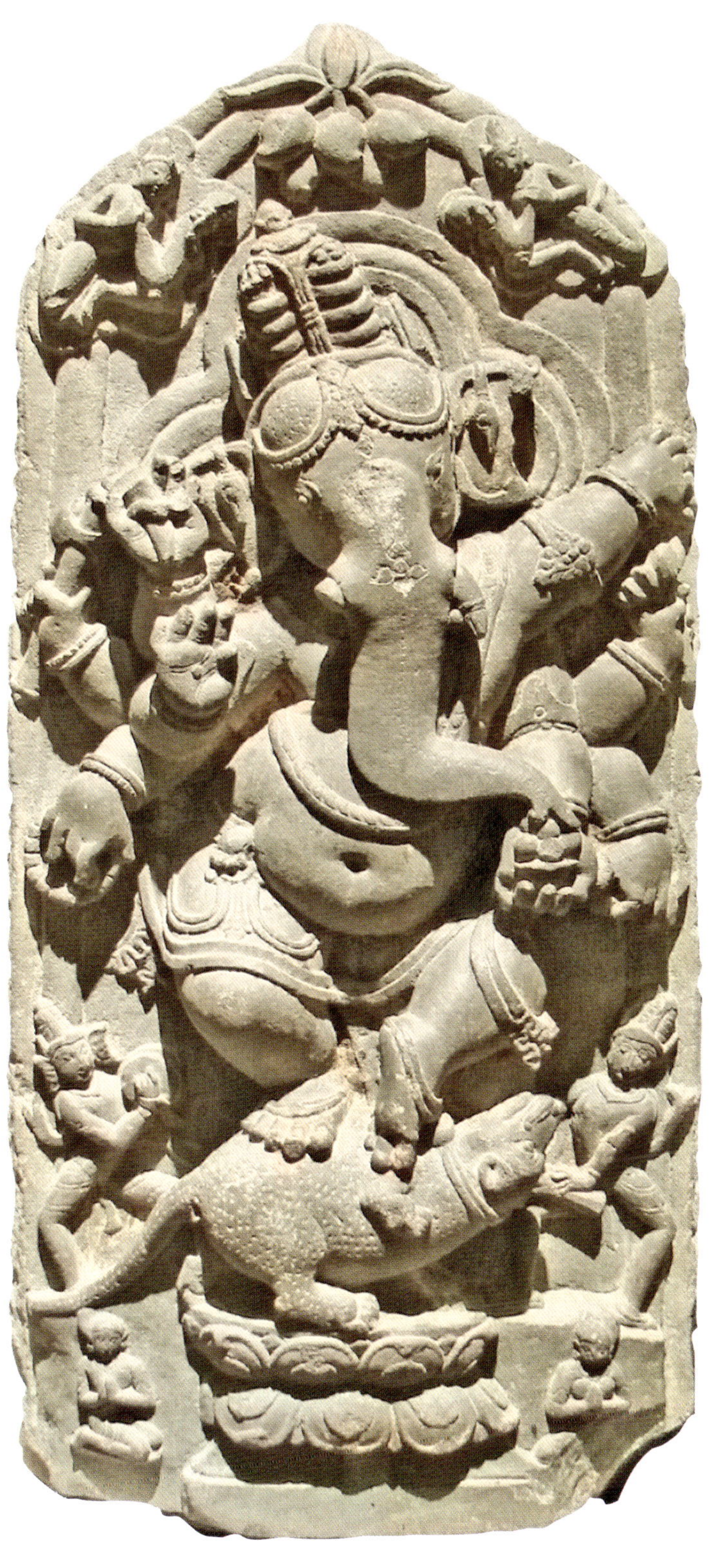

1.11. Relief of dancing Ganesha.
North Bengal, 11th century AD.
Slate, 22¼ × 9⅞ in. (56.5 × 25 cm).
Museum für Asiatische Kunst, Berlin.

in intellectual endeavors, removing obstacles. The appeal of such promises is understandable. And the combination of a rotund man and an elephant is understandably appealing. Quite a benign, positive therianthropic combination.

Sculptures of gods impart an aura of substantiality, of durability. Joseph Campbell suggested that "with the coming to flower in Memphis of an art in durable stone, the mythology arose also of a god who never dies."[2] Ganesha is a striking example of the independent importance of the artistic image. The folklorist Henry Glassie describes how, in Bangladesh, the myths about Ganesha are overshadowed by his image. The image of Ganesha does not illustrate the stories about him; rather, the story "illustrates the image."[3] The images of Ganesha are so appealing and revered that they substantiate the deity's existence.

The Minotaur is a fascinating example of the durability of an early therianthropic creature, up to his central role in a modern artist's creativity. This human with the head and tail of a bull first appears in a Greek myth, one memorably retold by Ovid. The Minotaur was the offspring of Pasiphaë, the wife of King Minos of Crete, and a bull. When the Minotaur grew and acquired a taste for human flesh, Minos had the architect-craftsman Daedalus build a gigantic labyrinth to hold him. Theseus was one of the Athenian youths destined to be devoured by the Minotaur, but, fortunately for him (and unfortunately for the Minotaur), Minos's daughter, Ariadne, fell in love with him as he was being brought to the Labyrinth. With advice from Daedalus, Ariadne gave Theseus a sword and a ball of thread, one end of which she tied to the entrance of the Labyrinth. Once inside, Theseus managed to kill the Minotaur and find his way out using the strand of thread.[4] Theseus carried Ariadne away from Crete and became an Athenian hero, appearing on numerous vase paintings of the Archaic period (plate 1.12).

The Minotaur lived to play an important role in the work of the twentieth century's greatest artist. For Pablo Picasso, the Minotaur had complex, deep, and personal associations, serving as an allegorical alter ego. Starting around 1928, the creature seemed to possess Picasso's creative mind, with many of his etchings, paintings, and sculptures featuring this mythical bull-man.

Early 1935 was a tumultuous time for both Europe and Picasso personally. Much of the continent was radically unstable, and fascism's growing strength deeply troubled the Spaniard. Picasso's marriage to his first wife, Olga Khokhlova, was floundering, and his young mistress, Marie-Thérèse Walter, was pregnant. Picasso's artistic output declined sharply, and he turned to writing poetry. He would later describe this period as "the worst time in my life."[5] But out of that time came one of the greatest etchings of the twentieth century, Picasso's *Minotauromachy* (plate 1.13).[6]

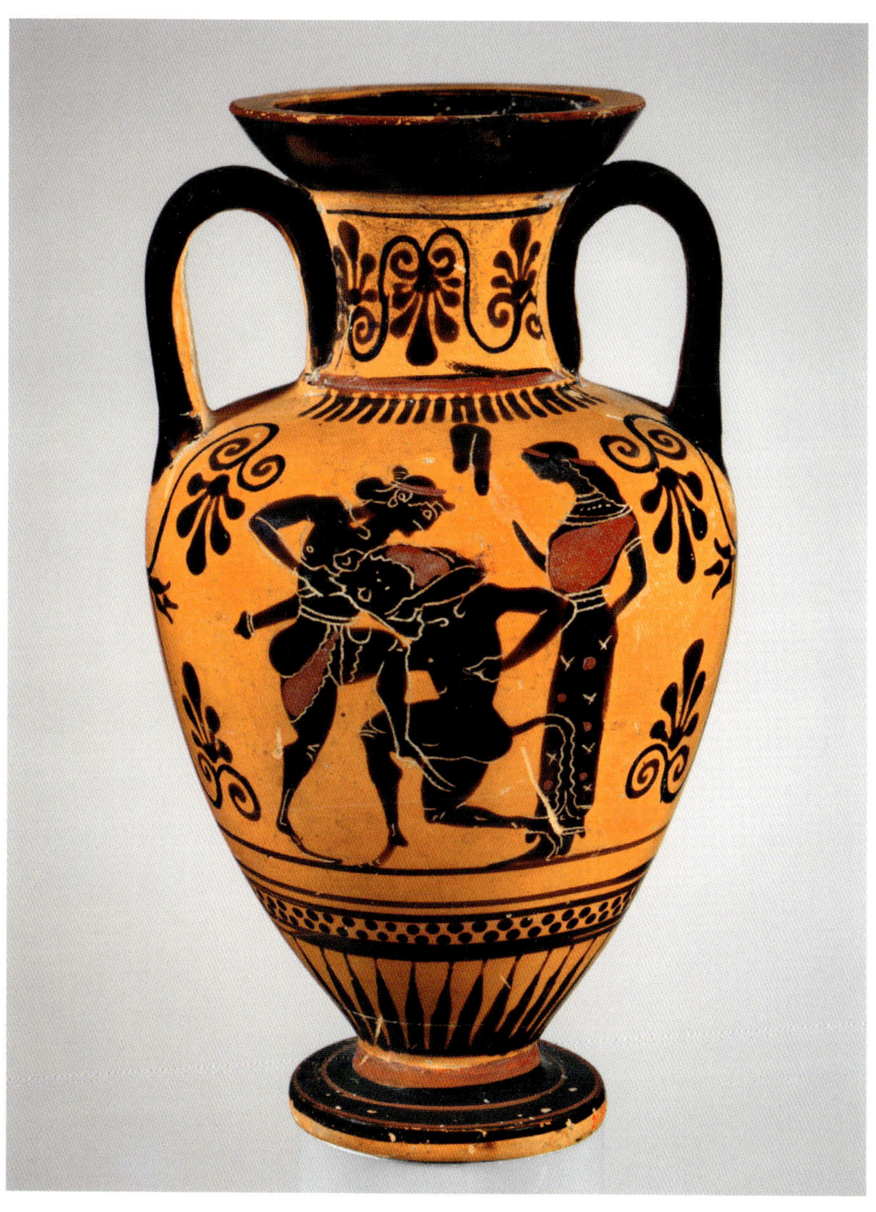

1.12. Neck amphora with Theseus slaying the Minotaur. Greek, Archaic period, c. 500 BC, attributed to the Edinburgh Painter. Height: 5¾ in. (14.6 cm). Metropolitan Museum of Art, New York.

There have been many interpretations of the *Minotauromachy*, but the major elements of the scene are clear. A young girl with a bouquet of flowers and a candle confronts—or leads—a huge, menacing Minotaur. Between them is a scene of violence: a wounded female bullfighter lies on her felled horse, which whinnies at the Minotaur with teeth bared. From a window above, two girls with doves, symbols of peace, peer down on the scene. A sailboat can be glimpsed on the far horizon. There is darkness and light, violence and peacefulness, suffering and hope, all dominated by the Minotaur.

Whatever the meaning of the *Minotauromachy*, it is powerful evidence of how the concept of the therianthrope can catalyze the creative imagination. Long before scientific explanations existed, early humans conceived of therianthropes in an attempt to understand and master the mysteries of the natural world, on which they were entirely dependent. And then they depicted these mythical beings on the walls of caves to make them real. Picasso's creative use of the Minotaur is related to those ancient images. He seeks understanding through the metaphorical power of artistic representation.

The *Minotauromachy* has been seen as prophetic of the Spanish Civil War, which began the next year. It also served as a visual source for Picasso's masterpiece mural, *Guernica*, in which the artist used some of the same imagery to agonize over that conflict.

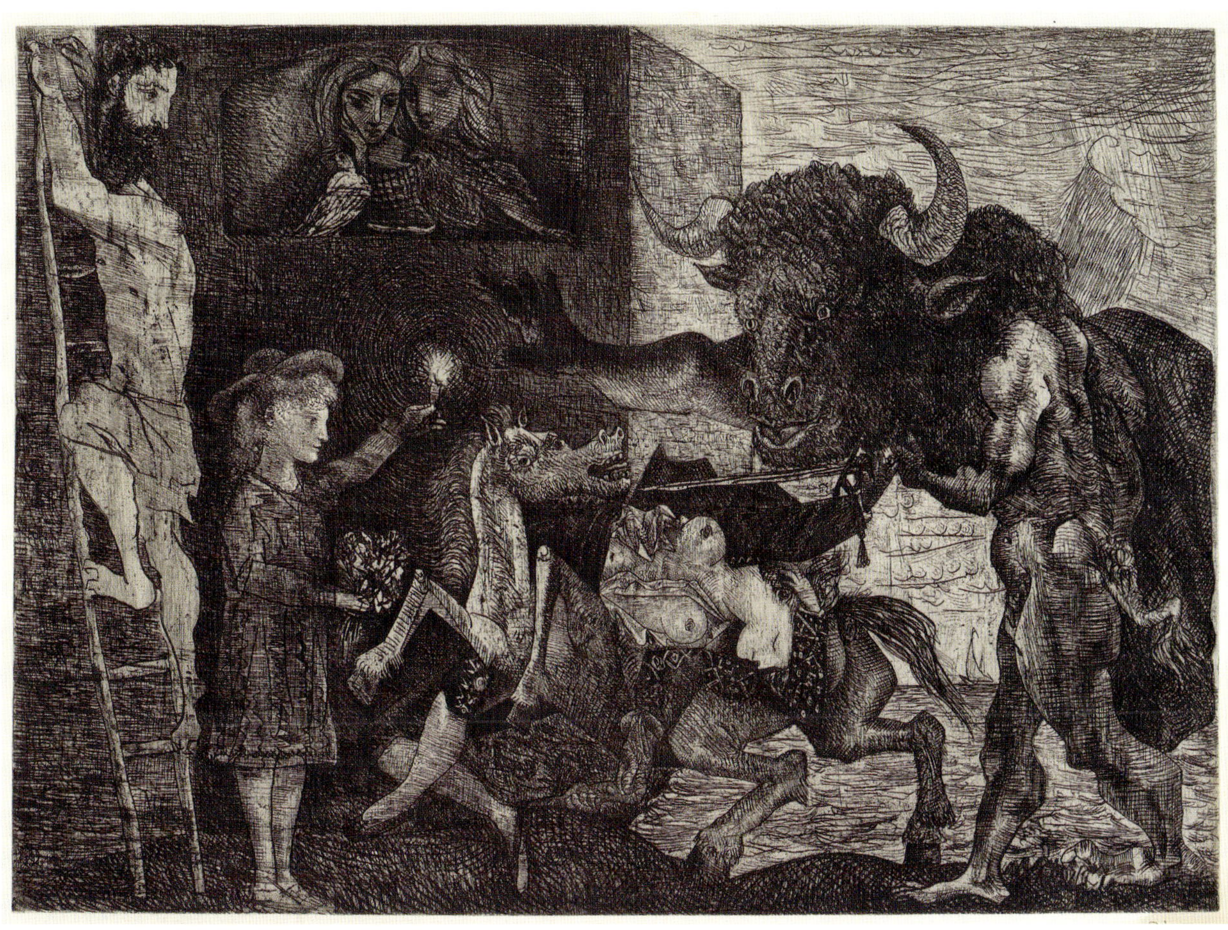

1.13. Pablo Picasso (1881–1973). *Minotauromachy*, 1935. Etching and drypoint, 19⅜ × 27⅜ in. (49.3 × 69.5 cm). Ashmolean Museum, University of Oxford.

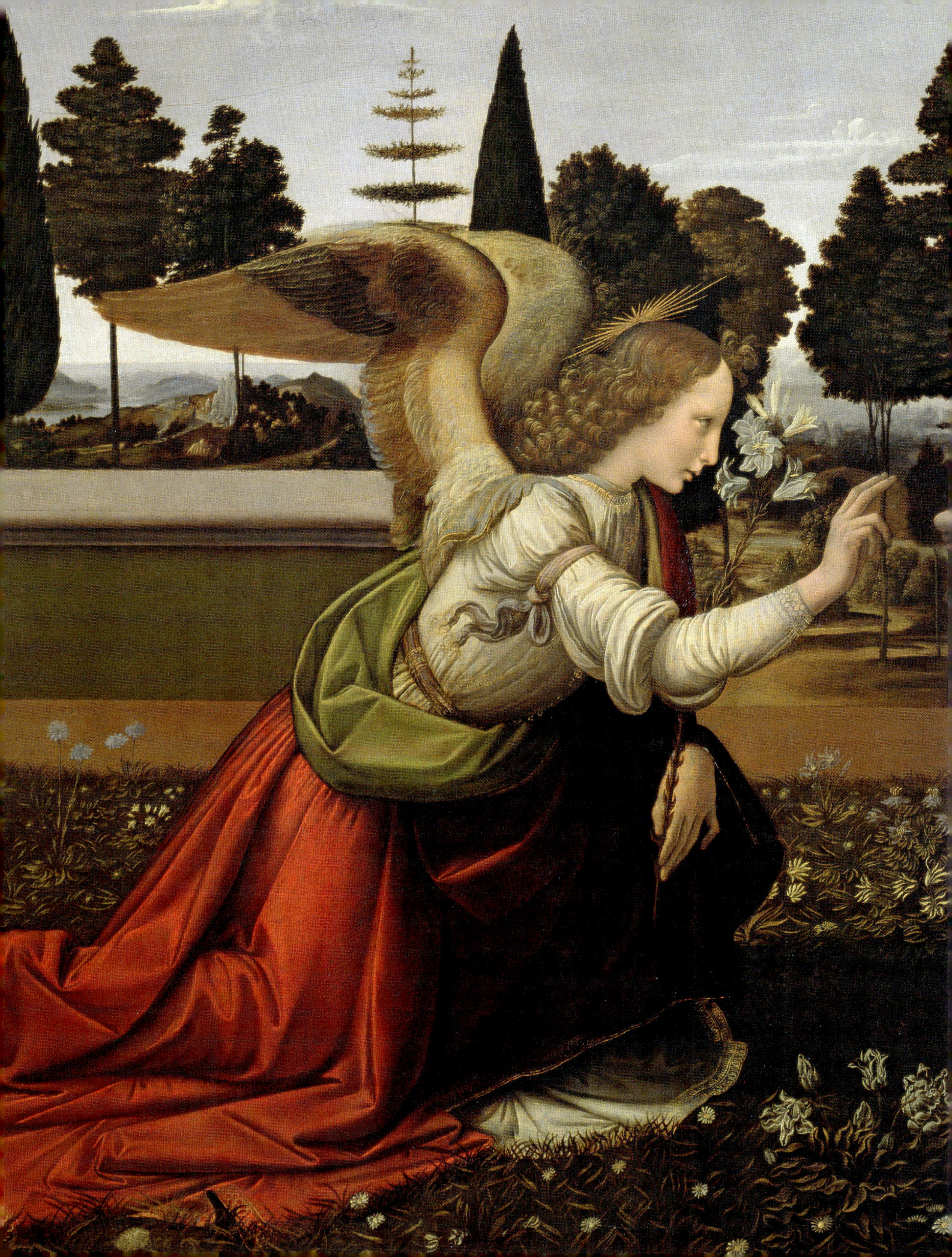

2
WINGED BEINGS

Detail of Leonardo da Vinci's *Annunciation*. See plate 2.11.

We have gotten so used to them, those human beings with wings, that we have forgotten how odd they are. Whoever first thought of that combination, those feathered things on the backs of humans? But of course, they weren't just humans. Maybe that was it: a device to say these were heavenly creatures, messengers from a different realm, a realm where it was normal for beings to have wings.[1]

Many therianthropes, including winged ones, existed in myths and fables well before they were recorded in writing. And they existed in human minds well before those myths and fables took shape. It is likely that one of the earliest mythological concepts was that of worlds other than our everyday one. Neanderthals, when they buried their dead with necklaces and tools, were expressing a belief in another world. "Otherworldly" experiences, from the earliest recorded, were often described as flights into a different realm. As Joseph Campbell put it, "The bird is symbolic of the release of the spirit from bondage to the earth."[2]

Early on, aspiration may also have played a part. Early hunter-gatherers had an intimate relationship with nature. They must have sensed that they shared certain basic requirements with other species: the need for food and water and shelter. And they must have been deeply aware of their own limitations compared with the animals on which they depended. They could not have helped being envious of the speed of the lion, or the eagle's ability to fly.

Birds were natural entrants into mythology, and the envy of flight endures. Envy combined with aspiration: If we only had wings!

Somewhere over the rainbow,
Bluebirds fly.
Birds fly over the rainbow.
Why, then, oh why can't I?[3]

Winged creatures were integral to the early development of religion. Creatures with wings were revered in one of the earliest civilizations, that of Mesopotamia in the Fertile Crescent. The gods of Mesopotamia had all sorts of forms: some were depicted with the body of a fish and the head of a man, others with the torso of a fish and human arms, legs, and head. And often, they had wings. Altars dedicated to winged gods have been found dating to 3000 BC, at the beginning of the Bronze Age. There were also winged goddesses. A notable example is Ishtar, an ancient Mesopotamian goddess associated with procreation, war, justice, and political power. In a cylinder seal dating to around 2200 BC, she is shown restraining a roaring lion (plate 2.1). We owe a great deal to such seals, which appeared in Mesopotamia as early as 6000 BC. Originally used to "sign" a document, the seal was carved into a stone cylinder (Ishtar's is in limestone) and rolled onto the moist clay of the document.[4] Ishtar survived to be mentioned in the Hebrew Bible, and her spirit influenced the development of the goddess Aphrodite in Greece, and Venus in Rome.

By the time of the reign of the Assyrian king Ashurnasirpal II (883–859 BC), there was a highly evolved panoply of gods. Prominent were the winged Apkallu, who, like the guardian angels to come, were protective spirits, particularly for the king. They were represented in aesthetically

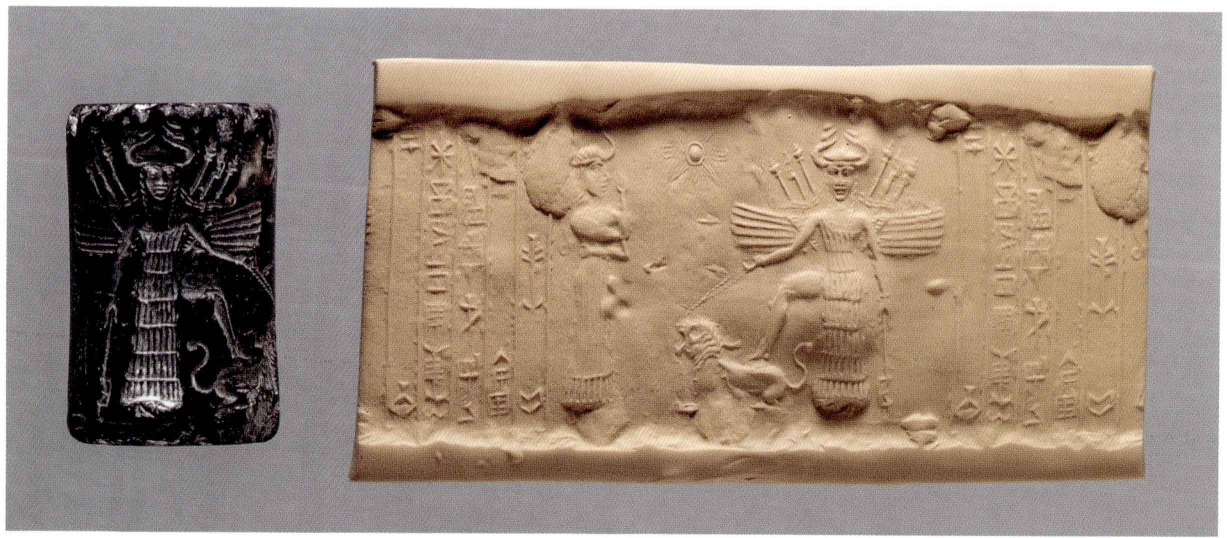

2.1. Cylinder seal depicting the goddess Ishtar with her foot on a lion. Akkadian, 2334–2154 BC. Limestone, 1⅝ in. (4.1 cm) high, 1 in. (2.6 cm) in diameter. Oriental Institute Museum, University of Chicago.

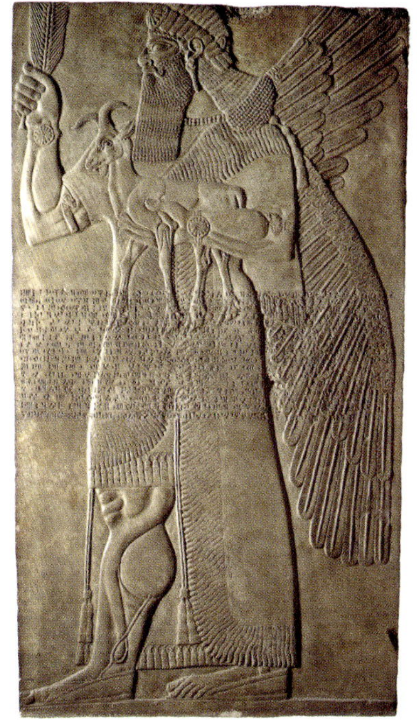

2.2. Bas-relief of an Apkallu. Neo-Assyrian, 875–860 BC. Gypsum, 88¼ × 50 × 4¾ in. (224 × 127 × 12 cm). British Museum, London.

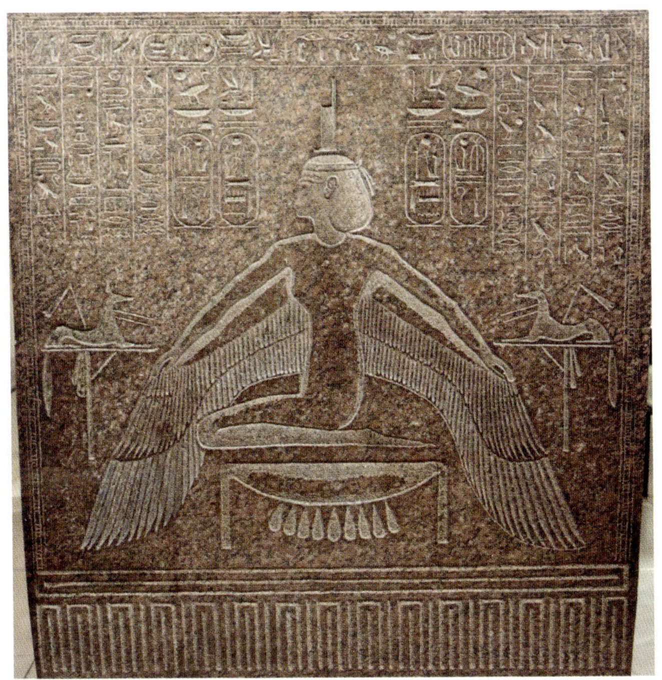

2.3. Winged Isis on the foot of the sarcophagus of Ramses III. Egyptian, 20th Dynasty, 1184–1153 BC. Granite, 70⅞ × 59 × 120⅛ in. (180 × 150 × 305 cm). Musée du Louvre, Paris.

sophisticated bas-relief panels in King Ashurnasirpal's Northwest Palace in Nimrud (ancient Kalhu) in modern-day Iraq. In one, an elegantly winged Apkallu is shown as a protector of agricultural productivity: he holds a goat in one hand and a sheaf of wheat in the other. His power is portrayed by an exaggerated rendering of his leg muscles (plate 2.2).

During the Bronze Age, the winged deities of Mesopotamia found their way to the then less-advanced civilizations of Egypt and Greece. One of the most widely worshipped Egyptian deities was the goddess Isis. Whether she was depicted with wings seemed to depend on the role she was fulfilling. They were appropriate when Isis was helping the dead enter the afterlife, as in her depiction at the foot of the twelfth-century BC sarcophagus of

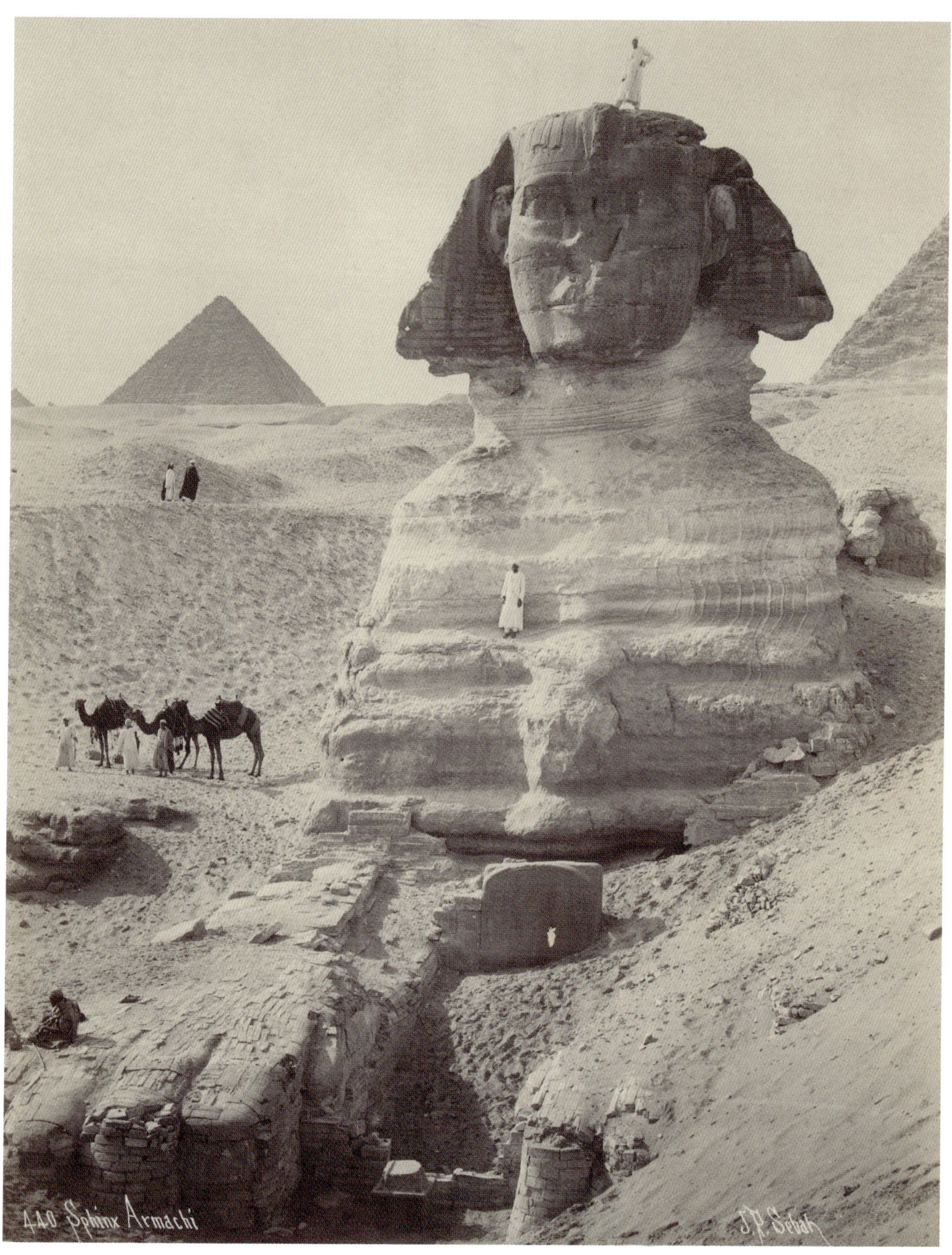

2.4. The Great Sphinx of Giza, c. 2558–2532 BC, as seen in a photograph of the late nineteenth century. Limestone, 60 ft. (20 m) high.

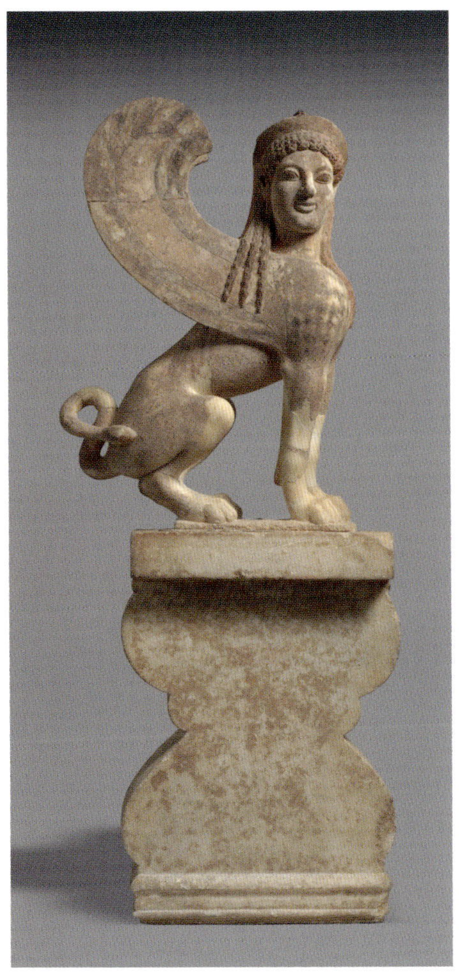

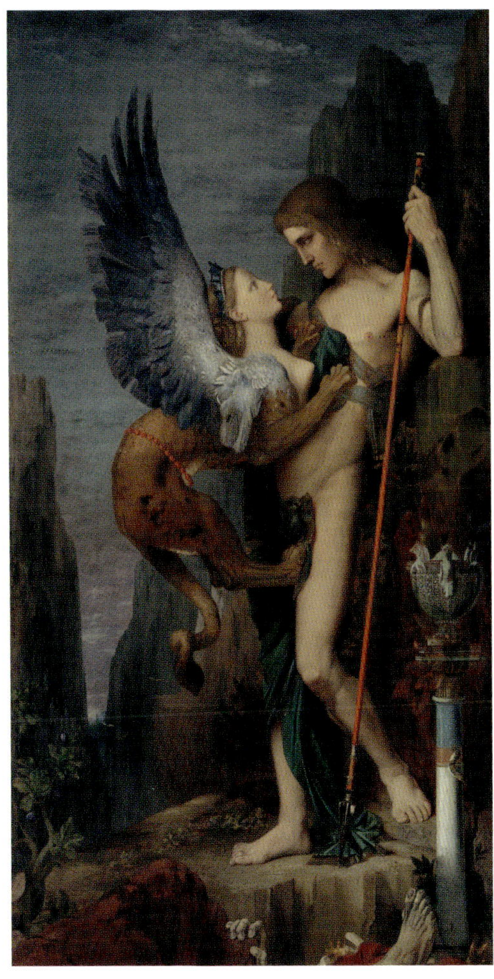

Ramses III (plate 2.3). Isis managed a more complete transformation into a bird when she searched for the remains of her murdered brother, Osiris. She brought Osiris back to life, manifesting the source of many mythical creatures: the desire to overcome the limitations of human existence, including mortality.

2.5. ABOVE LEFT: Marble capital and finial in the form of a sphinx. Greek, c. 530 BC. Marble, 56⅛ in. (142.6 cm) high. Metropolitan Museum of Art, New York.

2.6. ABOVE RIGHT: Gustave Moreau (1826–1898). *Oedipus and the Sphinx*, 1864. Oil on canvas, 81¼ × 41¼ in. (206.4 × 104.8 cm). Metropolitan Museum of Art, New York.

Some winged beings in ancient myths were combinations of more than two creatures. One of the best-known examples was the sphinx, a being with the head of a human, the body of a lion, and the wings of a bird. In ancient Egypt, the sphinx was a benevolent male, as manifested in the massive sculpture at Giza (plate 2.4). But in ancient Greece, the sphinx morphed into an attractive, and murderous, female (plate 2.5), at least for those who could not answer her riddle: What creature walks on four legs in

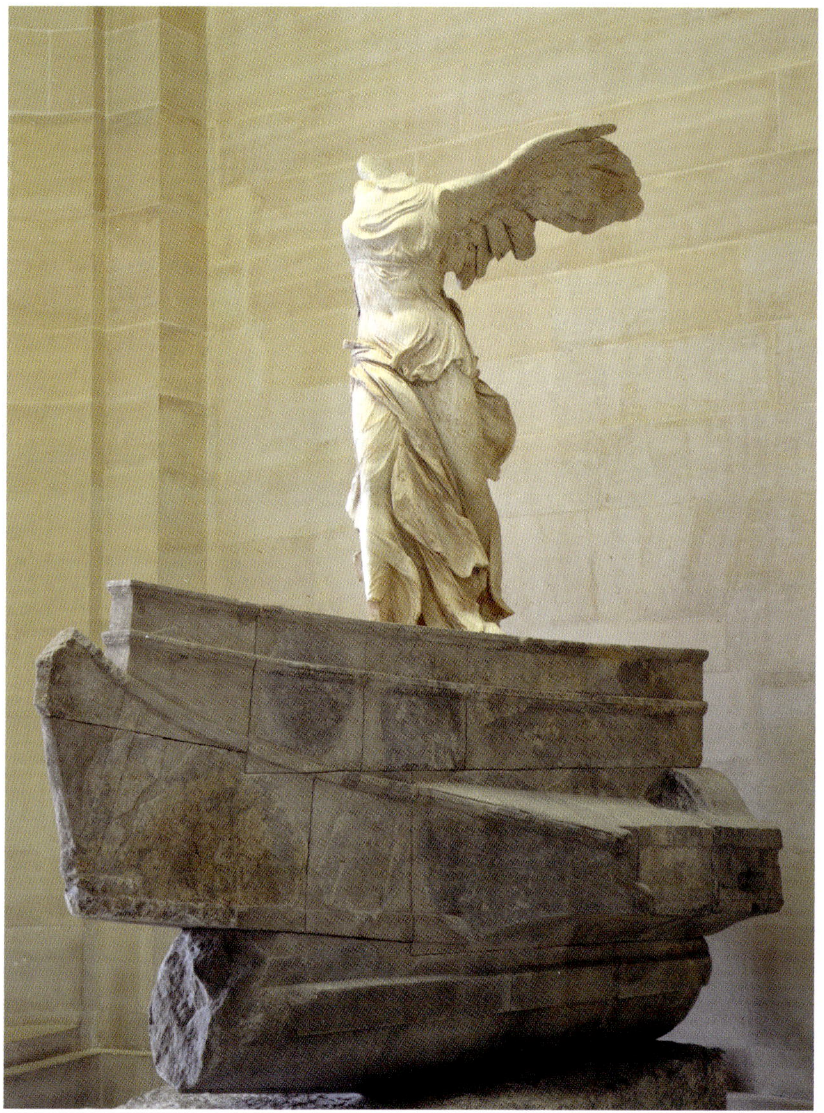

2.7. Winged Victory of Samothrace, 200–190 BC. Marble, 96 in. (245 cm) high. Musée du Louvre, Paris.

the morning, two legs at noon, and three legs in the evening? The answer: the human, who crawls as a baby, strides upright in maturity, and uses a cane in old age. From the Renaissance on, Western artists were attracted to the Sphinx of Greek myth and gave her a new reality in their depictions. When, in 1864, Gustave Moreau portrayed the Sphinx taunting Oedipus, she was as seductive as she was dangerous (plate 2.6).

Winged goddesses of a more conventional appearance and a more positive character also flourished in ancient Greece, and eventually became the subjects of majestic artistic representations. The most dramatic winged

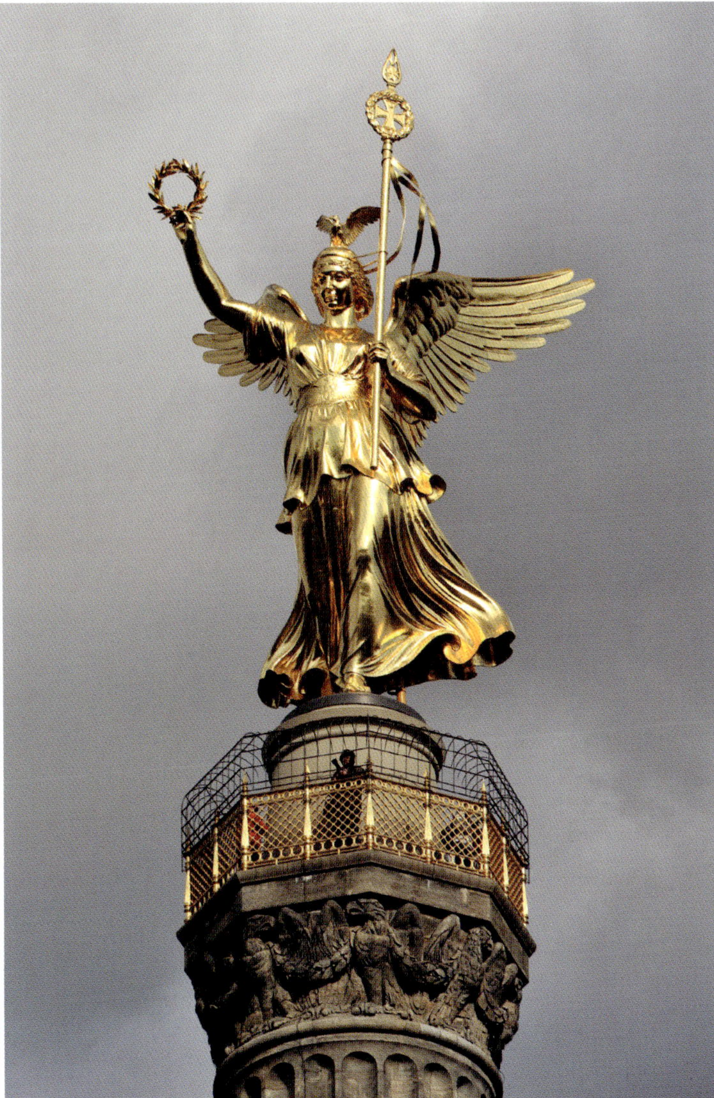

2.8. Friedrich Drake (1805–1882). *Victoria*, 1873. Gilded bronze, 28 ft. (8.5 m) high. Victory Column, Berlin.

figure in the history of art is the Winged Victory of Samothrace, now in the Louvre in Paris (plate 2.7). Most likely she was created by a sculptor from Rhodes about 200 BC to commemorate a sea battle. This dynamic work represents Nike, the Greek goddess of speed, strength, and victory. The convincing depiction of the wind pressing on Nike's body conveys a dramatic sense of movement, which is reinforced by her outstretched wings: because of their role in flight, wings always retain a sense of motion, and thus of life.

Certain therianthropes appeal to basic human instincts, and have persisted through space and time. They evolve to represent important ideals of subsequent cultures. Such was the case with Nike. In ancient Rome, Nike became Victoria. Over time her images came to symbolize the spirit of victory rather than an actual deity to be worshipped. That spirit prevailed into the modern era, as evidenced by the statue of Victoria commemorating the Prussian victory in the Dano-Prussian War of 1864 (plate 2.8).

Another figure who exemplifies the widespread appeal of the winged therianthrope is Garuda. Often represented as a man with the wings and facial features of a bird, Garuda appears prominently in Hindu, Buddhist, and Jain mythology. Initially his role was to transport the Hindu god Vishnu, but later Garuda was worshipped in his own right. He contributed not

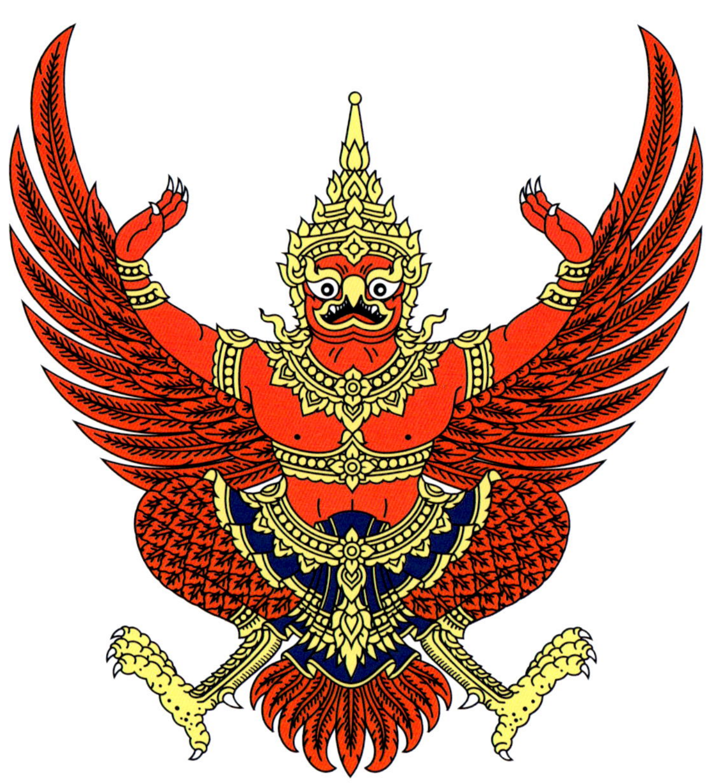

2.9. The national emblem of Thailand, a dancing Garuda with outstretched wings.

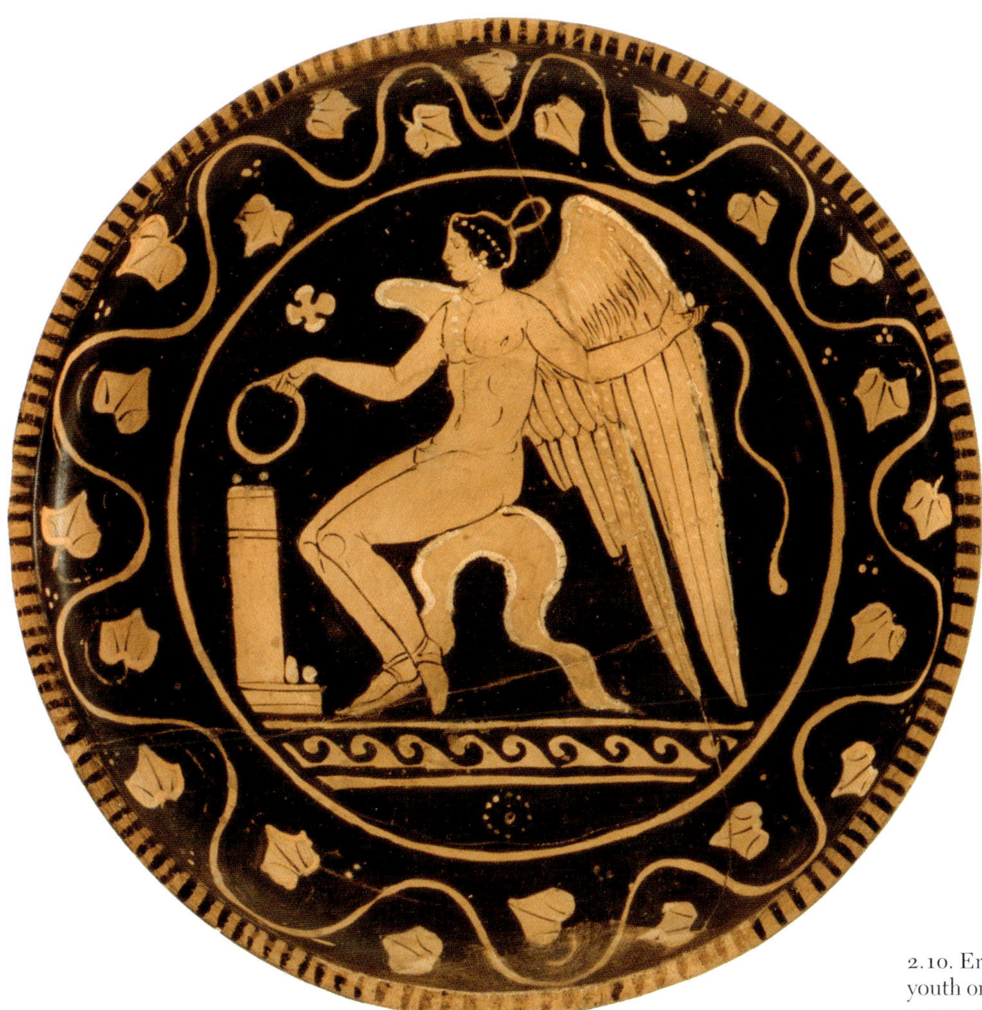

2.10. Eros depicted as a winged youth on a red-figure plate. Greek, c. 340–320 BC. Terra-cotta, 9.6 in. (24.4 cm) in diameter. Walters Art Museum, Baltimore.

only to the religious life but also to the national identity of India, Indonesia, and Thailand. The Indonesian national airline is called Garuda, and the Garuda officially symbolizes the government and people of Thailand (plate 2.9).

Wings can connote not only power and victory but also compassion and love. Even more resilient through time than representations of Nike and Victoria are representations of angels. Angels were born of necessity: if God existed in another, distant realm and had an ethereal form, he needed emissaries to communicate with people in the real world, and that was the role of angels. (The Greek word *angelo* means messenger). But according to Christian doctrine, angels are pure spirits without physical bodies, so art had to come to the rescue.

Artists have always played a crucial role in determining how we view mythological beings. Belief benefits from visualization, but a "pure spirit" defies representation. So, when European artists began to depict angels in the fourth century AD, they imagined a more literal form for the messengers of God, and gave them wings. Those wings were inherited from such predecessors as Ishtar in Assyria and Eros, the ancient Greek god of love (plate 2.10). From Eros, angels also inherited their elemental nature: the ancient Greeks considered Eros to be the primordial deity, older than all the others.

According to the Bible, angels performed several consequential acts in their role as messengers from God. One was the Annunciation. Through the centuries, numerous artists have depicted the occasion when the angel Gabriel appeared to Mary to announce that she would give birth to Jesus. These artists' aesthetic choices have determined how we envision this event. Early Renaissance artists depicted the Annunciation as taking place

2.11. Leonardo da Vinci (1452–1519). *The Annunciation*, c. 1472–76. Oil and tempera on panel, 39 × 85 in. (98 × 217 cm). Uffizi, Florence.

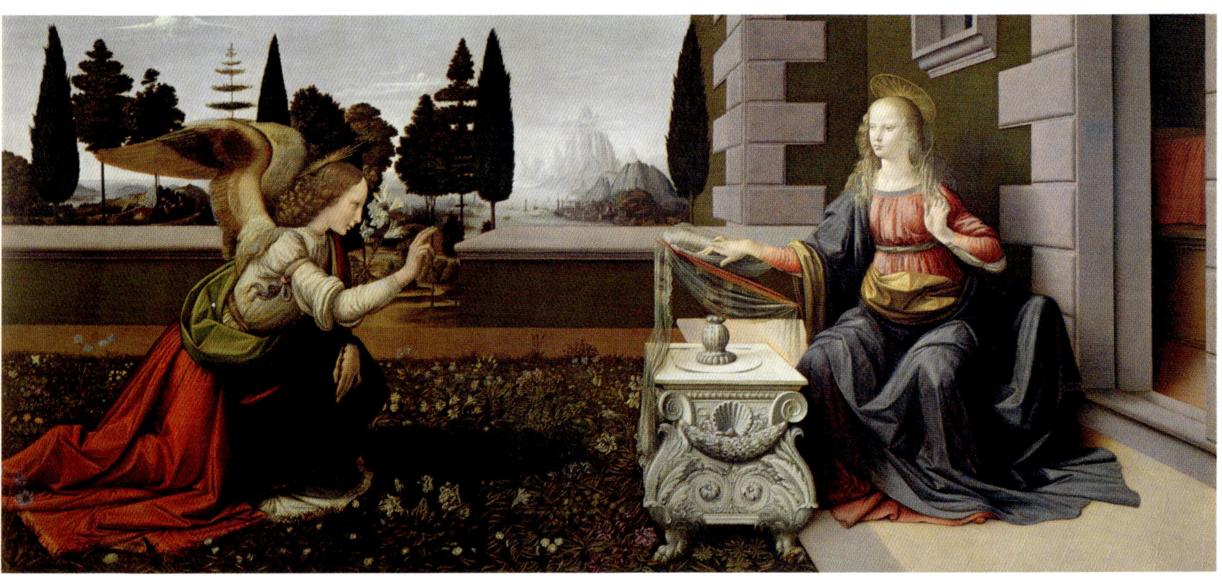

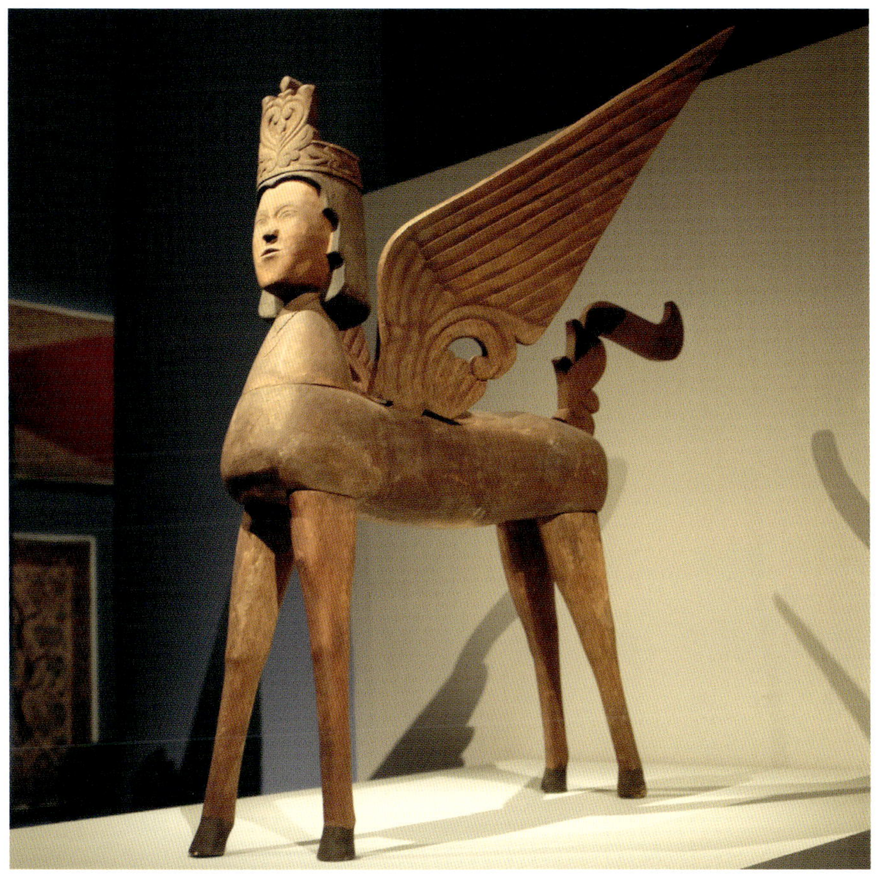

2.12. The Buraq, a mythical beast of Islamic tradition. Mindanao, Philippines, twentieth century. Wood and paint, 44⅛ × 40 × 43¼ in. (112 × 101.5 × 110 cm). Asian Civilisations Museum, Singapore.

indoors, interrupting Mary in her reading. In Leonardo's version, which he completed as a young man in collaboration with his mentor, Verrocchio, Mary is outside (plate 2.11). The young Gabriel appears as integral to nature, echoing both Leonardo's love of nature and the traditional role of angels in communicating nature's laws, defined by God.

Angels appear in virtually all religions, and usually exemplify positive characteristics. In Islam, belief in angels is one of the six basic articles of faith. As in Christianity, they are usually thought of as God's first creations. Although consisting of pure light, they have various functions, including communicating natural and ethical laws to humans. There is also another winged therianthrope in Islamic tradition, the complex creature that carried Mohammed into the heavens. The Buraq was a horse with wings and a human head, sometimes rendered as a male, sometimes as a female (plate 2.12). In heaven, Mohammed met Jesus, Adam, John the Baptist, and many others, and then ultimately God on his throne. All thanks to the Buraq.

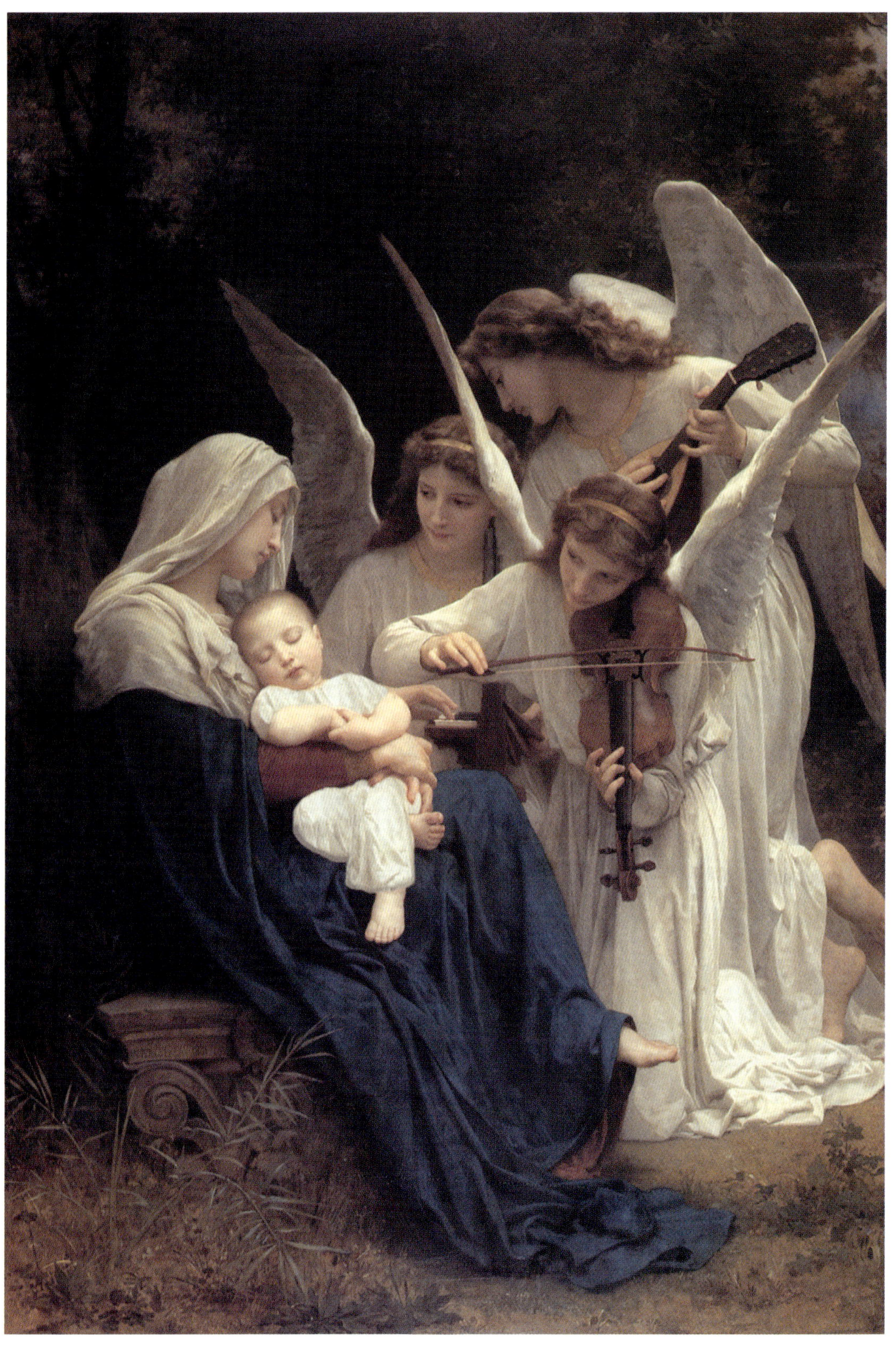

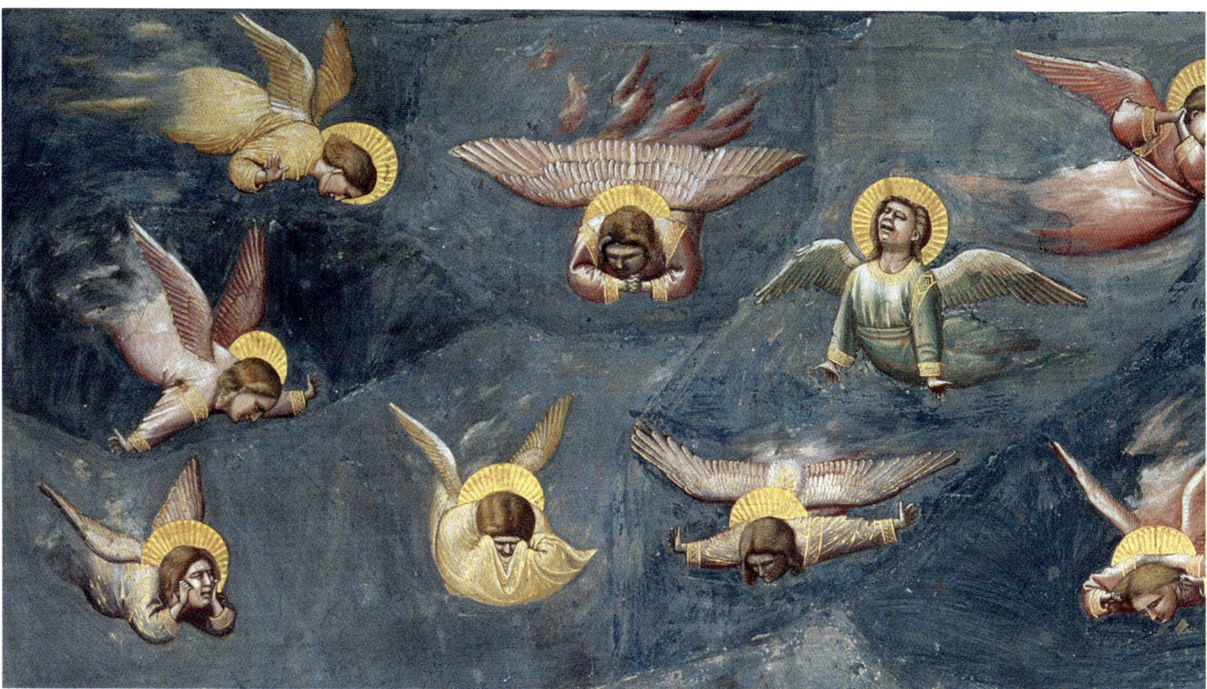

2.13. OPPOSITE: William Adolphe Bouguereau (1825–1905). *Virgin of the Angels*, 1881. Oil on canvas, 84 × 60 in. (213 × 152 cm). Forest Lawn Museum, Glendale, CA.

2.14. ABOVE: Giotto (c. 1266–1337). *The Lamentation of Christ*, c. 1305. Fresco. Scrovegni Chapel, Padua.

As artistic styles evolved, so did our notion of the appearance of angels, and their credibility. Absorbing a painting of angels by Bouguereau (plate 2.13) is quite different from standing in front of one of Giotto's many angelic images (plate 2.14).

Angels appear in many forms with many functions. In the Christian tradition, seraphim are the highest angelic class, serving as the caretakers of God's throne. They are represented as fiery creatures with six wings. The cherubim are another commonly mentioned class of angels. In the Jewish angelic hierarchy, cherubim are ranked quite low, whereas in Islam, the cherubim are the angels closest to God. But it is in medieval Christian iconography that a wondrously complex angelic form appears. Termed a tetramorph, this generous being has two pairs of wings and four faces

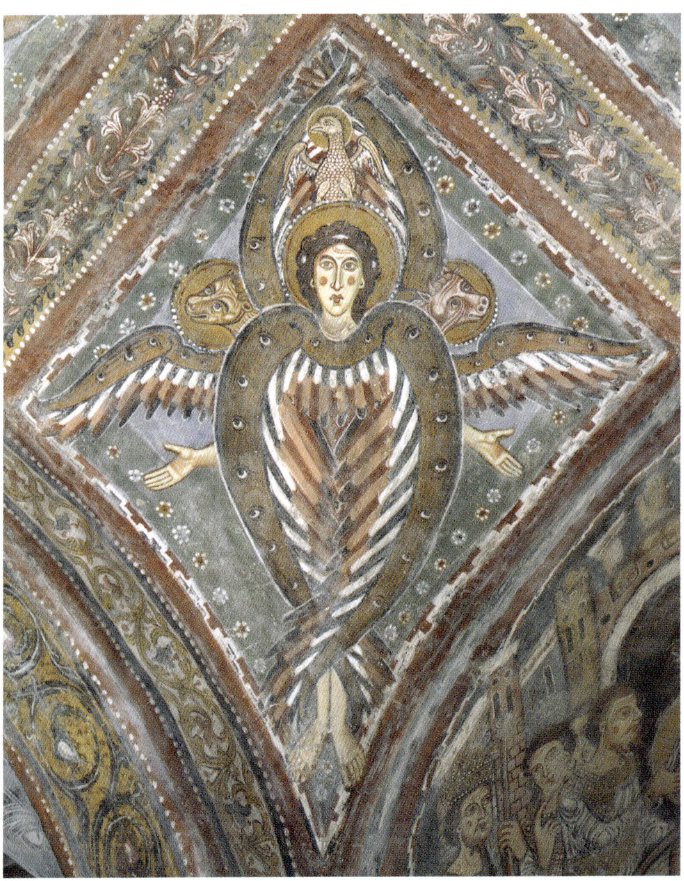

2.15. Tetramorph depicted in a thirteenth-century fresco, Cathedral of Anagni, Italy.

representing the four attributes of the Evangelists (plate 2.15): that of a lion (representative of all wild animals), an ox (domestic animals), a man (humanity), and an eagle (birds).

Eros, the Greek god of love and sex, appropriately had several conceptual offspring aside from the angels. In Rome, he became Cupid and took on softer characteristics. Although portrayed as the son of the goddess of love, Venus, and the god of war, Mars, he mostly took after his mother. One of the most enduring—and endearing—winged creatures in classical mythology, Cupid is the god of attraction and affection, and erotic love. He wields his bow and arrow to produce love and desire in his targets. Once again it is artists who have determined our image of Cupid. They have often chosen to convey his endearing nature by representing him as a pudgy youth. An example is Piero della Francesca's fifteenth century *Cupid Blindfolded* (plate 2.16). Blindfolded because love itself is blind.

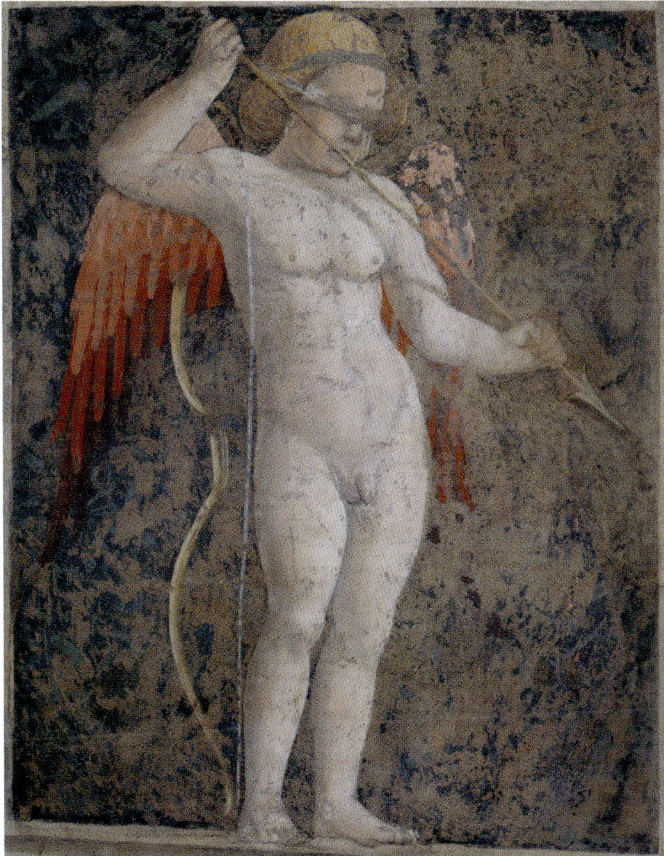

2.16. Piero della Francesca (1415–1492). *Cupid Blindfolded*, 1452–66. Fresco. San Francesco, Arezzo.

Lucas Cranach the Elder employed another technique to portray the appeal of Cupid: by illustrating a humorous story (plate 2.17). In Cranach's painting of about 1525, Cupid is stung by bees when he steals honey from their hive. He complains to his mother, Venus, that so small a creature shouldn't cause such painful wounds. Venus laughs, and points out the poetic justice: he too is small, and yet delivers the grand sting of love.

The cherubs or putti who feature in later Western art bear a physical resemblance to Cupid but are meant to represent angels. They appeared when painting had become more realistic, and were depicted as lifelike cuddly children with wings, perhaps to evoke the angelic qualities of children. The putti at the base of Raphael's *Sistine Madonna* exemplify their kind (plate 2.18). One account claims that Raphael's putti were inspired by two boys whom the artist had seen "looking wistfully into the window of a baker's shop."[5]

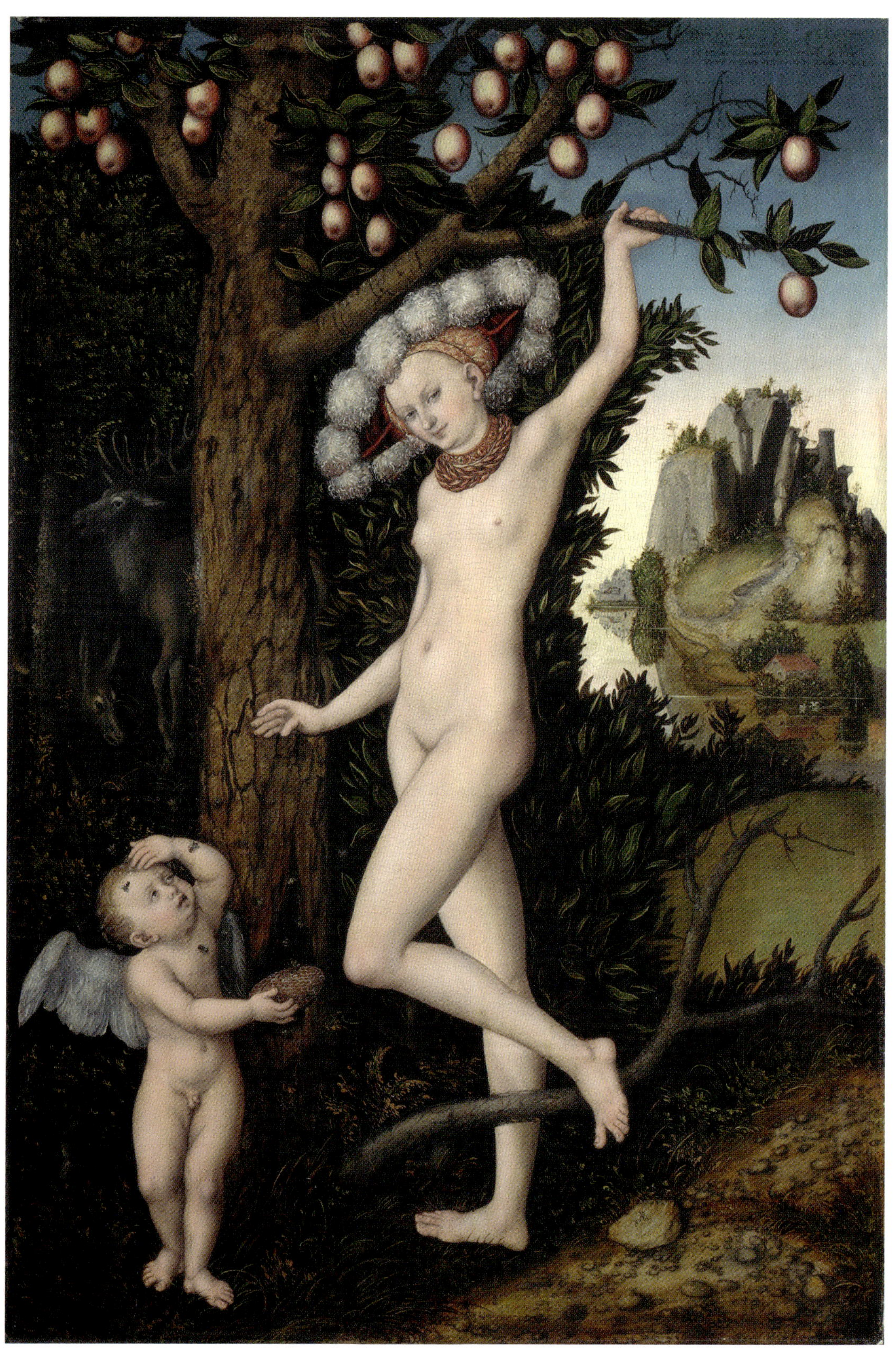

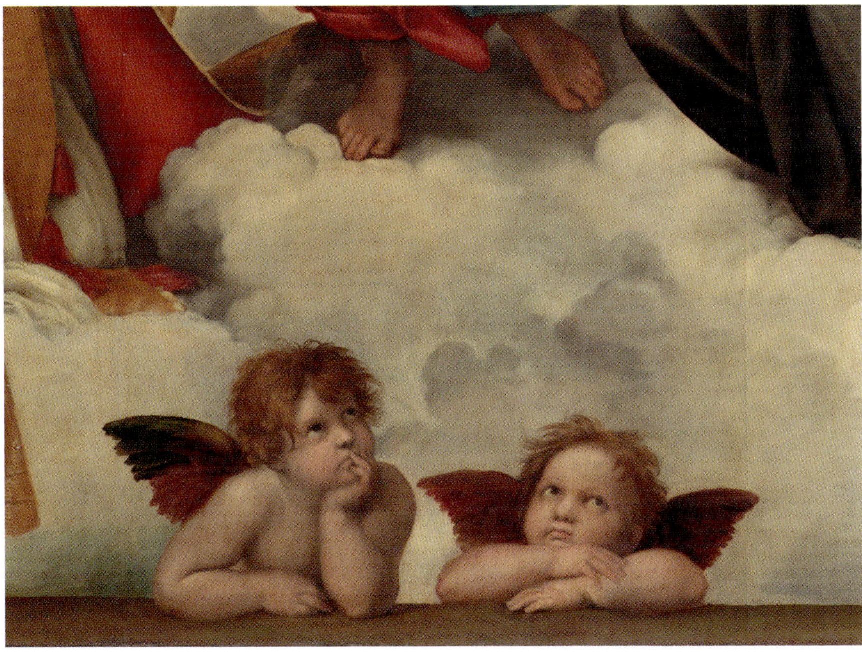

2.17. OPPOSITE: Lucas Cranach the Elder (1472–1553). *Cupid Complaining to Venus*, 1526–27. Oil on panel, 32 × 21½ in. (81.3 × 54.6 cm). National Gallery, London.

2.18. ABOVE: Raphael (1483–1520). Detail of putti from the *Sistine Madonna*, c. 1513–14. Oil on canvas, 104 × 77 in. (265 × 196 cm). Gemäldegalerie Alte Meister, Dresden.

The appeal of Cupid is widespread and long-lasting. He has a notional brother in Kamadeva, the Hindu god of human love or desire, but there are differences. Kamadeva doesn't have wings, and, more imaginatively, his bow is made of sugarcane, and his arrows are decorated with fragrant flowers.

Winged relatives of the angels are found in many different cultures and eras. In England, fairies first appeared in the thirteenth century as part of a broad secularization of miracle-working religious figures. In the fairy tales that grew up around them, they had both positive and negative attributes. Shakespeare's *A Midsummer Night's Dream* takes place partly in an enchanted forest where Oberon is the diminutive, wingless king of the fairies. It was only later, in nineteenth-century England, that fairies acquired their wings. In Luis Ricardo Falero's painting, the delicate lily fairy has wings akin to those of a butterfly, since English fairies were known to love flowers (plate 2.19).

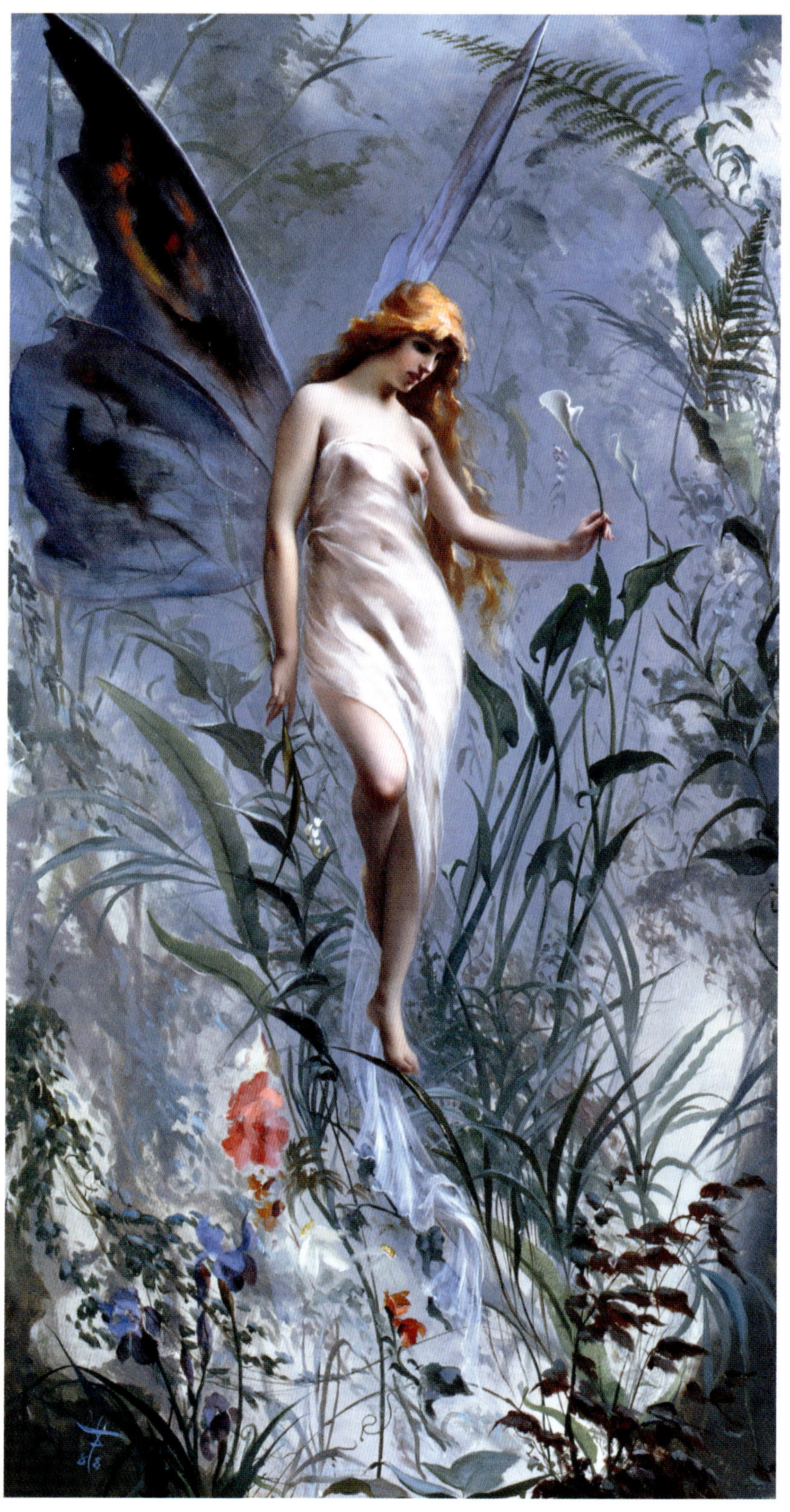

2.19. Luis Ricardo Falero (1851–1896). *The Lily Fairy*, 1888. Oil on canvas. Private collection.

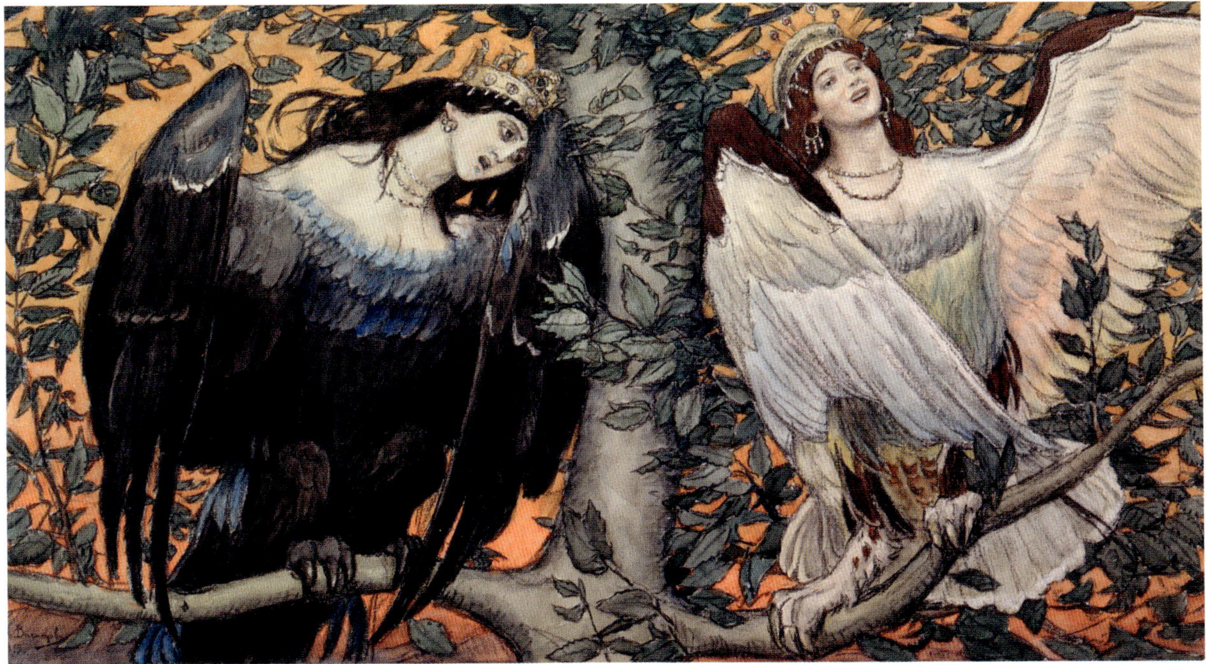

2.20. Victor Vasnetsov (1848–1926). *Sirin and Alkonost, Birds of Joy and Sorrow*, 1896. Watercolor. Art Gallery of Taganrog, Russia.

Angels generally have women's bodies, but Slavic myths offer a creative variation. Their Alkonost has the body of a bird and a woman's head, and she sings beautifully (plate 2.20). Those who hear her forget everything and never want anything else. In the power of her song, she is related to the sirens of Greek myth, and in her elevation of music, she is related to the heavenly Hindu musician Tumburu, whom we met in the first chapter. As all angel-like creatures, the Alkonost exemplifies the skein of connections that exists between therianthropes in different cultures and different times.

It is difficult to fully appreciate the impact that artists' portrayals of angels have had on people through the ages. One remarkable example is Paul Klee's *Angelus Novus*, an unusual male angel, and its effect on the philosopher and writer Walter Benjamin. Klee created this work in 1920 using an original technique, oil transfer drawing with watercolor, and Benjamin

2.21. Paul Klee (1879–1940). *Angelus Novus*, 1920. Oil transfer and watercolor on paper, 12½ × 9½ in. (31.8 × 24.2 cm). Israel Museum, Jerusalem.

acquired it the following year (plate 2.21). Benjamin felt a mystical identification with the drawing and frequently called it his most treasured possession. He described it as showing

> an angel looking as though he is about to move away from something he is fixedly contemplating. His face is turned toward the past. Where we perceive a chain of events, he sees one catastrophe, which keeps piling wreckage upon wreckage hurling it before his feet. A storm is blowing from Paradise; it has got caught in his wings with such violence the angel can no longer close them. This storm irresistibly propels him into the future to which his back is turned, while the pile of debris before him grows skyward.[6]

In the early 1930s, Benjamin and other progressive German Jews held out hope that when the Third Reich fell, the Soviet Marxist model would prevail. But by the late 1930s, that hope had withered. Benjamin was deeply depressed by the depredations of Nazism and through his writings attempted to make sense of the world's downward spiral. He couldn't, and soon after his release from an internment camp in France, he committed suicide.

Klee's *Angelus Novus* remains a powerful example of an artist adopting a mythical therianthrope and creating a striking new vision that can evoke deep feelings in a sensitive person. It is evidence of the relevance of therianthropes in modern times.

Over the centuries, winged angels evolved in art and in human imaginations. For some, they retained their heavenly connections and attributes. For others, they became vivid—if mythical—secular creatures. That evolution is reflected in the life of the pop artist Keith Haring, who grew from a boy raised in the Christian faith to an irreverent humanistic social activist (particularly with regards to AIDS education). One of his last images, created in 1990, the year he died, was of an angel (plate 2.22).

Angels were key to the brand image of one of the most culturally influential retailers of the later twentieth century. Victoria's Secret was founded in 1977 as a store where men could feel comfortable buying lingerie for their wives and girlfriends. A new owner reenergized the company in 1995 by creating the annual Victoria's Secret Fashion Show, a primetime television event in which the supermodels of the day strutted down the runway

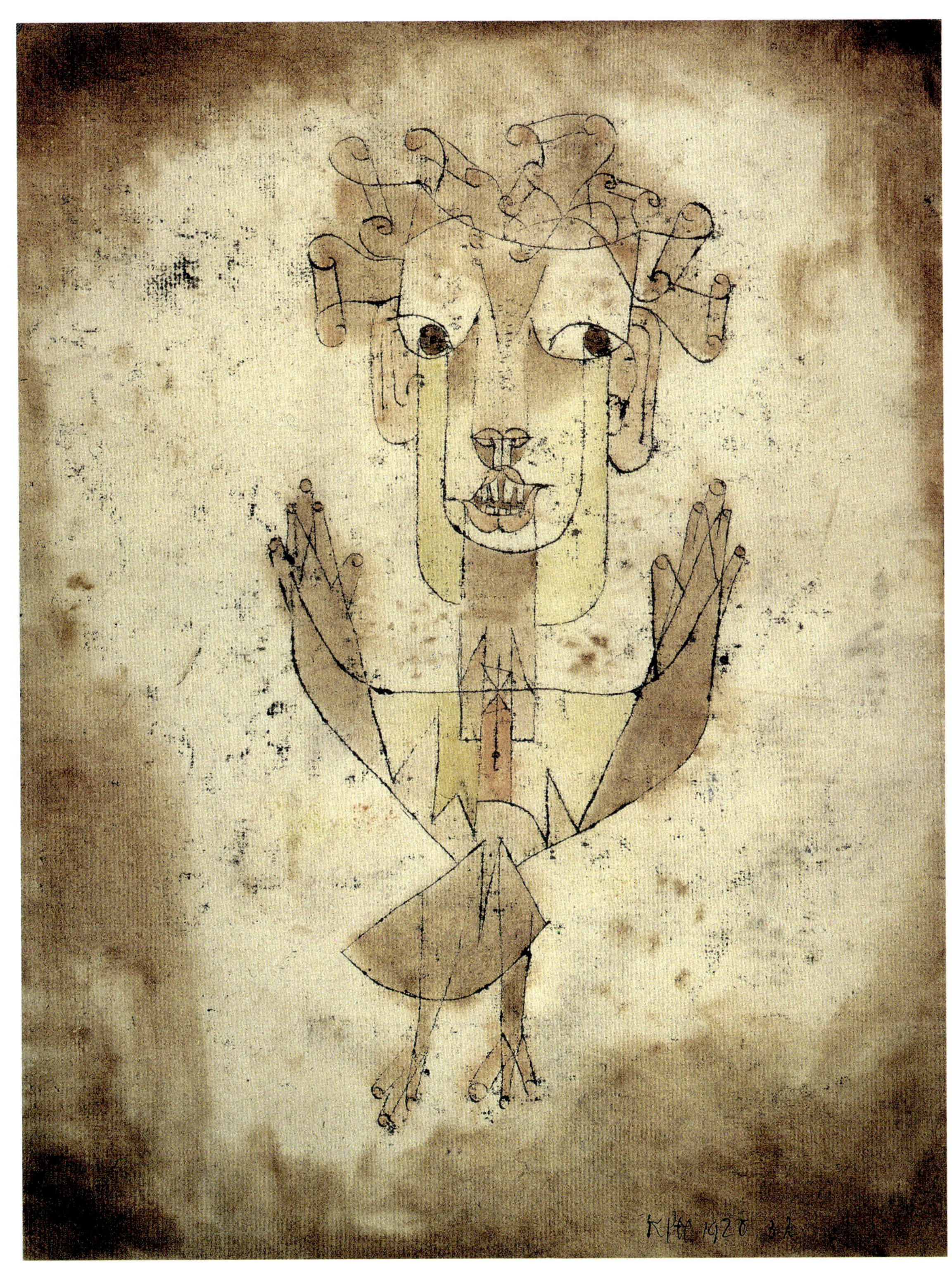

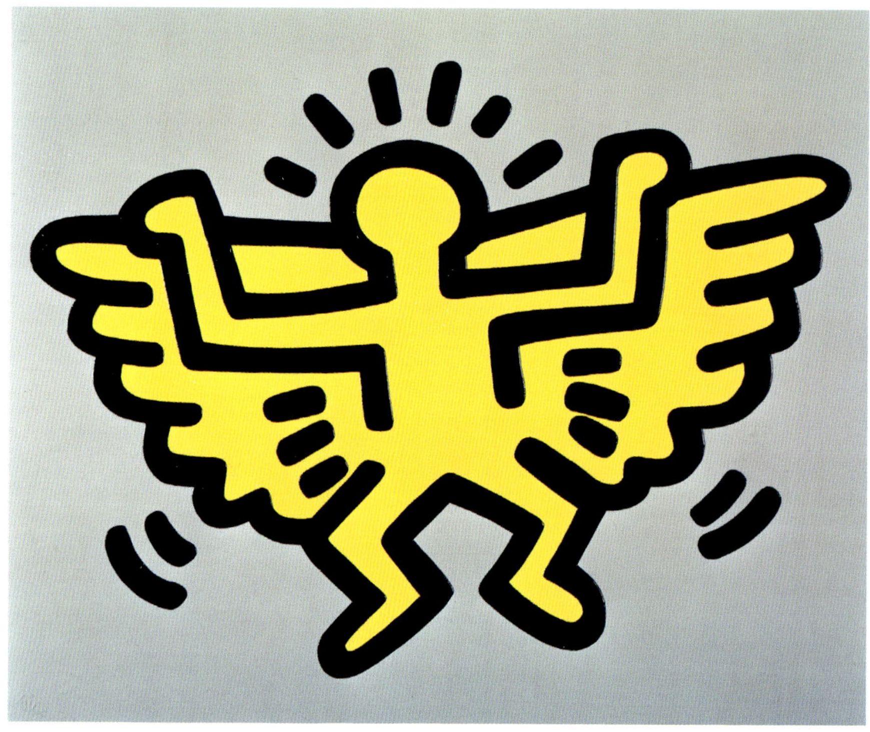

2.22. Keith Haring (1958–1990).
Icons ©—Winged Angel, 1990.
Silkscreen with embossing,
21 × 25 in. (53.3 × 63.5 cm).

wearing sexy, skimpy lingerie (plate 2.23). As a *New York Times* reporter noted, the company's name cleverly "referred to male fantasies of prim Victorian ladies who became naughty in the boudoir."[7] That concept of a dual feminine nature took visual form when, starting in 1998, the models in the Victoria's Secret Fashion Show began wearing elaborate angel wings. The effectiveness of the strategy depended on a prevailing sense of the positive connotations of angels.

The most recent chapter in Victoria's Secret's shape-shifting occurred in 2021. In response to falling sales and the tenor of the times, the company made a dramatic move away from supermodels and started hiring women "famous for their achievements and not their proportions."[8] They included Megan Rapinoe, the pink-haired soccer star and gender equity campaigner, and Eileen Gu, a seventeen-year-old Chinese American freestyle skier: angels, but without wings.

The desire for flight, and the freedom it implied, appeared early in the human psyche and has endured in modern popular media. The character of Peter Pan was invented by the Scottish novelist and playwright J. M. Barrie. Although he did not have wings, Peter flew, and that ability represented his free spirit. Peter appeared in many works in many media, but most memorably in the 1953 Walt Disney animated film. The thrill of flying was communicated in the lively lyrics of a song from the film:

> Think of the happiest things, that's the way to get your wings.
> Now you own a candy store. Look, you're rising off the floor.
> Don't wonder how or why.
> You can fly! You can fly! You can fly!

The same aspiration as that of stone age humans.

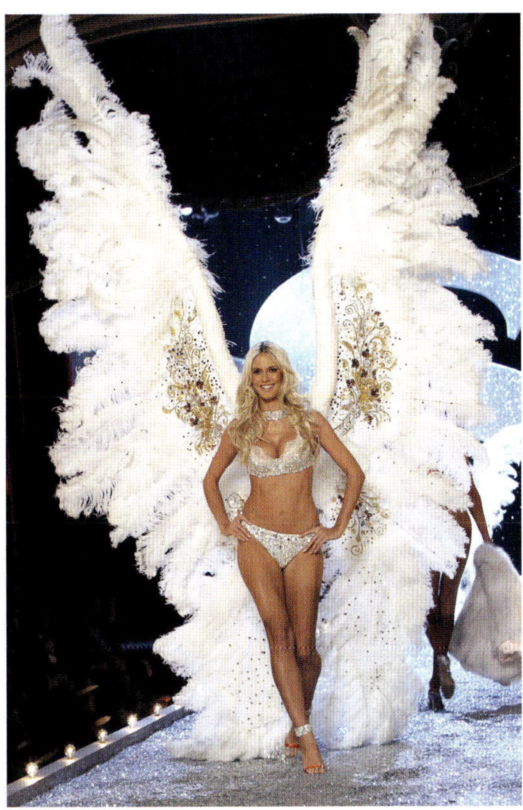

2.23. Heidi Klum in the 2003 Victoria's Secret Fashion Show.

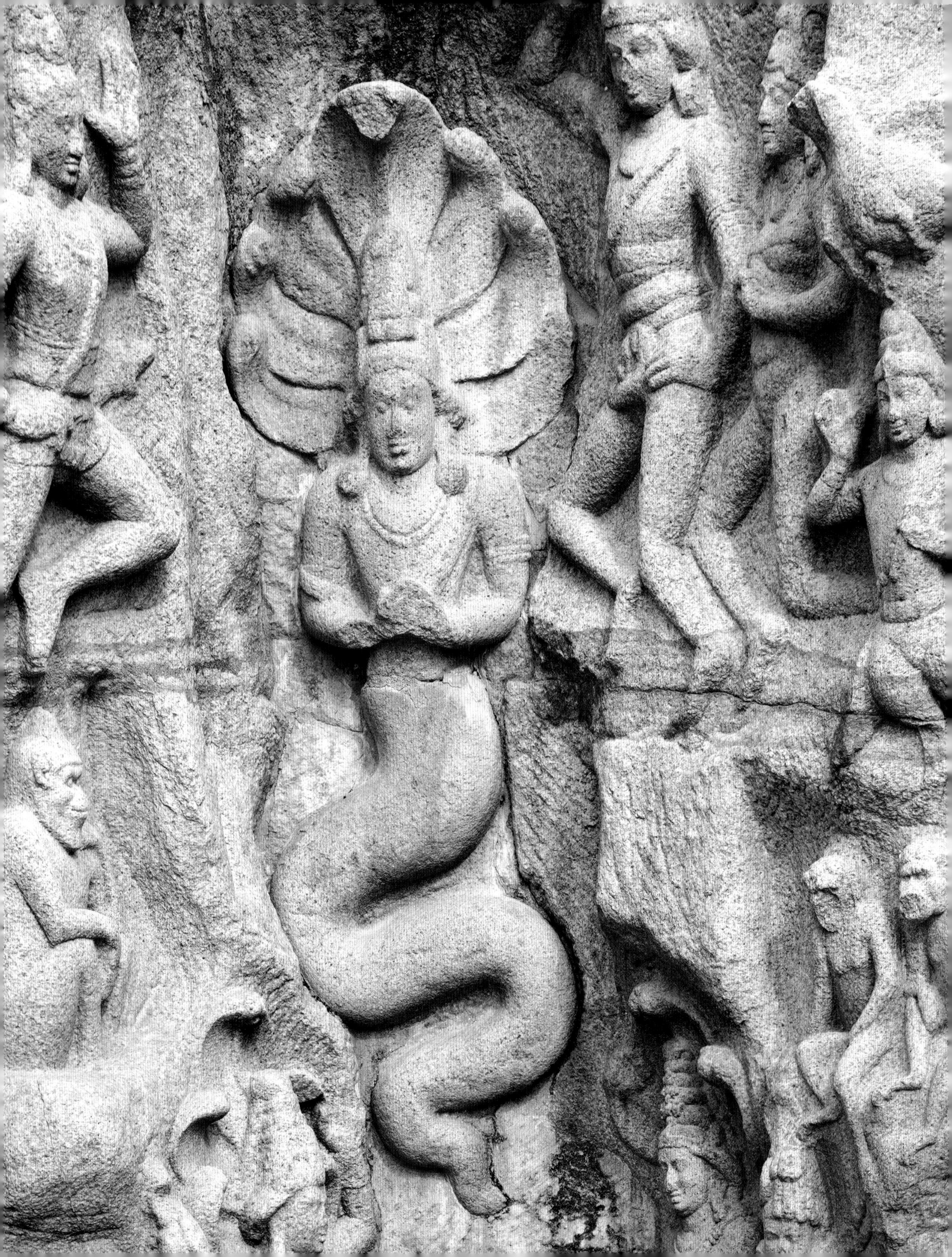

3
SERPENT-HUMANS

Detail of Naga in the Descent of the Ganges monument at Mahabalipuram. See plate 3.6.

We can understand how early humans could identify with tigers or eagles. We can imagine how they could aspire to the strength and speed of the tiger, or the eagle's freedom of flight; how, in dreams or altered states of consciousness, they could imagine taking on the attributes of the creatures they admired. But how about snakes? How did those slinky and shimmery creatures, to which many have an intrinsic aversion, enter into mythology? It may have been that the snake's shedding of its skin suggested reincarnation or that it seemingly emerges from an underworld. Or early humans' elevated respect for snakes may simply have derived from the fact that fear can produce reverence. In any case, serpents (a more general term that includes sea creatures) are some of the oldest and most widespread mythological symbols. Often, in their earliest manifestations, they can communicate with humans, and often they are part human.

It is difficult to communicate the complexity of early myths concerning therianthropes. Through time and in different cultures, they took different forms, evolved, and gave rise to other creatures. Take as an example the serpent-woman Echidna (plate 3.1), who has been called the "mother of all monsters" because of the multitude of her offspring as recounted by various Greek authors. There are five different versions of her parentage and several accounts of her character, although most describe her as vicious and a consumer of human flesh. Among her offspring, according to different texts, are the multiheaded dog Cerberus, who guarded the gates of Hades; another two-headed dog; a many-headed serpent who grew two more heads when one was cut off; a fire-breathing beast that was part lion, part goat, with a snake-headed tail; and the Sphinx, a monster with the head of a woman and the body of a winged lion. And each personality and offspring was described in—often gory—detail.

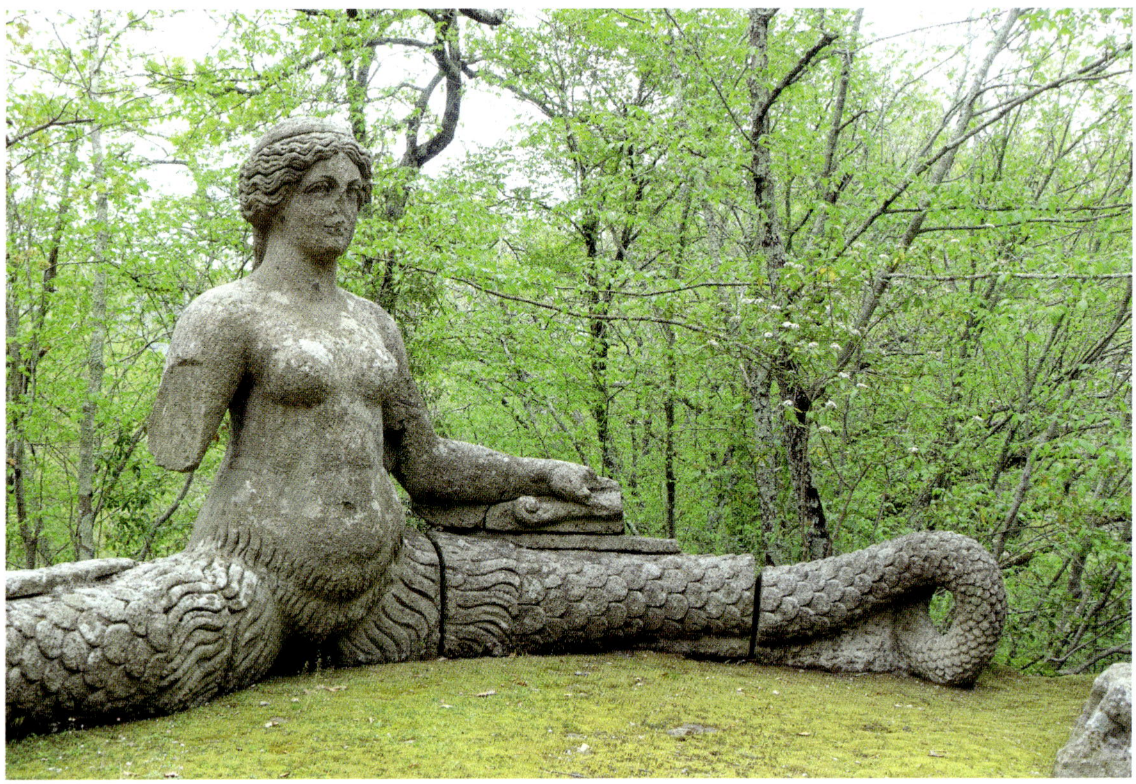

3.1. ABOVE: Simone Moschino (1553–1610). *Echidna*. Sacro Bosco, Bomarzo, Italy.

The many versions of particular therianthropes and the way in which they multiply and change through time demonstrate two phenomena: the abundance of creative storytellers at various times and in various cultures, and the large appetite in their audiences for myths about these creatures. The myths were important and must have reflected something deep within the imagination of both their creators and their consumers.

Mythological snake-humans range from the most evil of creatures, like Echidna, to the most kind and benevolent. The ancient Greek Lamia has at various times been both. According to myth, Hera learned that her husband, Zeus, was having a tryst with a beautiful woman, Lamia. Hera killed Lamia's children, and Lamia, in her rage and grief, was transformed into a child-eating monster, half woman, half serpent. Lamia's character continued to evolve through time, and in John Keats's poem *Lamia*, she has become a more positive—and alluring—enchantress, as shown in Isobel Lilian Gloag's painting inspired by the poem (plate 3.2).

3.2. OPPOSITE: Isobel Lilian Gloag (1865–1917). *The Kiss of the Enchantress*, c. 1890. Watercolor, 24⅜ × 12⅝ in. (62 × 32 cm). Private collection.

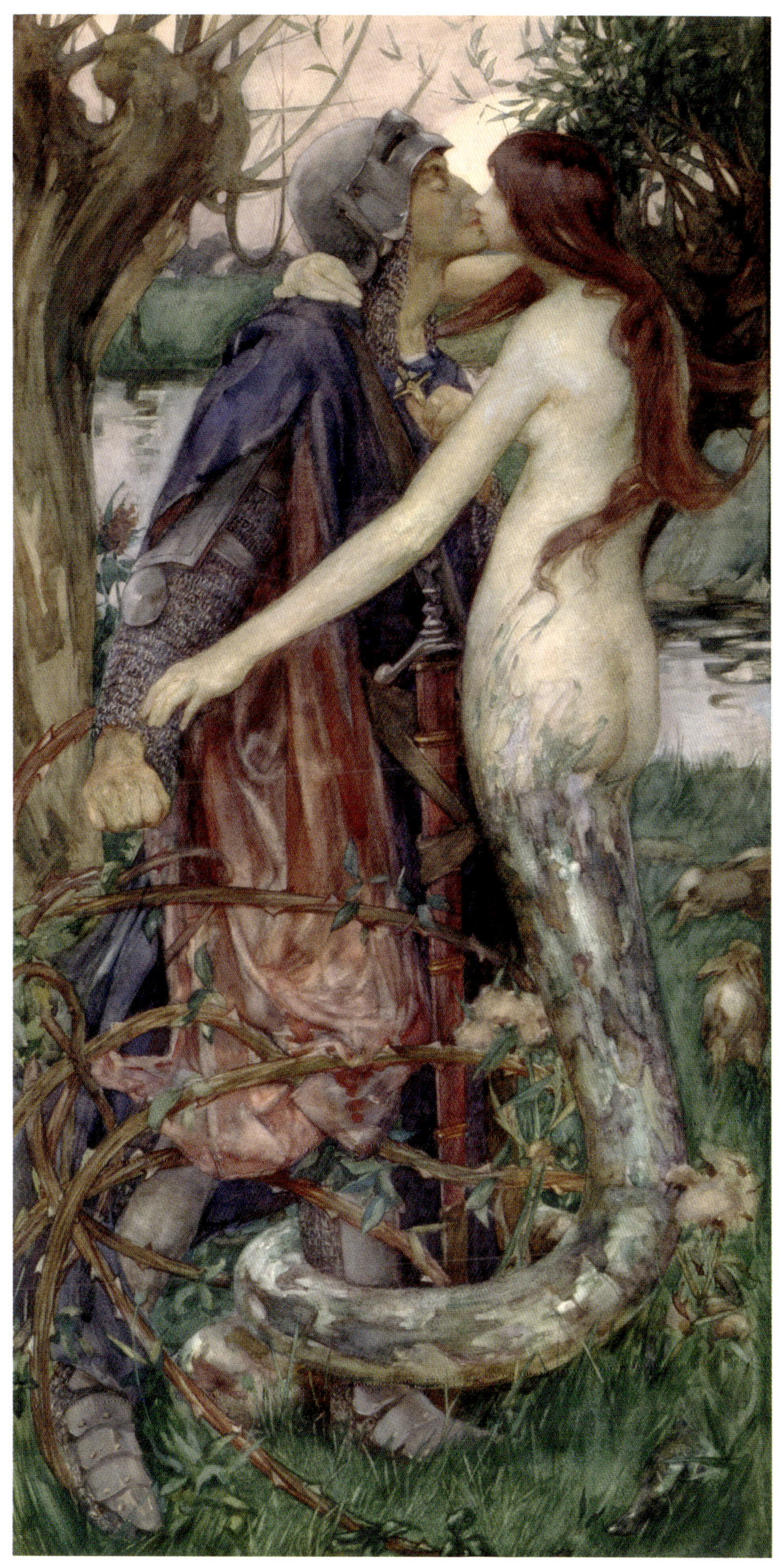

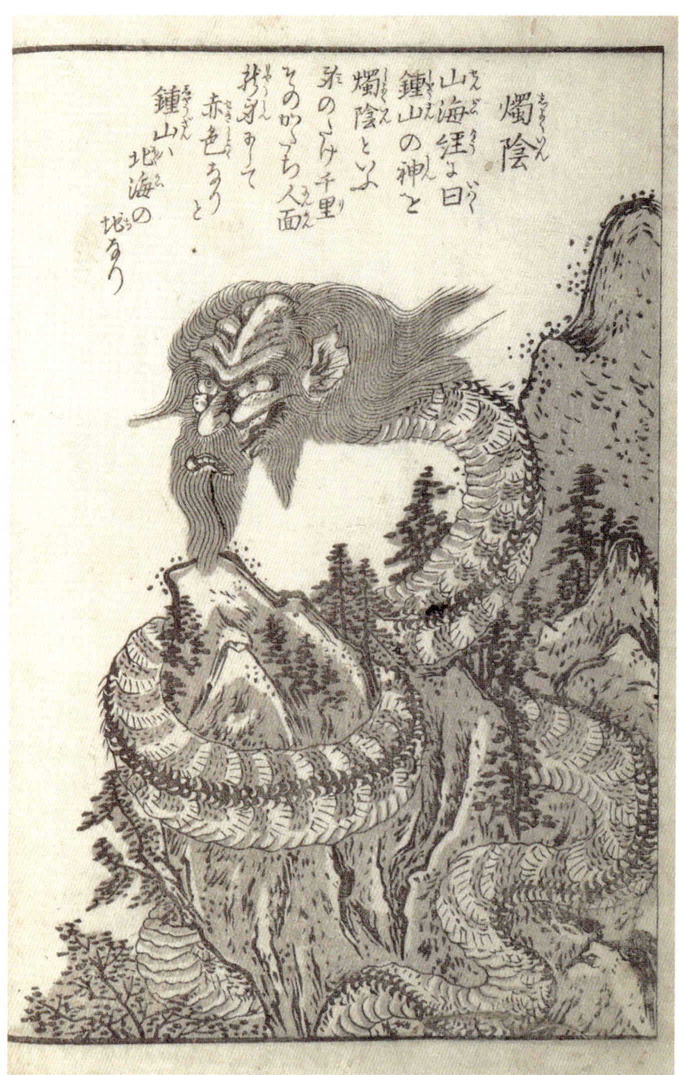

3.3. Toriyama Sekein (1712–1788). Zhulong, from *One Hundred Monsters Ancient and Modern*. Woodblock-printed book, 8⅞ × 6¼ in. (22.5 × 16 cm). Metropolitan Museum of Art, New York.

Early Chinese mythology contains some of the most prominent—and imaginative—combinations of snakes and humans. The deity Zhulong has a human face and a snake's body that extends for a thousand miles (plate 3.3). According to *The Classic of Mountains and Seas*, "When this deity's eyes look out there is daylight, and when he shuts his eyes there is night. When he blows it is winter, and when he calls out it is summer."

The name Zhulong means "torch dragon," connecting this therianthrope to the idea of the dragon, which is so important in Chinese culture. (The concept of the dragon may also have been inspired by large migrating crocodiles, now extinct.)

The most elevated snake-human deities in Chinese mythology are Fuxi, the imagined first emperor of China, and his sister Nüwa (plate 3.4). Fuxi's miraculous birth, as a divine being with a serpent's body, is said to have occurred in the twenty-ninth century BC. He was one of humanity's original ancestors and brought writing, fishing, and the domestication of animals to humankind. Fuxi is just one example of the mythological figures who are credited with bringing the means of survival and the elements of culture to our species. Well before the discovery of genetic and cultural evolution, myths explained human origins.

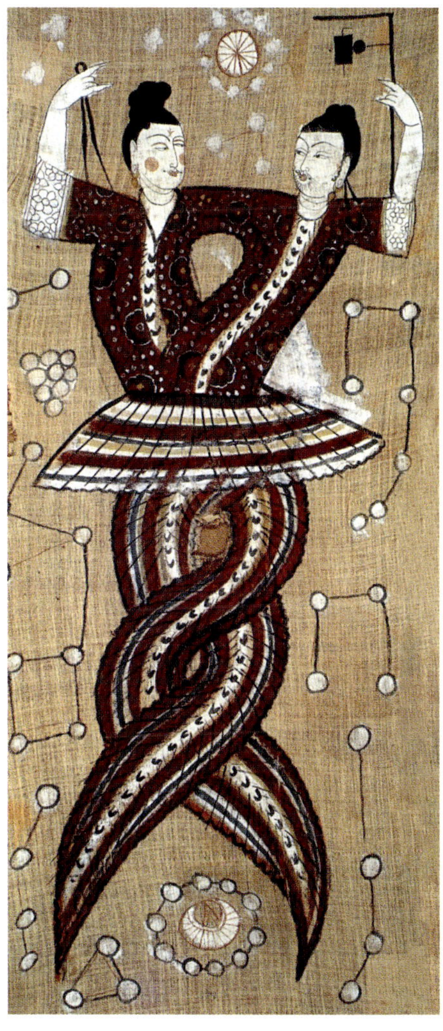

3.4. Hanging scroll of Fuxi and Nüwa. Chinese, Tang Dynasty, mid-eighth century BC. Color on silk, 72½ × 33½ in. (184 × 85 cm). Xinjiang Uighur Autonomous Region Museum, Urumqi.

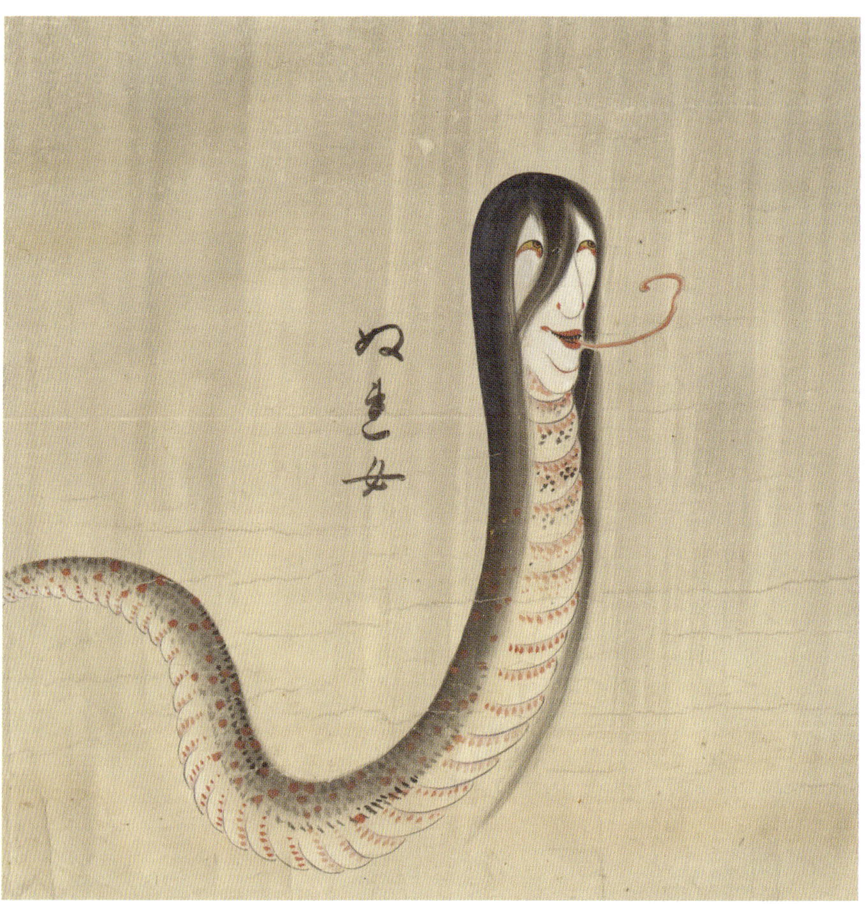

3.5. Nure-onna, detail of *Bakemono no e*, c. 1700. Scroll, 17⅜ in. × 50 ft. (0.44 × 15.25 m). Harry F. Bruning Collection of Japanese Books and Manuscripts, L. Tom Perry Collections, Harold B. Lee Library, Brigham Young University.

A broad assortment of serpent-humans populates early Japanese folklore. Although they have a wide variety of shapes, most are female, and best avoided. The Nure-onna, for example, has the head of a woman and the body of a snake (plate 3.5). There are many variants of the Nure-onna, but none is very appealing. Some have reptilian bodies a thousand feet long. They devour anyone who comes close, and even fell large trees with their monstrous tails.

Serpent-humans also play a prominent role in Hinduism and Buddhism. Nagas are a category of creatures that combine human and snake features, often those of the king cobra (plate 3.6). They appear in many early myths and can do either good or evil. Nagas participate in a rare confrontation between different therianthropes. The Mahabharata, an ancient Indian epic, tells the story of a legendary dynastic struggle in which the very numerous Nagas are locked in ceaseless battle with their half-sibling, the man-eagle Garuda.

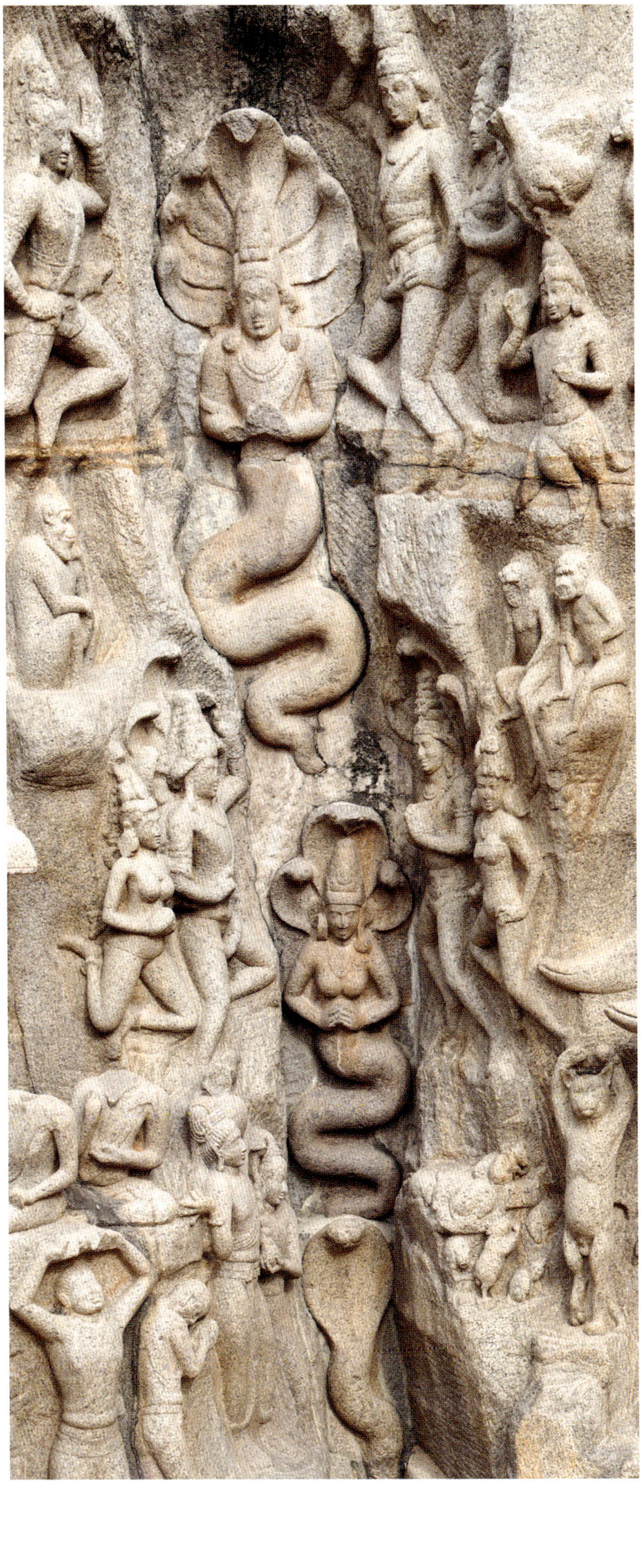

3.6. LEFT: Detail of Nagas in the Descent of the Ganges monument, 7th century AD. Relief carved in granite boulders. Mahabalipuram, Chengalpattu district, Tamil Nadu, India.

3.7. BELOW: Cecrops, the serpent-king of Athens. Engraving after a Greek vase found in Palermo, Sicily.

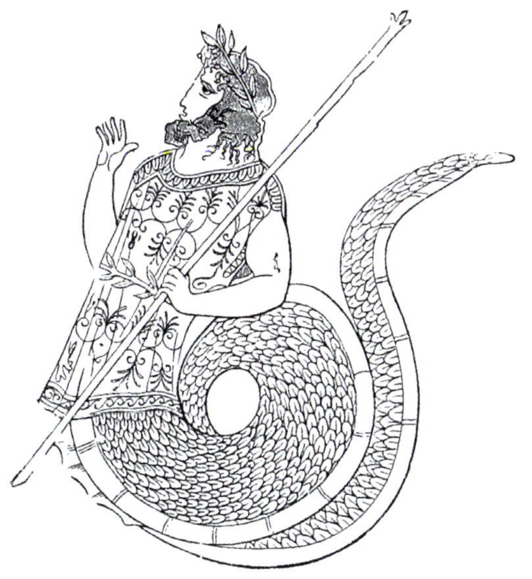

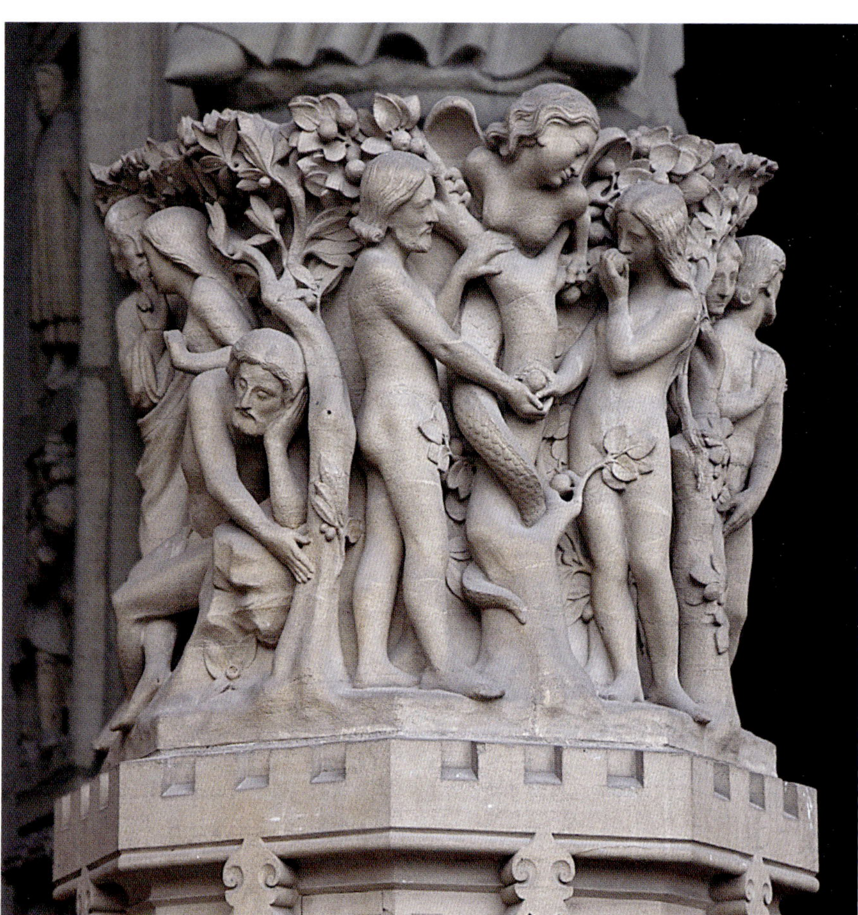

3.8. The temptation of Adam and Eve by the serpent, on the pedestal of the statue of the Madonna and Child on the western portal of Notre Dame, Paris, 1210–20.

In contrast to the elevated status of Chinese snake gods, the serpent plays a notably negative role in Judeo-Christian tradition. Like many later animal-humans, the Bible's snake-human probably derives from a creature in Greek mythology such as Cecrops, the serpent-king of Athens (plate 3.7).

According to the Bible, all was going well in God's creation of the world, including man and woman, until the serpent appeared. The serpent, the "most subtle" of all the wild creatures that God had made, tempted Eve to partake of the fruit of the forbidden tree of the knowledge of good and evil. Eve shared the fruit, and the loss of innocence, with Adam. In retribution, God condemned the snake to crawl on its belly and eat dust all the days of its life.

In some artistic renderings, the serpent in the Garden of Eden is a mere snake, but medieval Christian artists often depicted it with the head of a woman. The carving of the serpent's perfidy at the base of a statue of the Madonna and Child at Notre Dame in Paris is a stunning example of sculptural richness (plate 3.8). Not only does this eloquent work depict the temptation of Eve by a serpent with the bust of a woman and her sharing of the apple with Adam, but also (around to the left) the creation of Eve from Adam's rib and (to the right) the expulsion of the two of them from the garden.

The rather surprising appeal of snake-humans continued into the Middle Ages in Europe. Melusine appears in many legends in France, Luxembourg, and the Low Countries during that time. She is occasionally depicted as a mermaid, but usually as a woman who is a serpent from the waist down, and sometimes she has wings as well. There are several versions of Melusine's story, but many have a common element. When she agrees to marry a prince, a condition is that he not view her at certain times, as when she is giving birth or on Saturdays, because that's when she appears with her serpent tail. Of course he doesn't obey, and dire consequences follow. In one version she turns into a dragon and flies away forever (plate 3.9).

3.9. Melusine's secret discovered, from the Roman de Mélusine by Jean d'Arras, c. 1450–1500. Bibliothèque Nationale de France, Paris, MS Fr. 24383, fol. 19.

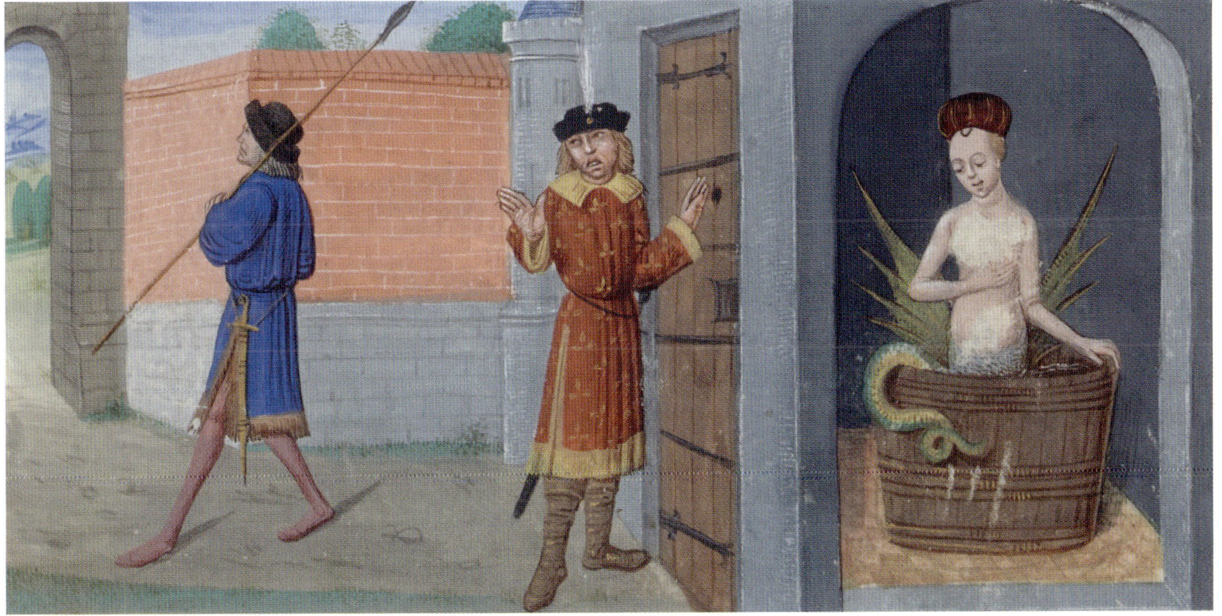

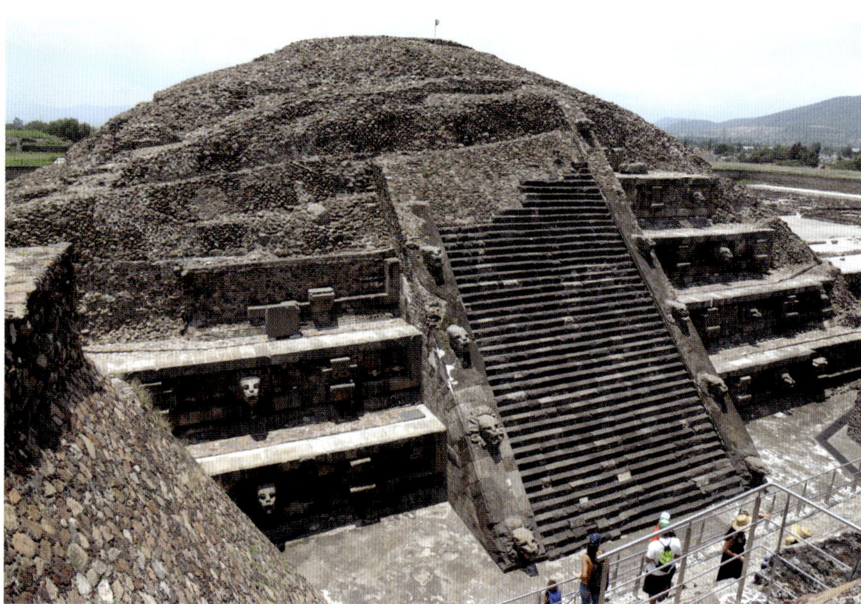

3.10. Temple of the Feathered Serpent, second century AD. Teotihuacan, Mexico.

We think of therianthropes as fanciful mythological figures, but through history many animal-humans have been seriously worshipped, even sacrificed to. In the 1980s, evidence of human sacrifice was found in the Temple of the Feathered Serpent, a pyramid of the second century AD at Teotihuacan in Mexico (plates 3.10 and 3.11). Known by the Aztecs as Quetzalcoatl, the feathered serpent went through various transformations, from an actual snake to a deity with human features. He also had various roles, from god of the wind and the dawn to protector of learning and knowledge to patron god of the Aztecs. The earliest depiction of Quetzalcoatl is at the Olmec site of La Venta and dates to about 900 BC.

Among the roughly two hundred human bodies found buried beneath the pyramid at Teotihuacan, many were of men attired as warriors with their hands tied behind their backs. It is speculated that they had been sacrificed at the dedication of the temple. All this to win favor with a therianthrope.

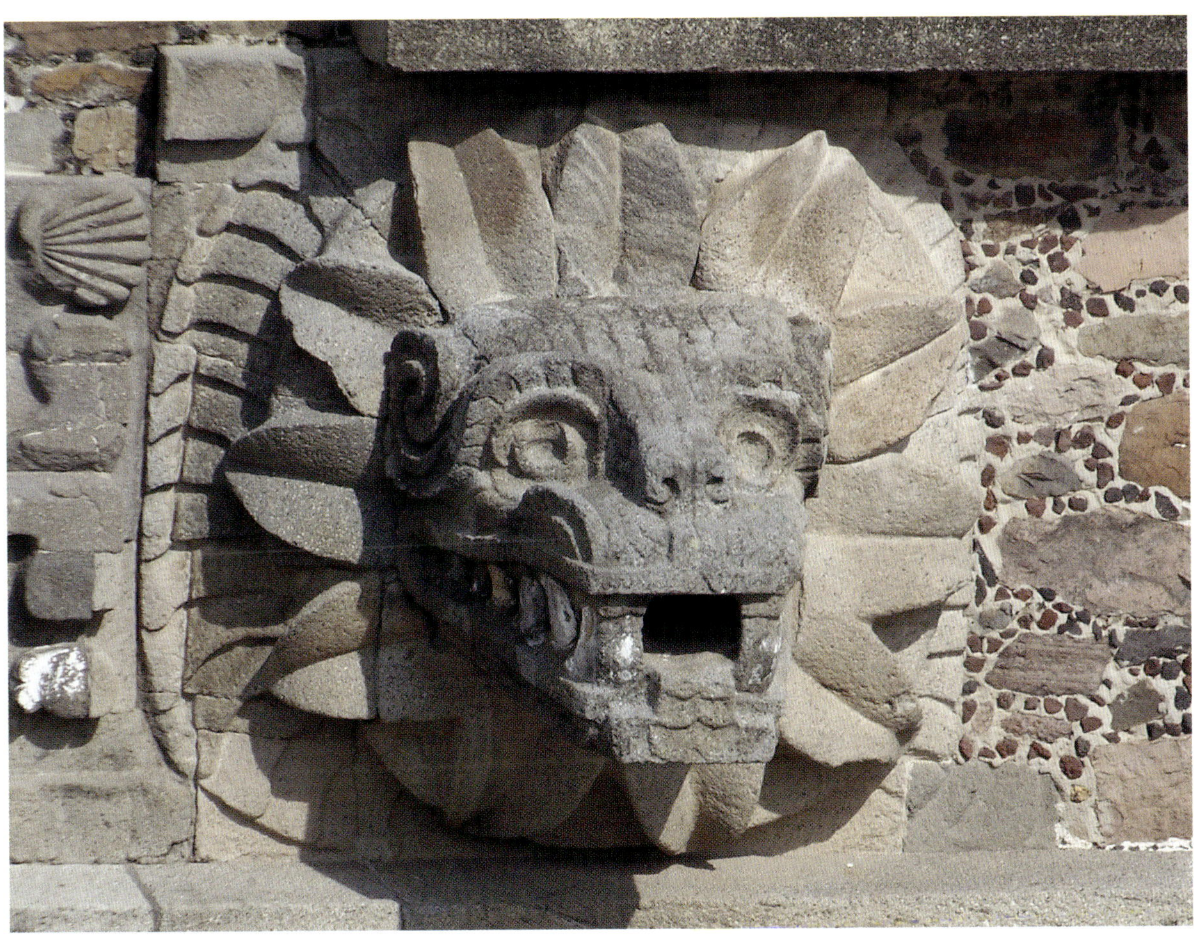

3.11. Feathered serpent head. Temple of the Feathered Serpent, second century AD. Teotihuacan, Mexico.

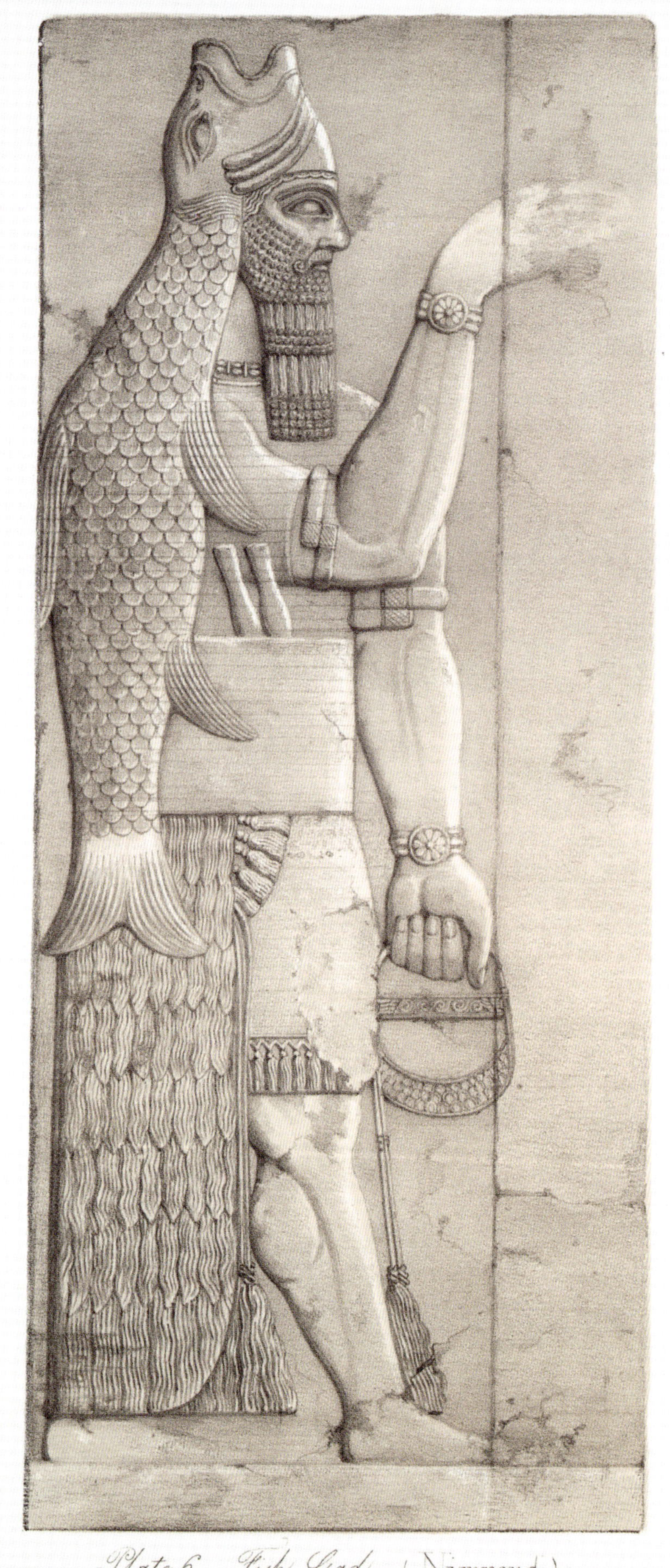

Plate 6 — Fish God (Nimroud)

4
MERPEOPLE

4.1. Drawing of a bas-relief of an Apkallu from the Temple of Ninurta at Nimrud, 865 BC. From *A Second Series of the Monuments of Nineveh*, ed. Austen Henry Layard (London, 1853).

There are all sorts of mythological combinations of humans and animals: we have already examined animal-headed humans, winged beings, and serpent-humans. But some combinations have been more popular than others over time and across cultures. Some are simply more appealing. They are favored by the creators of legends, by the artists who give them presence, and by humans generally.

It is reasonable that winged creatures, including winged humans, are widespread. After all, for early humans, indeed even for us today, wings represent an enticing form of freedom. And envy was a likely stimulus for imagining creatures. For some reason, merpeople, combinations of humans and fish, also appeared early in human history and are remarkably common in different cultures.[1] They exemplify the deep-seated appeal of therianthropes, and how the human imagination and art enrich and diversify them through time.

The prevalence of merpeople in myth may be related to the importance of water to human survival. It may also be related to the early and widespread accounts of dramatic floods. Accounts of a deluge imposed by a deity existed well before the tale of Noah's flood in the Book of Genesis (which dates to the sixth century BC). The Babylonian myth that has Gilgamesh as its hero originated in 2100 BC. In one version, a god decides to destroy the world with a flood because humans have become too noisy. But he alerts one devotee and instructs him how to build a boat so that life on earth can be saved.

There is disagreement among scholars as to whether the flood myths were inspired by actual floods, and if so, when and where those floods occurred. But unanticipated river floods must have had dire consequences for early farmers, and must have given rise to preventive rituals. It is also possible that the rising seas after the last Ice Age could have stimulated a myth that continued in later cultures. Sea levels rose gradually for millennia after the last glacial maximum around 21,000 years ago. The rise was more rapid, however, around 15,000 years ago (in a "meltwater pulse"). An early origin of the great flood myths would be consistent with their widespread occurrence. We find such myths in ancient Egypt, Greece, China, India, and Scandinavia, and floods also feature in the creation myths of the Toltec, Aztec, and Mayan cultures.

Remarkable evidence of early fish-human worship has been found at Lepenski Vir on the banks of the Danube River in Serbia. The site was inhabited by a hunter-fisher-gatherer society from as early as 9500 BC. Boulders carved with fish-human hybrids have been found near the burials of children and adults dating to around 6000 BC (plate 4.2). This may indicate a belief in the concept of human metamorphosis into a kind of fish-human being.

When we think of combinations of fish and humans, we usually think of mermaids, but mermen seem to predate mermaids. As with many therianthropes, the first recorded merman appeared with the invention of writing

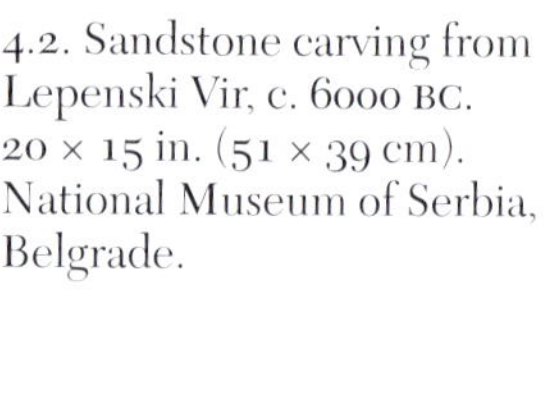

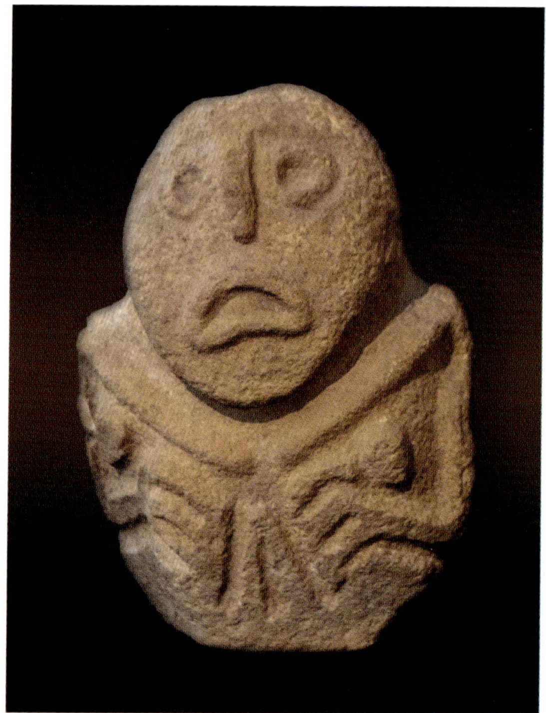

4.2. Sandstone carving from Lepenski Vir, c. 6000 BC. 20 × 15 in. (51 × 39 cm). National Museum of Serbia, Belgrade.

in Mesopotamia.[2] Sumerian religion refers to an era "before the flood" when the god Enki sent seven demigods, called Apkallu, to bring civilization to mankind. One of the Apkallu was the fish-human god Oannes, who emerged from the ocean every day to teach humans about geometry, science, art, and written language. He also taught them how to compile laws, and how to construct temples and cities: just about everything, in fact.

The Apkallu represented in a bas-relief from the Temple of Ninurta at the Assyrian city of Nimrud, dating from around 865 BC, represents the god as a man wearing the skin of a fish (plate 4.1). It is reminiscent of the not-implausible theory that certain therianthropes originated with humans garbing themselves in animal hides. For example, it has been claimed that the Lion-Man represents a human wearing the head and skin of a lion in preparation for a hunt.

Even if mermaids are not as old as mermen, they appear even more widely in mythologies around the world. While mermaids may well have existed in oral traditions, the first written record of a mermaid, the Assyrian goddess Atargatis, appeared well after Oannes. As a human, Atargatis fell in love with a fellow mortal, a shepherd, and unintentionally killed him. Ashamed, she jumped into a lake intending to drown herself, but survived when she was transformed into a mermaid. Mermaids have represented many things and have had many roles in their multiple incarnations, but Atargatis became a goddess of fertility, reflecting the lush bounty of the ocean. She may have been an inspiration for the Greek goddess Aphrodite, and her story is reflected in the tales of mermaids in other cultures.

Along with their meanings, representations of merpeople have evolved over time. The Babylonian sea god Oannes, for example, had a man's head below his fish head and both a fish tail and human legs. The appearance of Oannes became more reasonable (if a fish-man can ever be reasonable) when he became Triton in Greek mythology, the son of Poseidon and Amphitrite. In ancient Greek art, Triton was depicted as a pure and powerful merman: half-man, half-fish. Triton was unusual in that he was also identified with music, or at least sound, as he was shown playing his conch shell like a trumpet to calm or agitate the seas. In later antiquity, *triton* became a generic term for a merman.

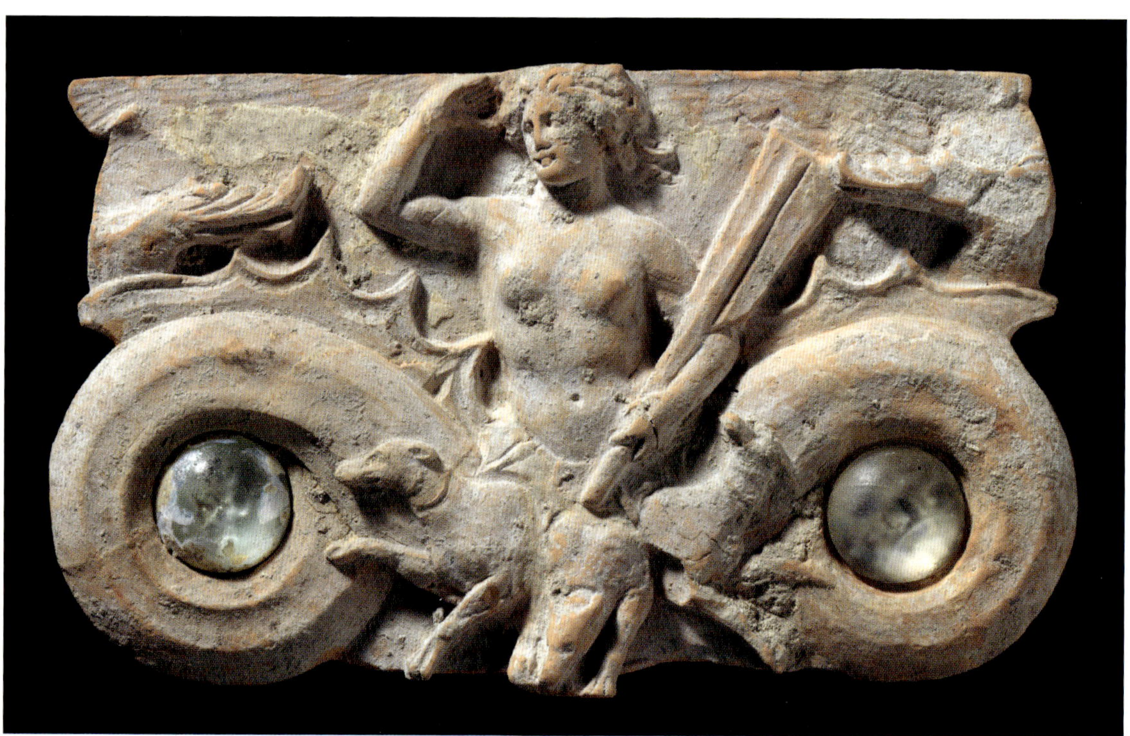

4.3. Plaque with a representation of Scylla. Greek, from southern Italy, fourth century BC. Terra-cotta with glass inlays, 5¾ in. (14.5 cm) long. Metropolitan Museum of Art, New York.

Therianthropes change over time and some even become embedded in modern parlance. "You are an angel!" If you want to describe having to choose between two risky moves, you can say "I was between a rock and a hard place," but you can also say (if you don't mind sounding snobbish) "I was between Scylla and Charybdis." In Homer's *Odyssey*, Odysseus had to navigate carefully between a huge whirlpool, identified with the sea monster Charybdis, on one side, and the hybrid monster Scylla on the other. Scylla was a horrific beast with a huge appetite for human flesh (plate 4.3). In her original manifestation she was part woman, part fish, with six heads each with three rows of teeth "full of black death." It's a wonder of therianthropic evolution that this monster developed into the lovely thing we now know as a mermaid.

Mermaids exist in the mythology of various regions of Japan. They vary in form and character, but several are vicious and use a baby to attract their victims. One variant carries with her a small bundle that is apparently a child. She offers the child to an interested woman, but the bundle turns into a heavy stone. Having disconcerted her victim with this trick, the mermaid uses her long tongue to suck the blood from her body.

In Western culture, mermaids played a role well beyond their mythological status. During the Middle Ages, they were used by the Christian church as instruments of persuasion. In sculptures in British churches, mermaids were presented as sexually attractive, lustful, and dangerous. They represented not only the sinful temptations of the flesh, but served to denigrate femininity and to reduce the status of women. The church may have considered mermaids as fictional, if useful, symbolic creatures, but the sculptures of mermaids persuaded many worshippers that they were real—and dangerous. A thirteenth-century bestiary shows a mermaid pulling a sailor into the water while her *onocentaur* (man-donkey) ally shoots an arrow from his bow (plate 4.4). Another sailor covers his ear to avoid hearing the alluring song of the mermaid, which is here conflated with the siren of Greek myth.

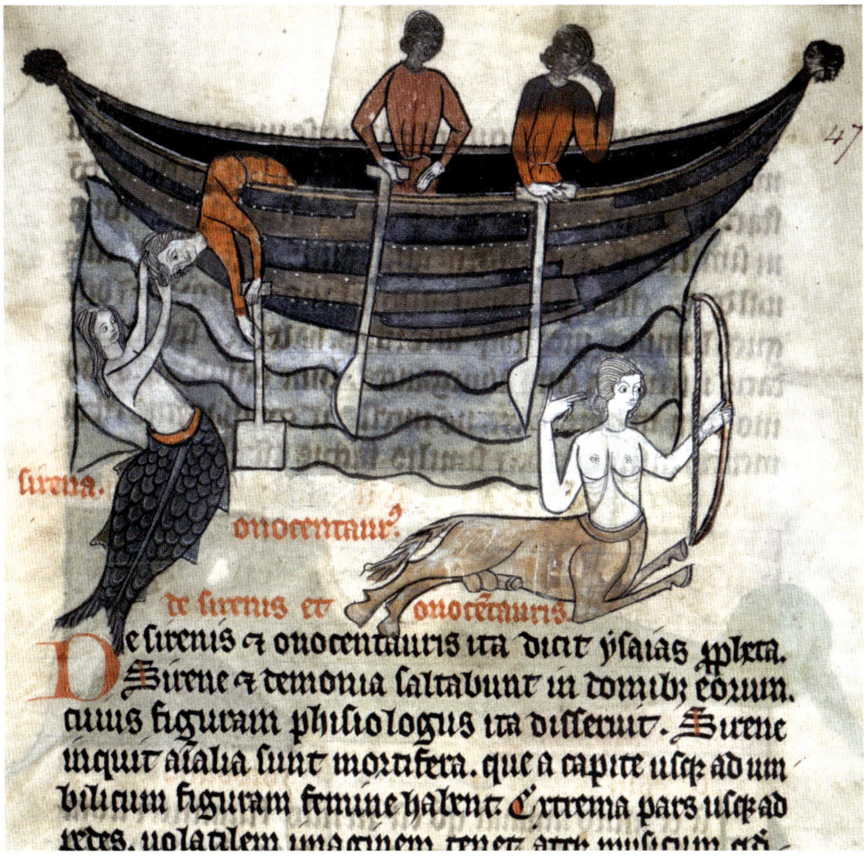

4.4. A mermaid and an onocentaur, from a northern French or Flemish bestiary, c. 1280–1300. British Library, London, Sloane MS 278, fol. 47.

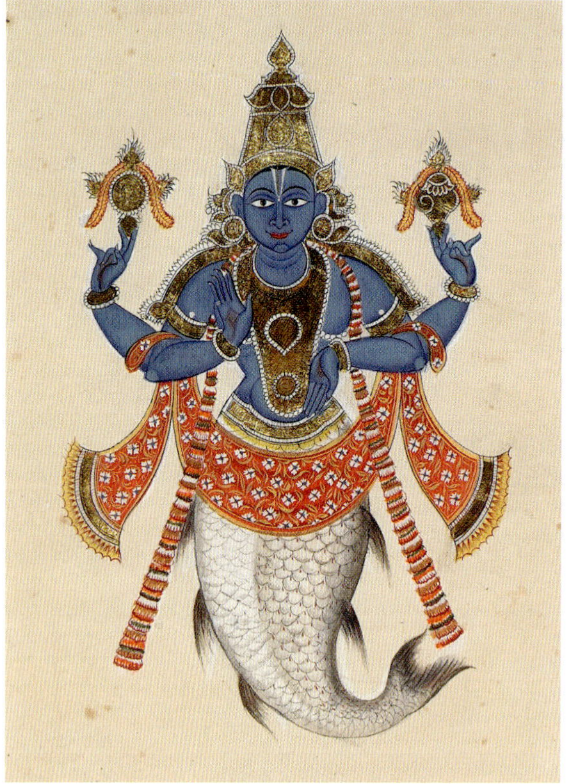

4.5. Matsya, avatar of Vishnu. Southern India, c. 1820. Paint and gold on paper, 11¾ × 8⅝ in. (28.5 × 21.8 cm). British Museum, London.

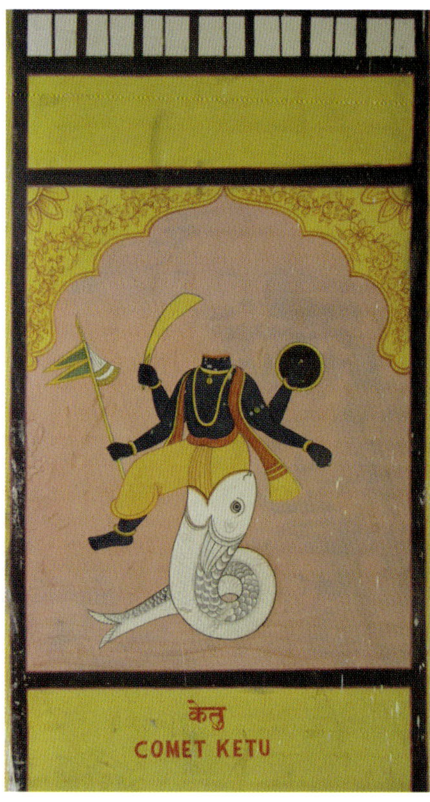

4.6. Contemporary mural of the planet Ketu. Jawahar Kala Kendra, Jaipur.

The concept of the merman had a broad appeal in India. The term *avatar*, derived from the Sanskrit word for "descent," is now used to refer to the embodiment of a concept in human form. Originally, however, it referred to an incarnation of the Hindu deity Vishnu. A principal avatar of Vishnu was Matsya, who took various fish-like forms, including that of a merman (plate 4.5). He was one of many mermen who warned a favored subject of an impending deluge, and thus helped save humanity.

One of the most imaginative, and oddest, fish-human combinations is Ketu, who appears in Hindu mythology and astrology. Referred to as a "shadow" planet, Ketu has a strong influence on human behavior, for both good and evil. But when it does harm, it is to induce a more spiritual outlook in the person affected. While various therianthropes have sported all sorts of animal and bird heads on human bodies, Ketu has no head at all, but the strong tail of a fish (plate 4.6).

A more conventional mermaid appears in the *Ramayana*, an epic poem originally composed in Sanskrit in ancient India and adapted into hundreds of versions in multiple languages throughout Asia. In the Thai version of the *Ramayana*, the mermaid Suvannamaccha is a prominent character. In one episode she undertakes to foil Hanuman's plans to build a bridge to an island fortress, but falls in love with him instead (plate 4.7). Suvannamaccha is popular to this day in Thailand, and her image is hung in houses and shops as a good luck charm.

In the West, the belief in merpeople only strengthened during the Renaissance, with mermaids and tritons often appearing in literature as well as in paintings and sculptures. As adventurers from Europe began to explore other lands, merpeople seemed to be obligatory discoveries. Christopher Columbus was just one of the many early explorers who vividly described sightings of mermaids. Most of the elaborately decorated maps

4.7. Mural of Suvannamaccha and Hanuman in the *Ramakien* (Thai *Ramayana*) mural cycle at the Wat Phra Kaew, Bangkok.

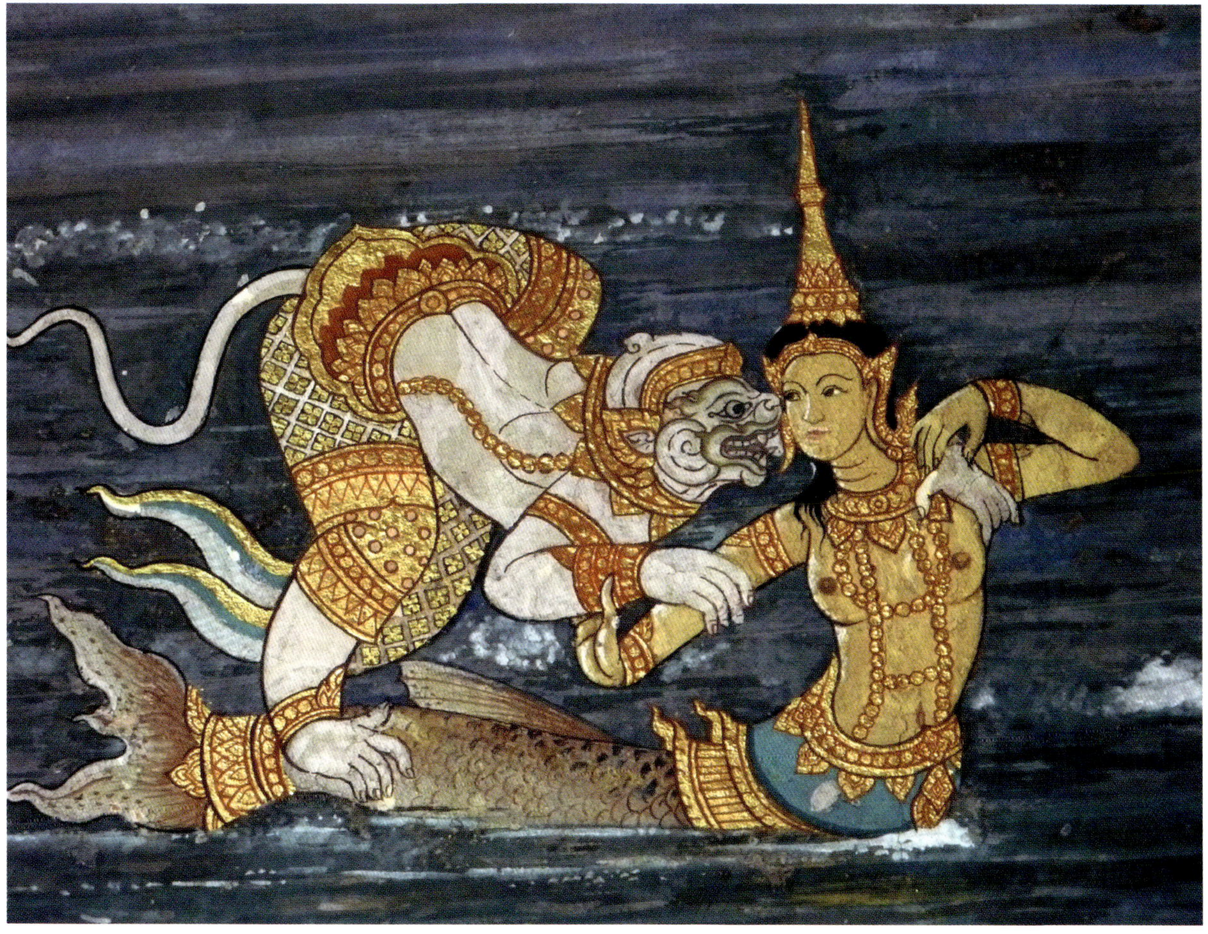

that included merpeople were not intended for navigation but to demonstrate the enlightenment of their wealthy owners (plate 4.8). Art once again encouraging a belief in therianthropes.

The belief in merpeople even survived the skepticism of the Enlightenment. Benjamin Franklin himself wrote in his *Pennsylvania Gazette* of a "sea monster" spotted off Bermuda. The creature had the upper body of a boy of about twelve, and the lower body of a fish.[3] Some naturalists, including the eminent Carl Linnaeus, even speculated that humans could have descended from merpeople.

For Western artists, the appeal of mermaids was irresistible. It certainly was for the Pre-Raphaelite painter Edward Coley Burne-Jones, who felt that a picture should be "a beautiful, romantic dream of something that never was, never will be—in a light better than any light that ever shone" (plate 4.9).[4] Burne-Jones's younger contemporary John William Waterhouse carried the romantic style of the Pre-Raphaelites into the early twentieth century. Waterhouse's portrayals of sirens and mermaids combined beauty, exoticism, and the aura of myth (plate 4.10).

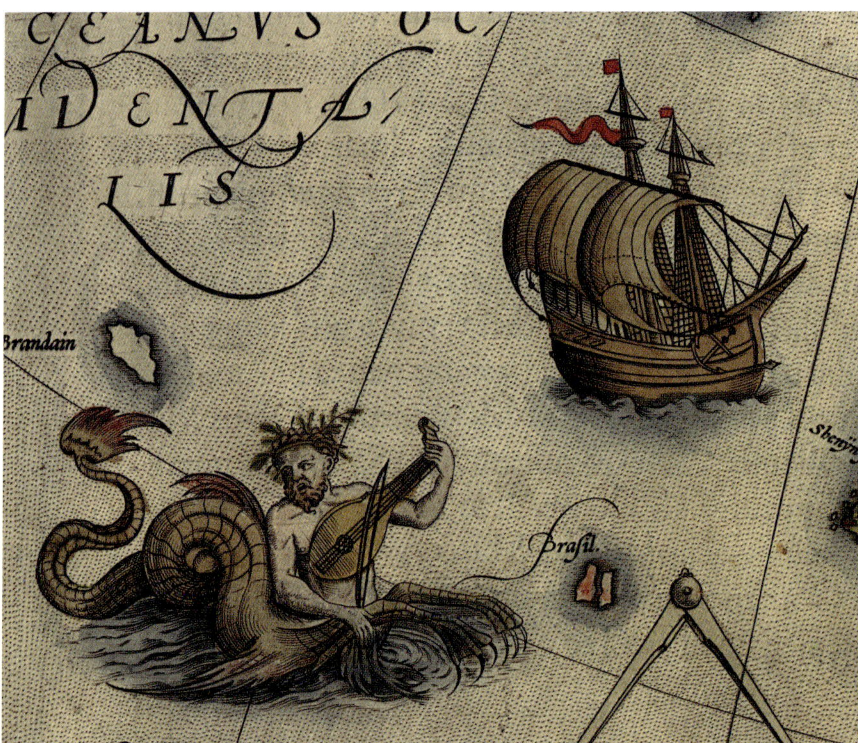

4.8. An ichthyocentaur playing a viol, from a map of Scandinavia in Abraham Ortelius's *Theatrum orbis terrarum* (Antwerp, 1570).

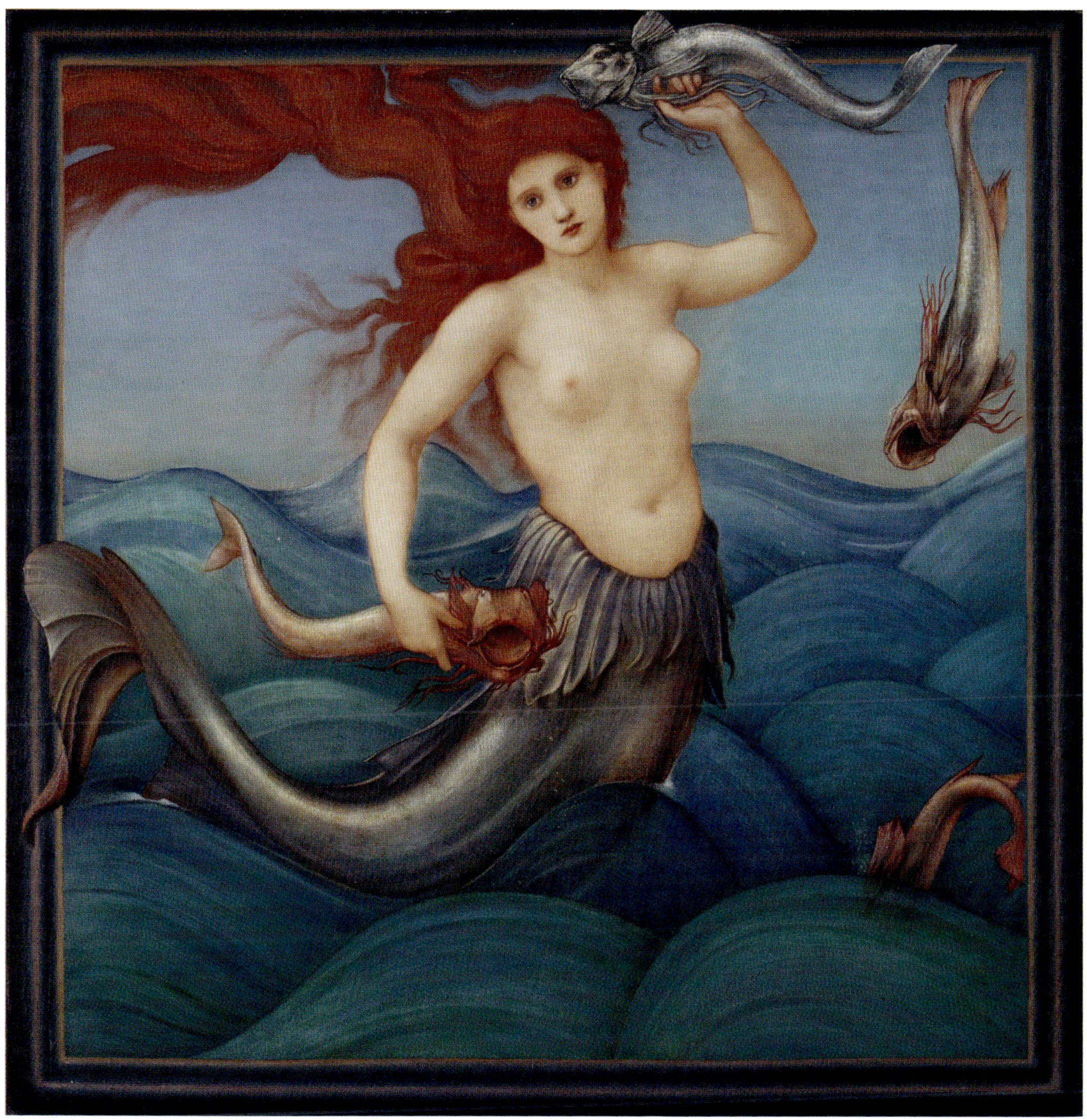

4.9. Sir Edward Coley Burne-Jones (1833–1898). *A Sea-Nymph*, 1881. Oil on canvas, 47¾ × 47¾ in. (121.3 × 121.3 cm). Minneapolis Institute of Art.

The siren is one of the many therianthropes whose physical form has changed with time and cultures. In ancient Greek art, sirens were portrayed as various combinations of birds and women. And they were dangerously attractive. In Homer's *Odyssey*, Odysseus's crew manages to resist the sirens' alluring song only by plugging their ears with wax. Over time, sirens were increasingly represented as mermaids—as we have already seen in the miniature from a medieval bestiary above—but were no less cunning.

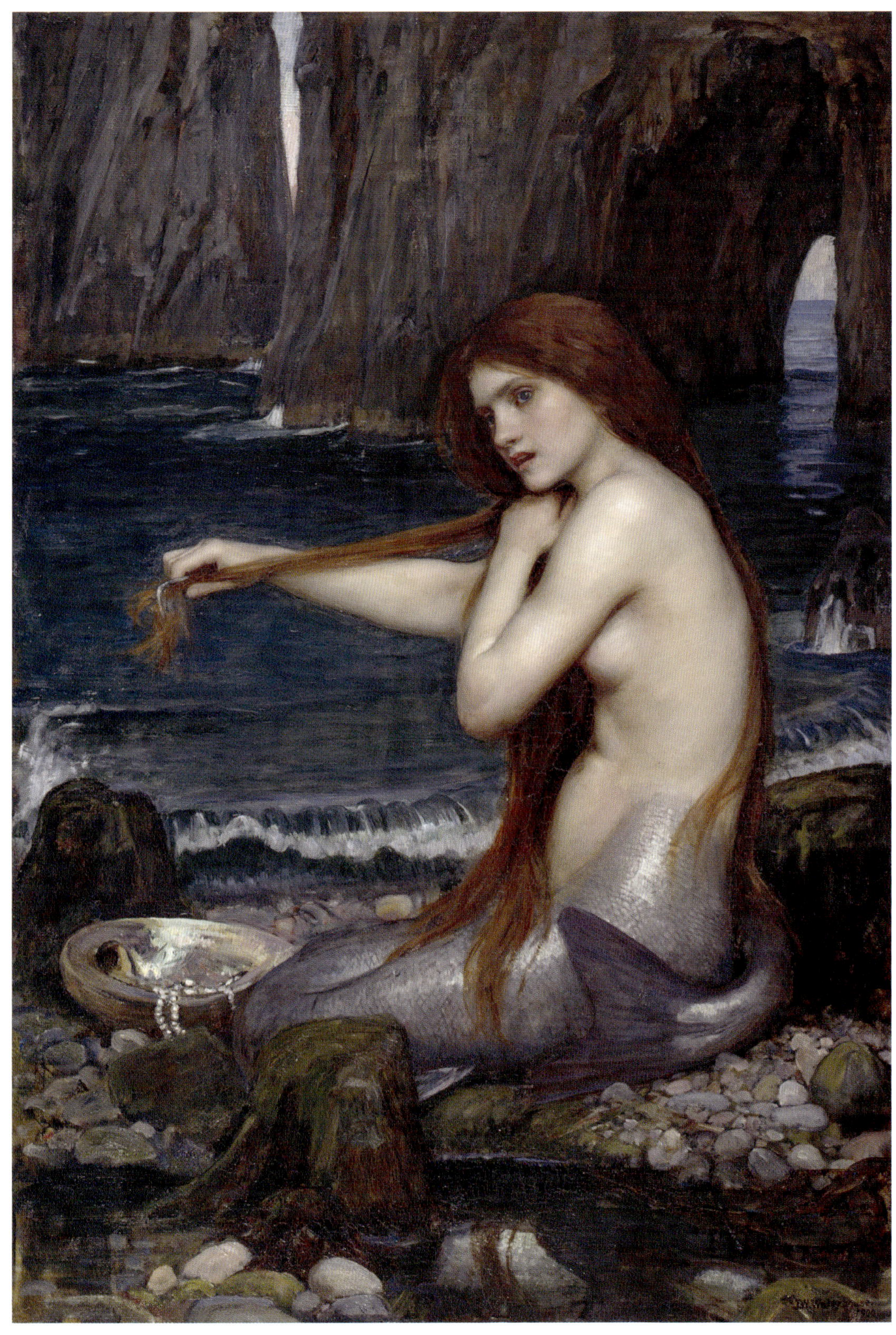

We consider mermaids to be fictional creatures, but for most of human history, since ancient Mesopotamia, they have been considered both real and divine. That unlikely combination of a fish and a woman appears in cultures around the world, from the Syrian goddess Derketo to the water spirits of the Karoo desert in South Africa to the merrows of the Irish coast.

4.10. OPPOSITE: John William Waterhouse (1849–1917). *A Mermaid*, 1900. Oil on canvas, 40 × 26¼ in. (96.5 × 66.6 cm). Royal Academy of Arts, London.

The protector of the world of water, the beautiful provider of spiritual and material well-being to her believers, Mami Wata was an early presence in East and West African belief systems who later traveled to the Caribbean and parts of South America. In Trinidad she became Mama Dlo, the healer and protector of the water and the animals that call it home, but she was no protector of humans. Like a siren, she rests beautifully at the shore, gently dipping her fingers in the water. But when she spies a polluter or fisherman, she bursts into action—her hair turns into snakes, and she strikes the offender dead. She protects the sea; she is the sea (plate 4.11).

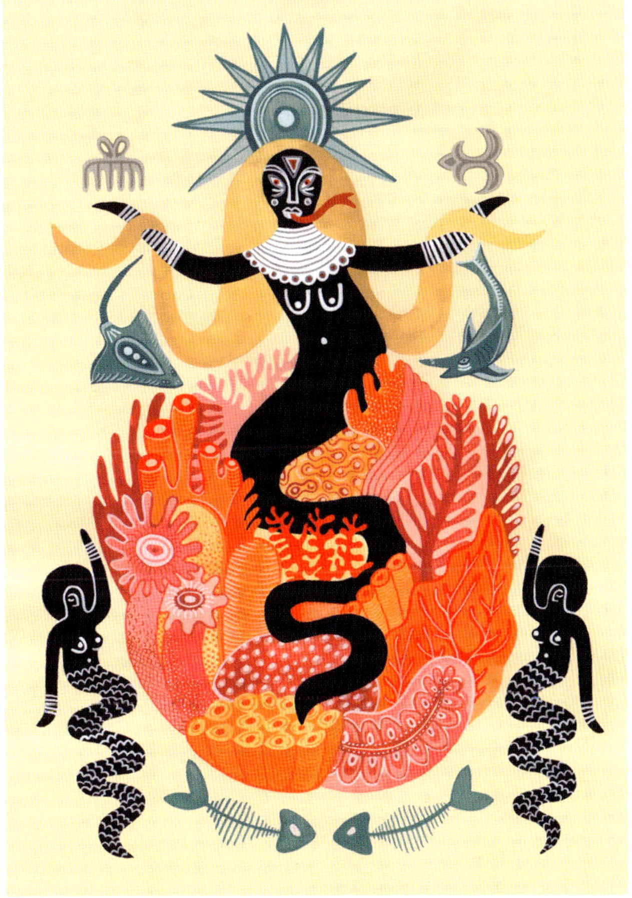

4.11. Sophie Bass (b. 1991). *Mama Dlo*, 2016. Gouache on paper, 11¾ × 8¼ in. (30 × 21 cm).

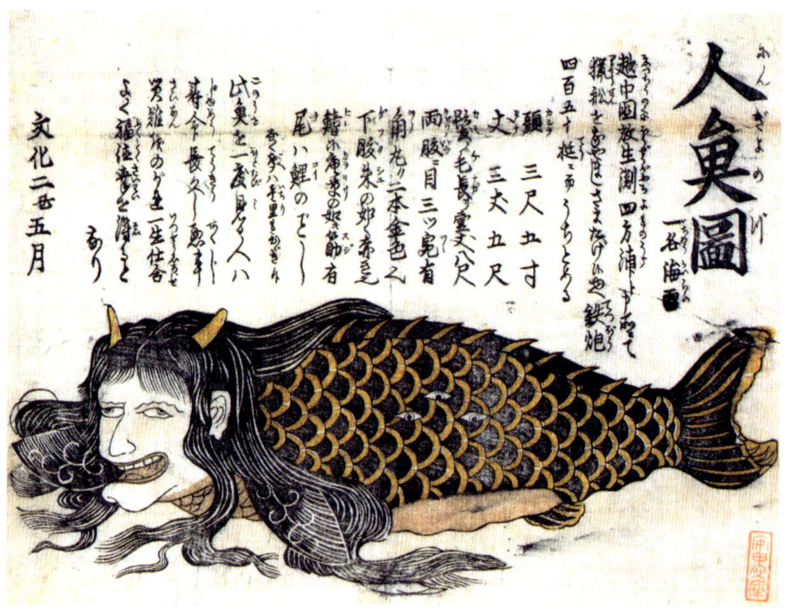

4.12. A woodblock-printed bulletin of 1805 depicting a *ningyo* allegedly caught in Toyama Bay. Tsubouchi Memorial Theatre Museum, Wasada University, Tokyo.

The mermaids of different cultures do not all look alike, nor are they all beautiful and seductive. The Japanese *ningyo* (literally "human-fish") was sometimes represented as having an unlovely female head on a fish's body. In 1805, a news bulletin declared that a thirty-five foot long ningyo had been killed in Toyama Bay (plate 4.12). It had a pair of golden horns, a red belly, three eyes on each side of its torso, and a carp-like tail.

As with other forms of animal-humans, some sea creature–human hybrids were shape-shifters, able to transform from one form to another—either of their own volition or as willed by another. In the folklore of Scotland's Northern Isles, selkies could transform from seals to humans by shedding their skin.

In myth and literature, mermaids appear with a variety of attributes. Some are evil, luring sailors to their deaths. Others are deities bringing fertility to women. Remarkably, modern humans retain a sense of connection with mermaids. But there seems to be a sadness, a loneliness attached to them. That sense was communicated by Hans Christian Andersen's fairy tale "The Little Mermaid" of 1836 (which inspired Walt Disney's animated musical). It tells of the complex trials of a beautiful mermaid who dreams of becoming human and falls in love with a human prince only to suffer dire consequences.

The sadness of mermaids evokes human sympathy. Who hasn't experienced sadly infeasible aspirations? That sense is communicated in a work by John Collier, painted in 1909 (plate 4.13).

Andersen's tale was also adapted into an early twentieth century ballet that, in turn, inspired the bronze statue of the Little Mermaid in the Copenhagen harbor, which is widely known and loved (plate 4.14). Out there in the harbor, it too communicates a certain loneliness. These sympathetic modern mermaids are quite a distance from the fearsome Scylla of Greek myths.

4.13. BELOW LEFT: John Collier (1850–1934). *The Land Baby*, 1909. Oil on canvas, 55¾ × 44¼ in. (142.2 × 112.4 cm). Private collection.

4.14. BELOW RIGHT: Edvard Eriksen (1876–1959). *The Little Mermaid*, 1913. Bronze on granite, 49¼ in. (125 cm) high. Langelinie, Copenhagen.

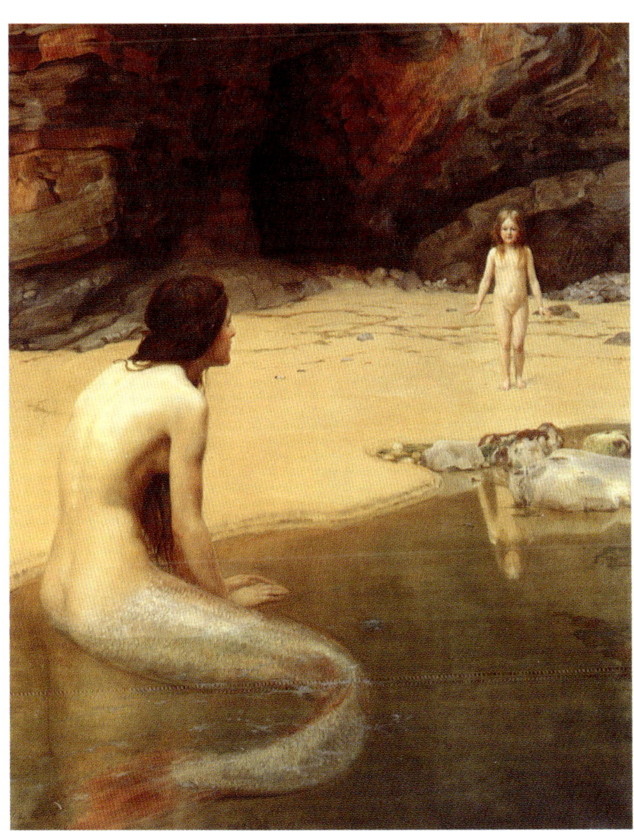

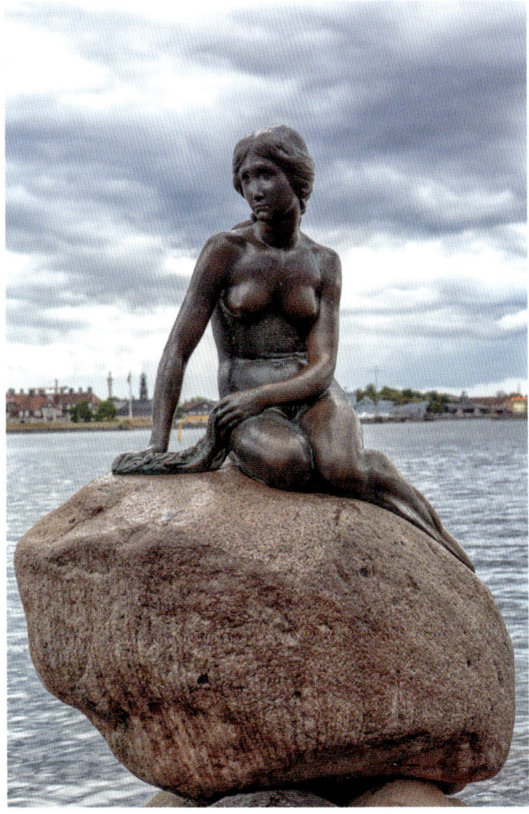

It was not only humans who were given fish tails. In classical mythology, the hippocampus (whose name was derived from the Greek *hippos*, "horse," and *kampos*, "sea monster") was depicted as a composite creature with the head and foreparts of a horse and the tail of a fish. In mosaics, hippocampi are often depicted with green scales, fin-like manes, and long, serpentine tails. The eighteenth-century Trevi Fountain in Rome shows Triton battling a hippocampus (plate 4.15).

It may seem odd that the region of the brain associated with memory is also called the hippocampus. Humans and other mammals have two hippocampi, one in each side of the brain. They have that name because they are shaped like the small fish of the genus *Hippocampus* that are commonly known as seahorses. The ancients believed that seahorses were the juvenile form of their mythical fish-tailed horses of the sea, their hippocampi.

The list of fish-tailed creatures goes on. There are fish-tailed lions (*leokampos*), fish-tailed bulls (*taurokampos*), fish-tailed goats (*aigikampos*) and fish-tailed leopards (*pardalokampos*). The hybrid creatures of myth seem

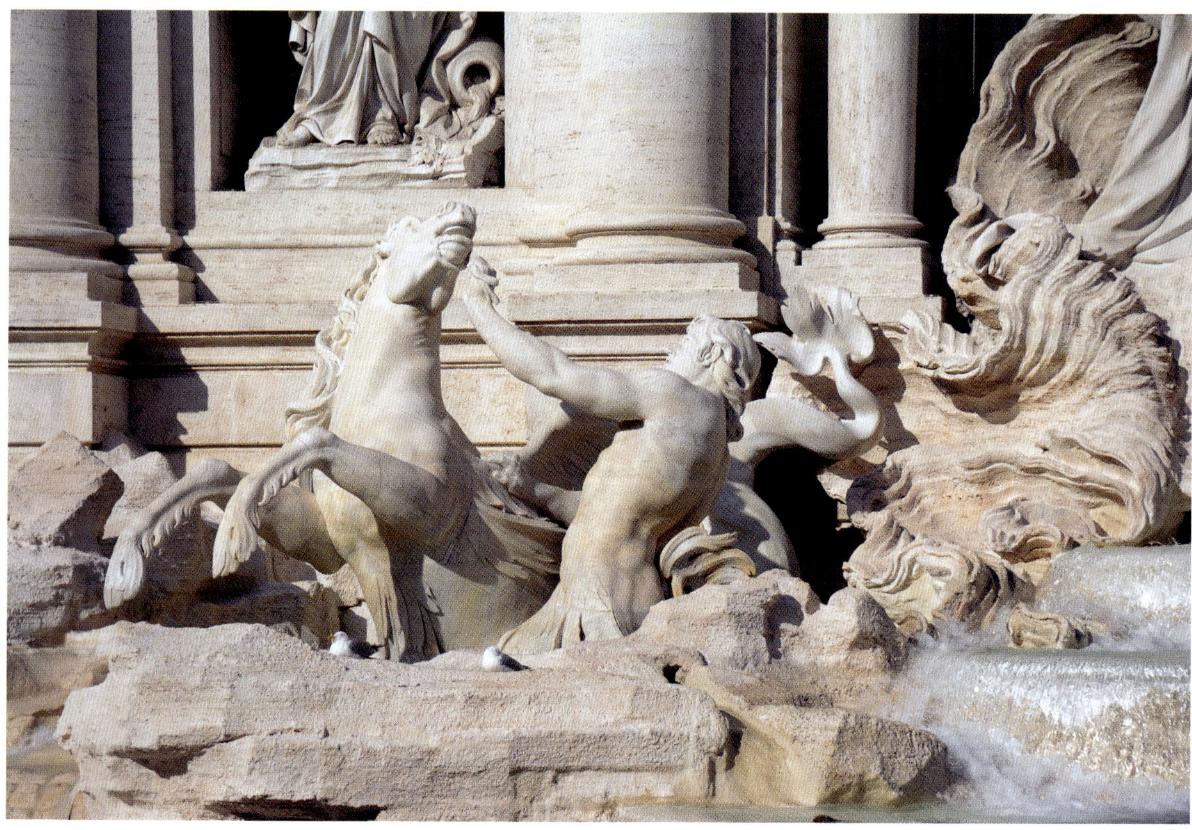

4.15. Triton and hippocampus in the Trevi Fountain in Rome, designed by Nicola Salvi (1697–1751) and constructed 1732–62.

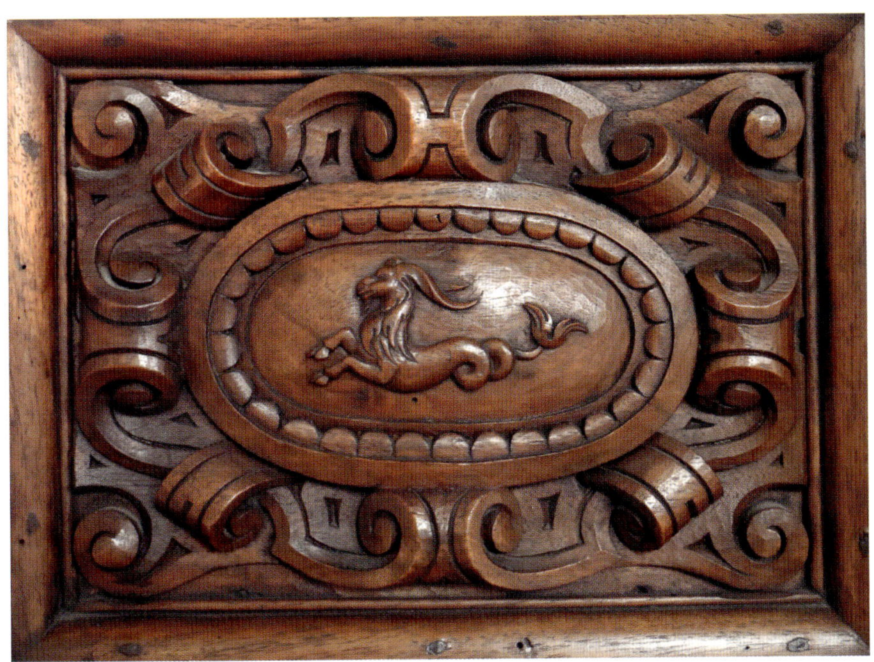

4.16. Wood carving of Capricorn, the rising sign and personal emblem of Cosimo I de' Medici (1519–1574), Grand Duke of Tuscany, in the Biblioteca Medicea Laurenziana, Florence.

to have been born at once deep inside us and "out there," in the other world. Fittingly, they have often inspired the names of constellations. Since the Bronze Age in Mesopotamia, the constellation Capricornus—one of the ten constellations of the zodiac—has been associated with a horned, fish-tailed goat (plate 4.16).

Sighting of mermaids by credible observers continued into the beginning of the nineteenth century. But the belief in mermaids was struck a blow in England in the 1820s, when con men exhibited rough-hewn "mermaid" bodies. The creature that the showman P. T. Barnum exhibited in New York in 1842 was found to have been created by crudely joining a monkey's head to the body of a fish. Incidents like these led the public to associate mermaids with profit-seeking hoaxes. Mermaids were then set free to return to the realm of myth, where they were represented by artists and loved forever after, as in a fairy tale.

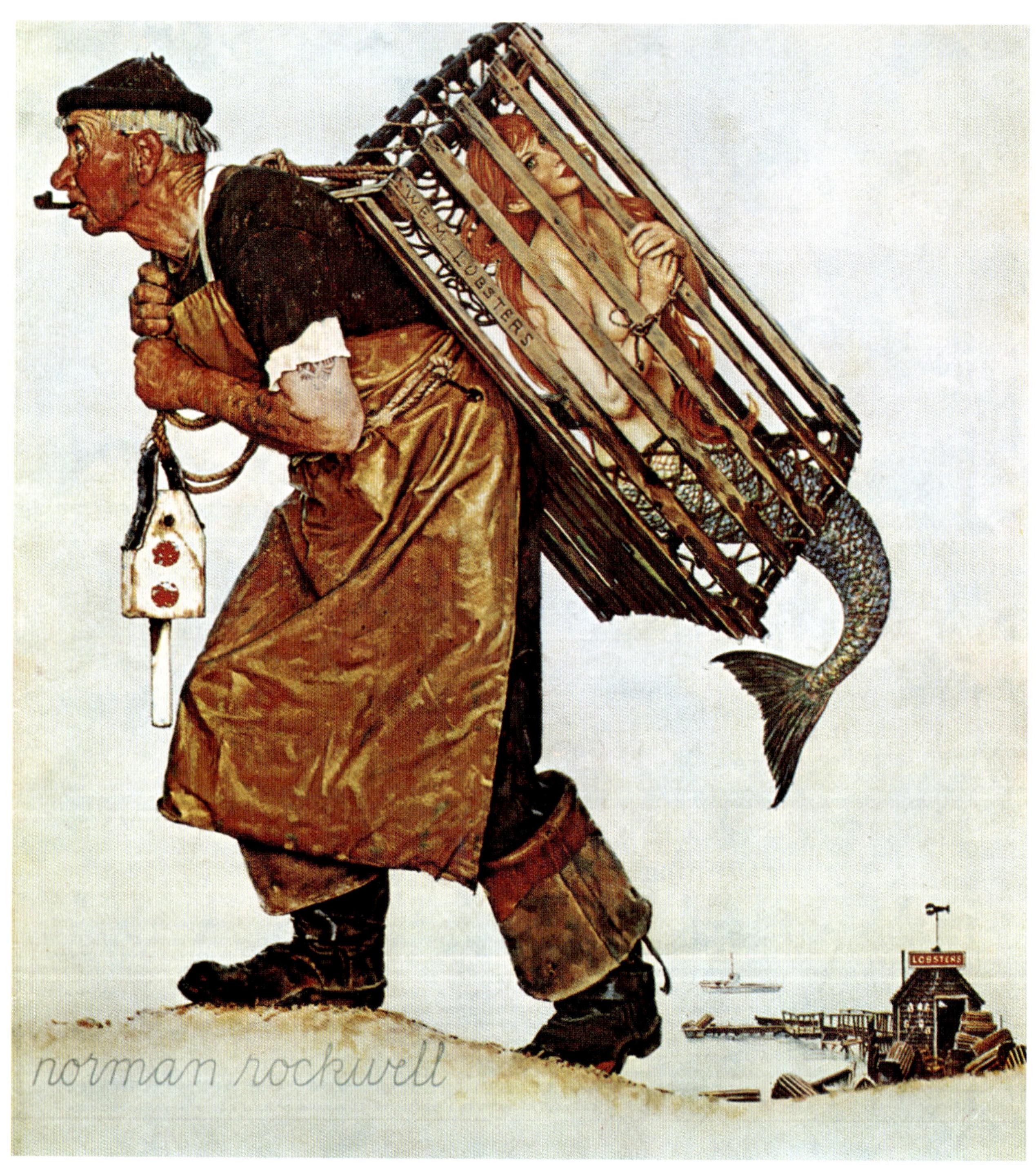

4.17. Norman Rockwell (1894–1978). *The Mermaid*, cover of the *Saturday Evening Post*, August 20, 1955.

Indeed, mermaids became, in the words of Vaughn Scribner, "the most recognized, universal, and beloved mythical creatures in the world."[5] Mermaids have become a common presence in popular culture. Norman Rockwell's cover for the *Saturday Evening Post* depicting a lobsterman hauling a mermaid home in one of his traps (plate 4.17) recalls the propensity of fifteenth-century explorers to find merpeople wherever they traveled, even close to home. And it reflects the appeal of mermaids ever since.

Like many ancient therianthropes, mermaids have been used as symbols of commerce as well. You can see one on almost every block in some cities, on the appealing Starbucks logo (plate 4.18). The company is named after the first mate in Herman Melville's *Moby Dick*, Starbuck. The designer of the Starbucks logo, Tony Heckler, wanted to maintain the nautical theme and found a concise representation of a siren in an old Nordic woodcut. The hope, perhaps, was that the twin-tailed mermaid would lure customers as her ancient predecessors had lured sailors, but to a cup of coffee rather than a painful demise.

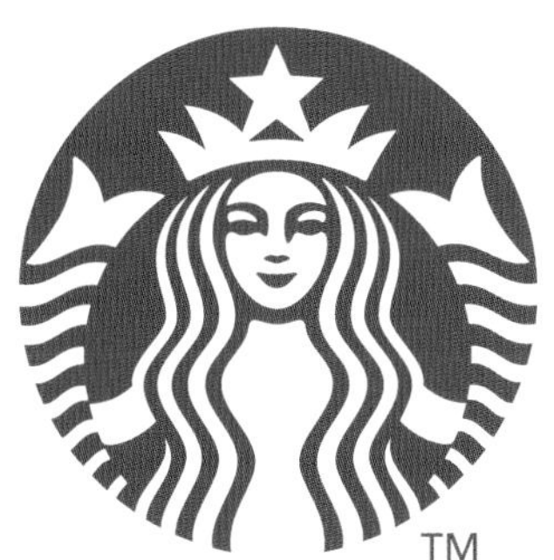

4.18. The version of the Starbucks logo used since 2011.

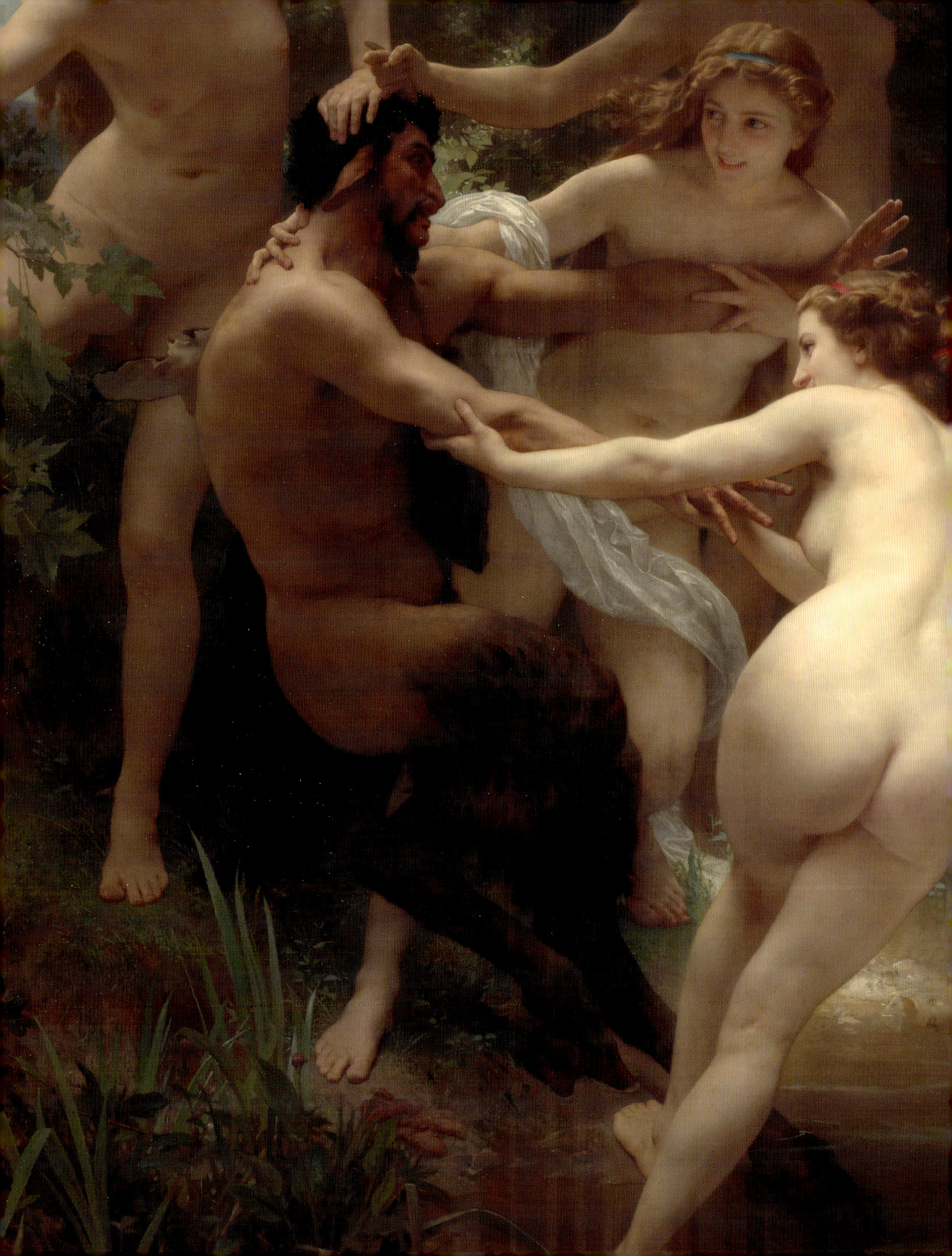

5
FROM CENTAURS TO FAUNS

Detail of William Adolphe Bouguereau's *Nymphs and Satyr*, 1873. See plate 5.11.

Among the many therianthropes with human heads and the bodies of land animals, horse-humans are the most prevalent. Horses appear prominently in the earliest figurative art—and they are represented with clear admiration. Nearly a third of the animals in Upper Paleolithic cave paintings are horses, and one of the first animal sculptures, dating from 30,000 BC, is an accurately rendered horse found in the Vogelherd Cave, near Stetten, Germany (plate 5.1). The beauty of the horse is communicated by the pure curves of its neck and upper haunch.

It is possible that groups of early humans adopted the horse as a totem. It is also reasonable to believe that early humans desired to mount those wild horses and benefit from their strength and speed, or become like them. That aspiration was satisfied in their mythology in the form of a centaur, a creature with the upper body of a human and the lower body and legs of a horse. There is another theory of the origin of the centaur: that it arose from the first reaction of a non-riding culture, such as that of the Minoans, to nomads who were mounted on horses. To those unfamiliar with riders on horseback, they might appear as half-man, half-animal. In any case, centaurs have galloped widely through mythology, taking on a variety of characteristics.

The ancient Greeks were amazingly adept at creating animal-human creatures—and taking them seriously, believing in them. They not only invented a huge variety of therianthropes but also imported imagined creatures from other cultures. A relative of the centaur, the manticore, can be traced back to Persia, where its name meant "man-eater" (plate 5.2). It was not a pleasant creature. It had the head of a human, the body of a lion, and a tail with a sting like that of a scorpion. With its triple row of sharp teeth, it devoured its prey whole, including clothes and belongings,

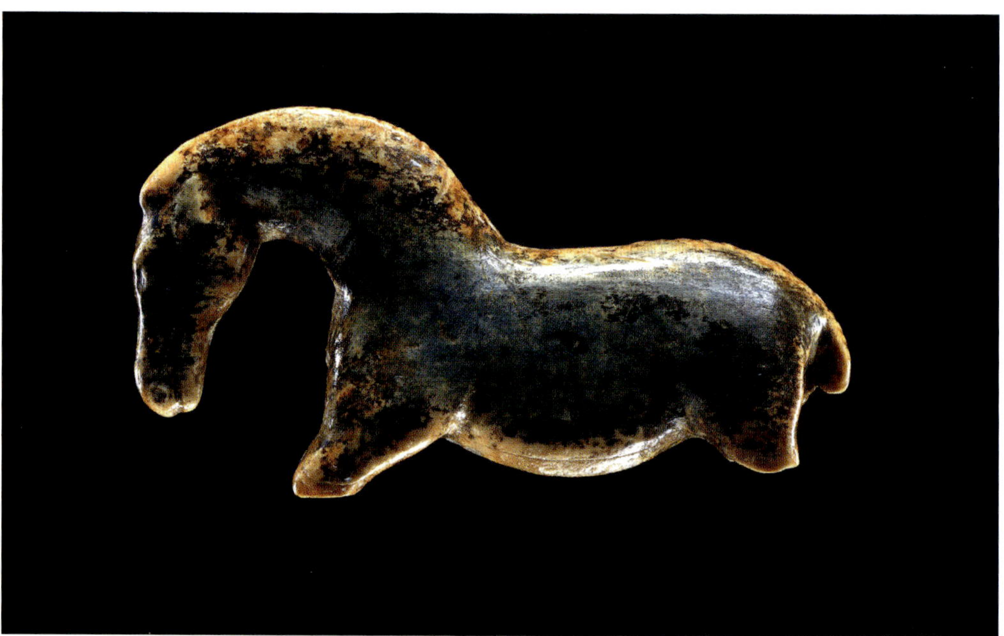

5.1. Horse figurine from the Vogelherd Cave, c. 30,000–29,000 BP. Mammoth ivory, 1⅞ × 1 × ¼ in. (4.8 × 2.5 × 0.7 cm). Museum der Universität Tübingen, Germany.

leaving no trace of its victims. Oddly, although the manticore couldn't talk, it could sing, or at least "make musical sounds." Perhaps that was a connection to sirens.

The manticore lived on to appear in bestiaries during the Middle Ages. There, it had an instructional role: all the creatures described in the bestiary had been created by God to illustrate, through their characteristics and behavior, moral teachings for mankind. That interpretation echoes the practical role that therianthropes had played for early humans.

There are degrees of believability in therianthropes. Although centaurs were related to manticores in Greek mythology, somehow centaurs were more believable, more real. And while they had a bad reputation, their faults were closely related to human weaknesses. They were usually presented as wild, lusty, and violent when drunk. Their credibility was also reinforced by artistic representations. Several centaurs appeared on the Parthenon, in architectural elements called metopes (plate 5.3). Carved around 447 BC, some show the battle between the Centaurs and the Lapiths, a legendary people in Greek mythology. As is often the case with

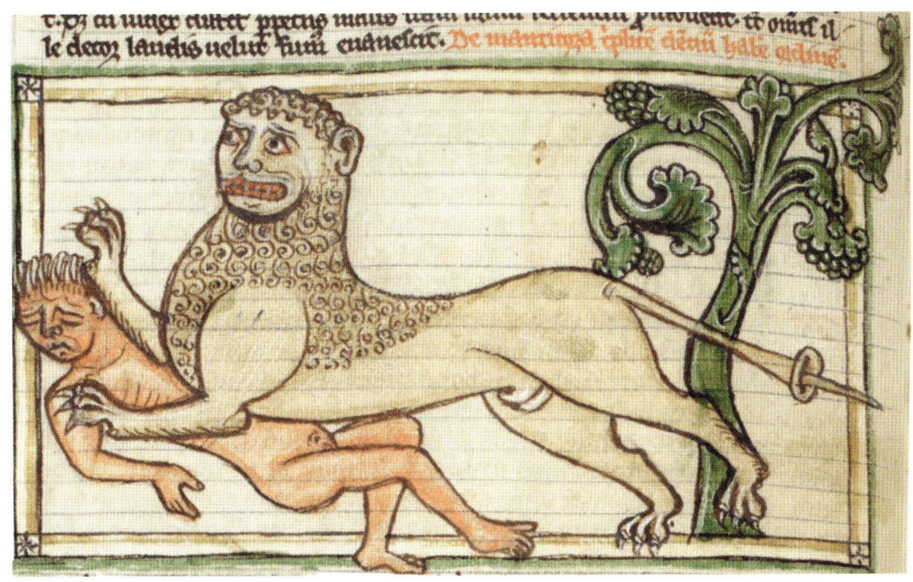

5.2. LEFT: Manticore from an English bestiary, c. 1236–50. British Library, London, Harley MS 3244, fol. 43v.

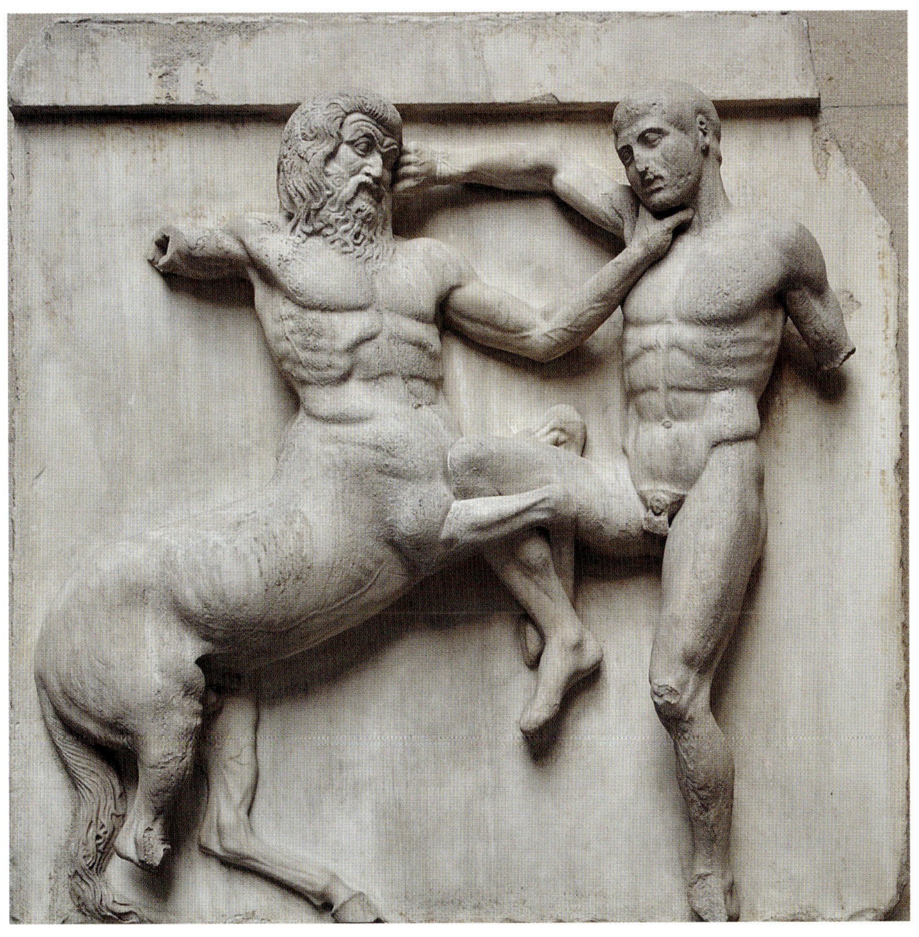

5.3. BELOW LEFT: South metope 31 from the frieze of the Parthenon, c. 447 BC, depicting a Centaur battling a Lapith. Marble, 47 in. (120 cm) high. British Museum, London.

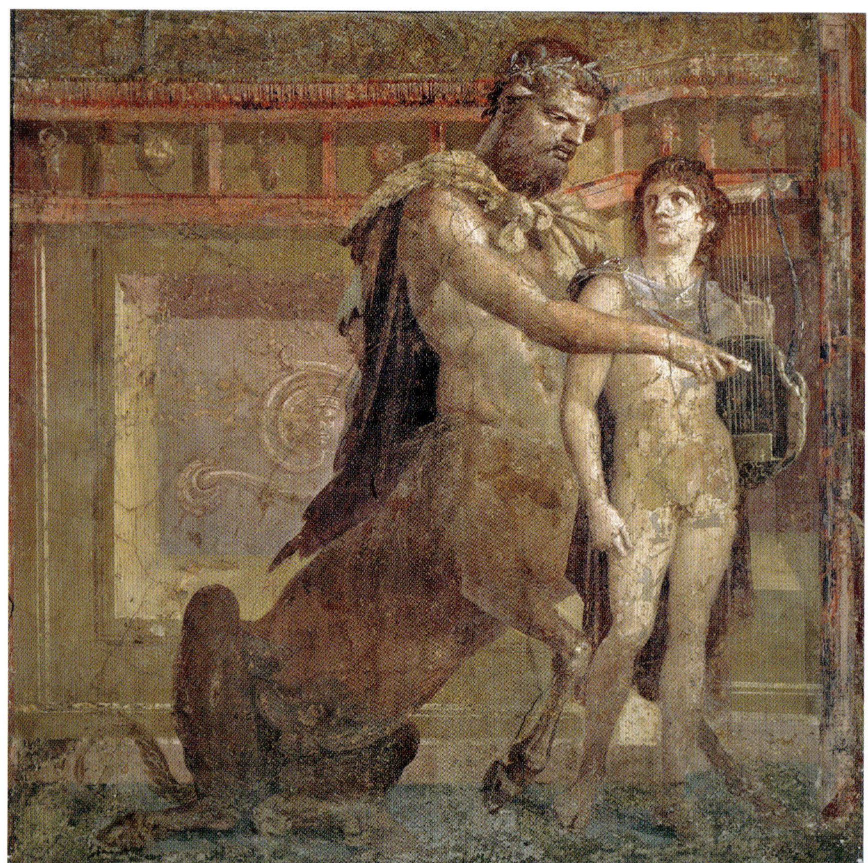

5.4. Fresco from Herculaneum depicting the education of Achilles by the centaur Chiron. 50 × 49¼ in. (127 × 125 cm). Museo Archeologico Nazionale, Naples.

Greek sculpture, there is a story behind the art. The Centaurs attend a royal wedding and become inebriated and characteristically rowdy. They thank their Lapith hosts by attempting to carry off all the women there, including the bride. The resulting battle, won by the Lapiths, would symbolize the grand conflict between the civilized Greeks and the "barbarians," between the noble and the ignoble.

Chiron was a notable exception to the usual centaur character. He was intelligent, civilized, and an engaging teacher. His foster father, Apollo, taught him the elements of a civilized life, including music, archery, prophecy, herbs, and medicine. Chiron, in turn, was the tutor of Achilles and the god of medicine, Asclepius (plate 5.4).

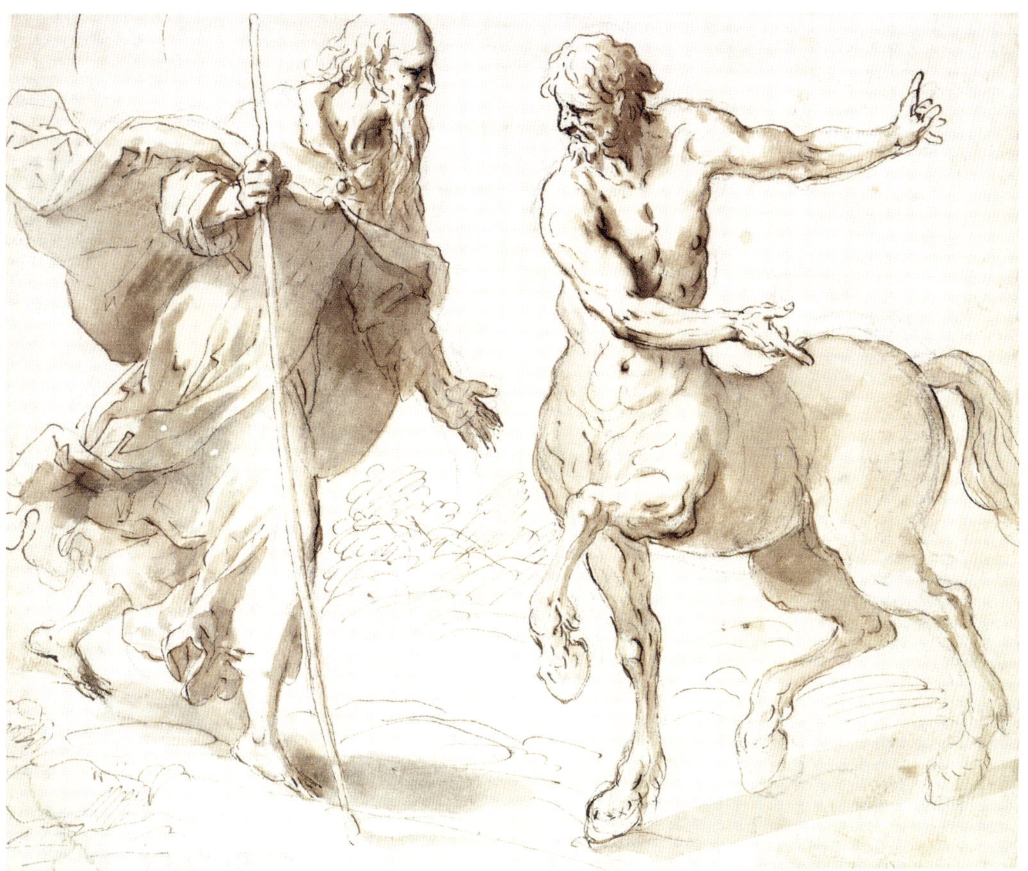

5.5. Jacopo Palma il Giovane (c. 1548–1628). *Saint Anthony Abbot Asking the Centaur the Way*. Brown chalk, pen and brown ink, and brown wash on paper, 8⅝ × 10⅜ in. (22 × 26.4 cm). Private collection.

Centaurs in the Christian tradition were descended from their Greek ancestors. Anthony was an Egyptian monk who entered the eastern desert around AD 270 to find another hermit, Paul of Thebes. There, he encountered a centaur and a satyr, irreligious demons. Anthony's prayers and faith managed to convert them both, and the centaur showed him the way to find Paul (plate 5.5). After his death, Anthony was revered as Saint Anthony Abbot or Saint Anthony the Great and is known as the father of all monks.

In his explorations of Asia in the late thirteenth century, Marco Polo reported seeing all sorts of unfamiliar and even fantastic creatures. Some were real animals that he referred to by the names of mythical beasts: for

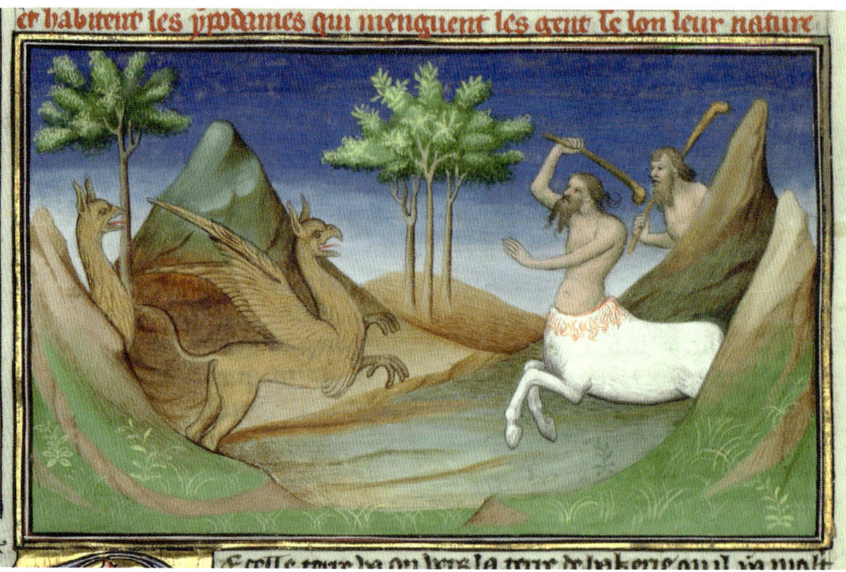

5.6. The centaurs and griffins of Bactria, from a French translation of Marco Polo's travels included in the illuminated manuscript known as Livre des merveilles du monde, c. 1410–12. Bibliothèque Nationale de France, Paris, MS Fr. 2810, fol. 211v.

example, he called the rhinoceros a "unicorn," but hastened to add that this creature was very different from the graceful horned horse his readers might imagine. However, the artists who illuminated the manuscript copies of Marco's *Travels* did not always feel themselves constrained by the details of his text: in one miniature, a centaur is seen attacking a griffin, a creature with a lion's body and an eagle's head and wings (plate 5.6).

One might say that all of the thousands of different therianthropes that populate mythology are irrational, but some are more irrational than others. There is a variant of the centaur called an *onocentaur*. First mentioned by Pythagoras, it is part human and part donkey, part male and part female, and instead of four legs it has only two (plate 5.7). Its unsettling, imbalanced design demonstrates that some animal-human combinations make less aesthetic, and physical, sense than others.

There are also female centaurs called Centaurides in Greek mythology (plate 5.8). The Greek rhetorician Philostratus the Elder declared:

> How beautiful the Centaurides are, even where they are horses; for some grow out of white mares, others are attached to chestnut mares, and the coats of others are dappled, but they glisten like those of horses that are well cared for. There is also a white female Centaur that grows out of a black mare, and the very opposition of the colours helps to produce the united beauty of the whole.[1]

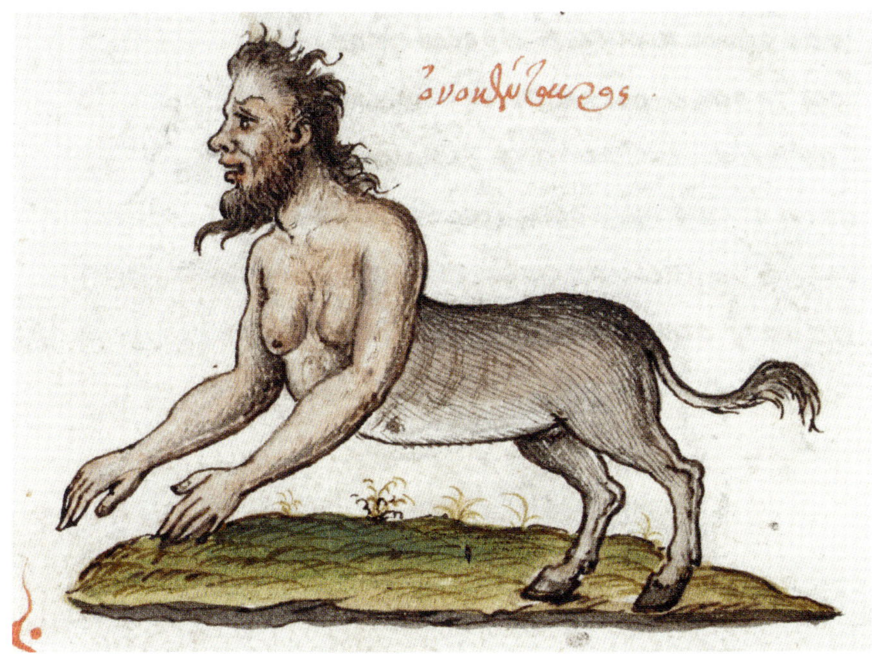

5.7. LEFT: An onocentaur, from a manuscript of *De animalium proprietate* by Manuel Philes. British Library, London, Burney MS 97, fol. 19v.

5.8. BELOW: Roman mosaic of the second century AD depicting Venus flanked by Centaurides. Bardo National Museum, Tunisia.

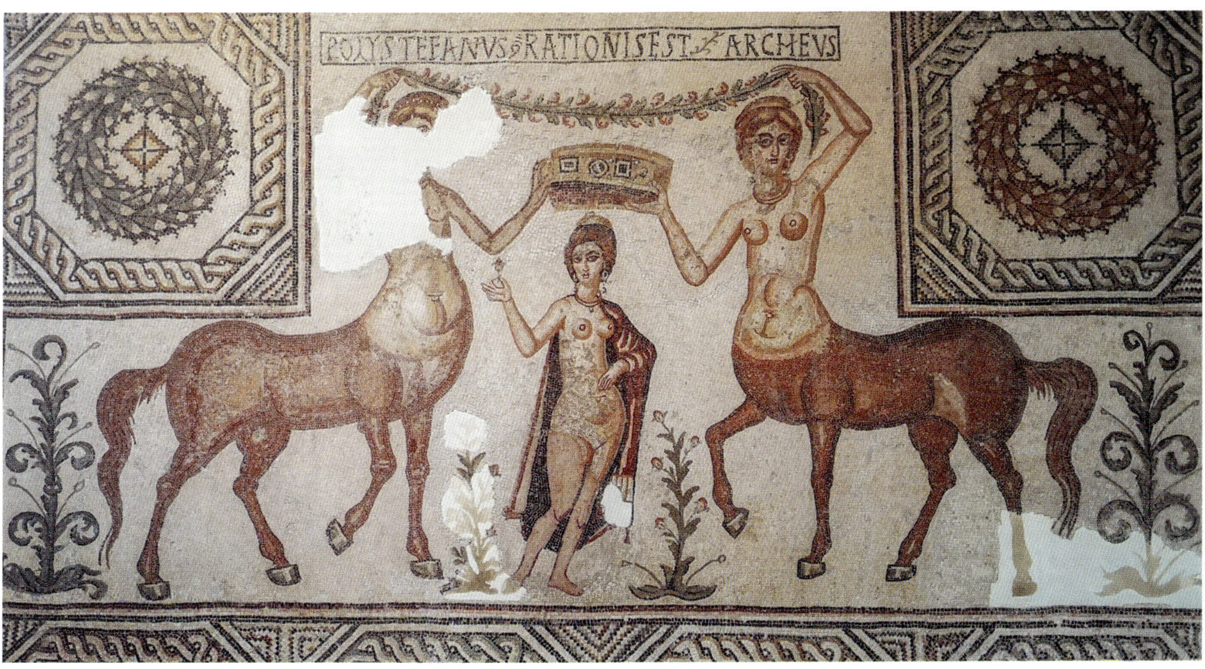

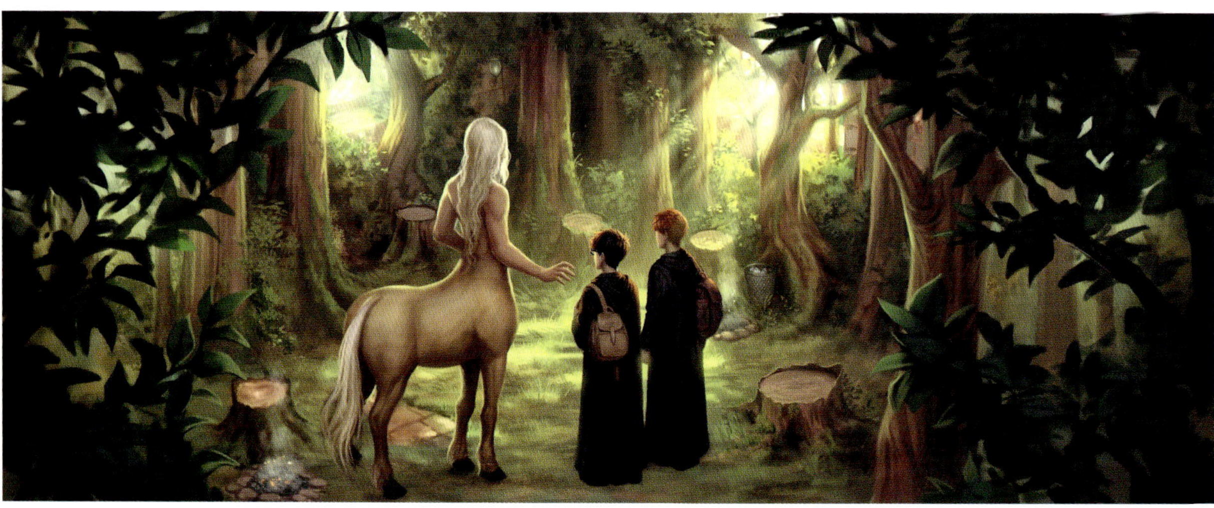

5.9. Firenze with Harry Potter and Ronald Weasley.

Like many therianthropes, the centaur has had a long cultural life, extending into the present. Recently, a centaur named Firenze had a prominent role in the Harry Potter books (plate 5.9).[2] In the first volume of the series, Harry ventures into the Forbidden Forest that lies to the east of Hogwarts, his wizarding school, and encounters the villain Voldemort. Firenze, who lives in the forest, saves Harry, carrying him on his back to safety. For this helpful deed, Firenze is censured by his fellow centaurs, who consider themselves too noble to be ridden by a lowly human.

Closely related to centaurs are deer-humans, which were among the therianthropes welcomed in modern and contemporary art, by Surrealism in particular. A prominent example is found in the work of the Mexican Surrealist painter Frida Kahlo. Her *Wounded Deer* of 1946 symbolizes the physical and emotional difficulties of her life and draws on ancient pre-Columbian, as well as Buddhist and Christian, mythology (plate 5.10). When she was eighteen, Kahlo suffered serious injuries in a bus accident, including to her right leg. She created *The Wounded Deer* late in her life, after a major surgery to address the lingering effects of the accident. Kahlo was aware that the right foot was associated with a deer in certain pre-Columbian cultures. Soon after Kahlo made this painting, her lower right leg was amputated as a result of gangrene.

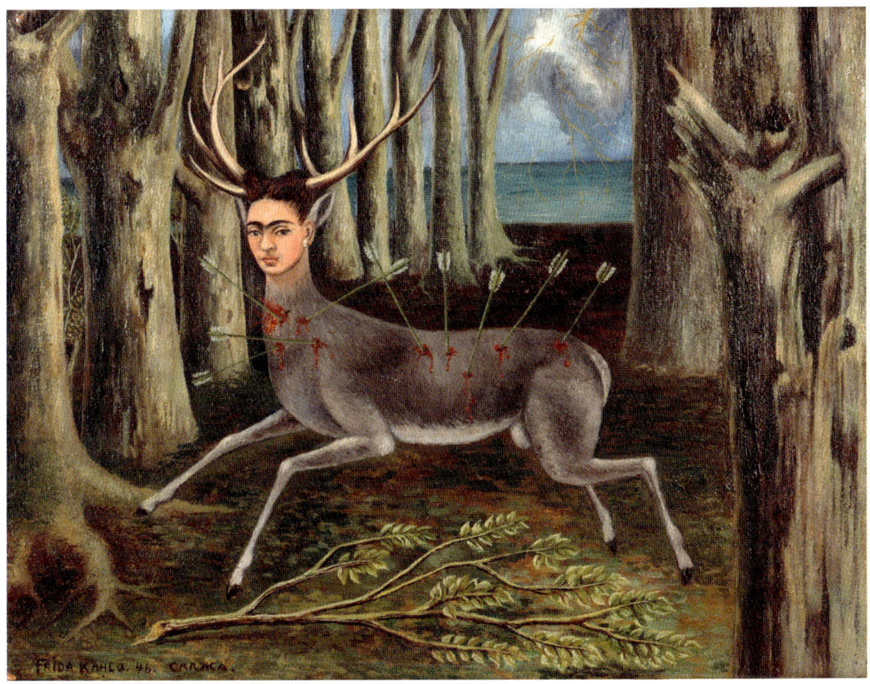

5.10. Frida Kahlo (1907–1954). *The Wounded Deer* or *The Little Deer*, 1946. Oil on Masonite, 8⅞ × 11¾ in. (22.4 × 30 cm). Private collection.

Some mythological figures seem to have emerged from a fear of certain animals, such as snakes. Others, such as horse-humans and bird-humans, seem to have derived from admiration and envy. Still others seem to represent extremes of certain human impulses. Satyrs would fall into that category. Products of the ancient Greek imagination, satyrs initially had the body of a man and the long tail and pointed ears of a horse, and evolved to be closer to half-man, half-goat. They loved women and wine, and neither in moderation. Satyrs seemed to revel in their ribaldry and were usually depicted in a state of outlandishly large arousal. The appeal of satyrs to men was understandable: "If a godlike creature could do all of that, then it's okay for me."

Art makes myth real. An excellent example is William-Adolphe Bouguereau's *Nymphs and Satyr* of 1873 (plate 5.11). In Bouguereau's romantic yet realistic painting, the nymphs manage to cool the ardor of the lascivious satyr by taking advantage of a weakness: he doesn't know how to swim, but the nymphs are pulling him into the water. Thus the engaging, lively tension that pervades the painting. And by being aesthetically engaging, the painting draws us into the world of nymphs and satyrs.

The Hellenistic Greeks created a toned-down descendant of the satyrs in the figure of Pan, who had the body of a man and the horns, ears, and legs of a goat. Pan was the god of the wild, of mountains, of shepherds and their flocks. In Roman mythology, fauns are a further benign evolution in the centaur-satyr family, similar in appearance to Pan (plate 5.12). The faun was a nature spirit with a shy and peaceful nature. He would definitely be looked down upon by his great-grandfather the satyr.

Horse-humans would seem to be a straightforward idea, at least in the world of therianthropes. But the variety of creatures that have descended from the Vogelherd Horse testifies to the creative power of the human imagination. And to the aesthetic power of the artists who have made them real to us.

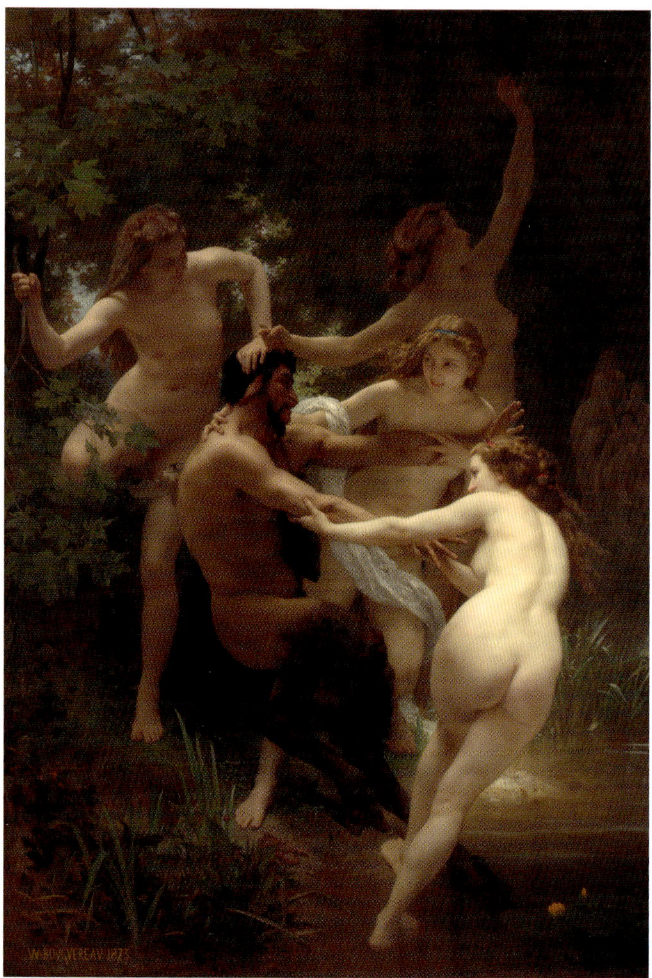

5.11. William Adolphe Bouguereau (1825–1905). *Nymphs and Satyr*, 1873. Oil on canvas, 102½ × 72 in. (260.4 × 182.9 cm). Clark Art Institute, Williamstown, MA.

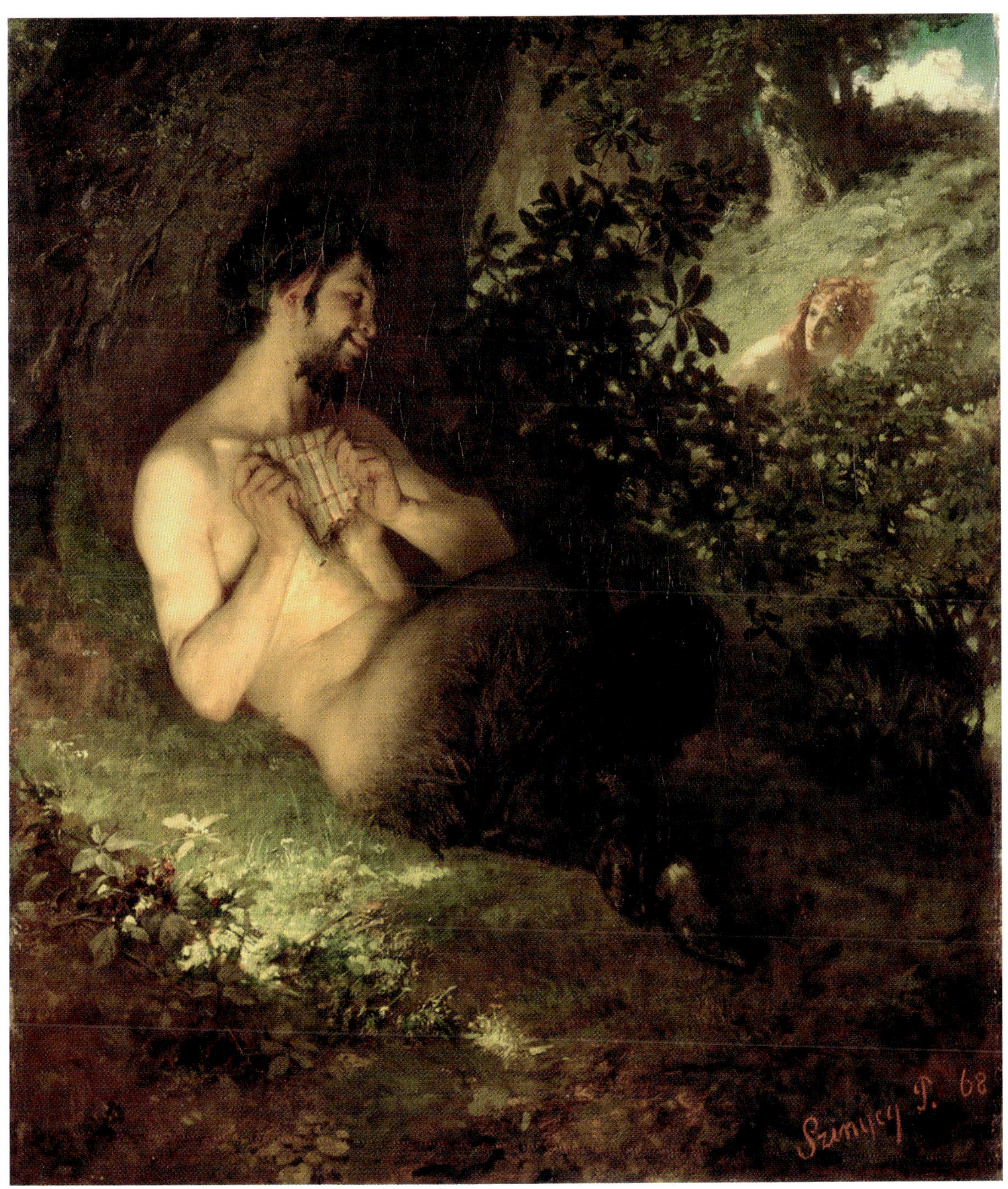

5.12. Pál Szinyei Merse (1845–1920). *Faun and Nymph*, 1868. Oil on canvas, 41¾ × 36 in. (106 × 91.5 cm). Hungarian National Gallery, Budapest.

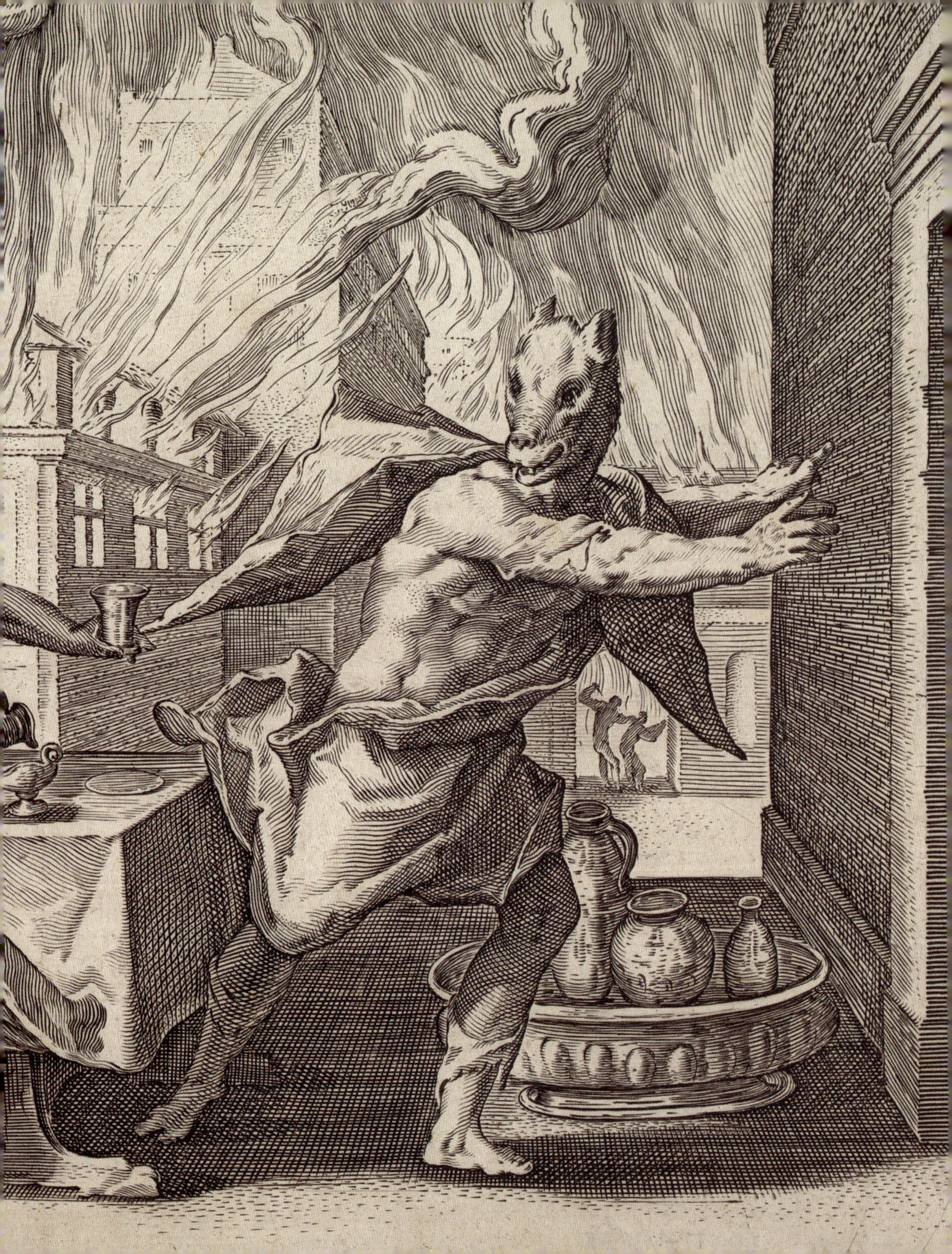

6
SHAPE-SHIFTERS

Detail of *Lycaon Changed into a Wolf*, by the workshop of Hendrick Goltzius. See plate 6.6.

Some animal-humans, like angels and sphinxes, have forms that remain constant throughout their lives. Others, however, are capable of transformation. They are called shape-shifters, and they have a rich history in myth and folklore. In early visual art, it's difficult to distinguish a shape-shifter from a static therianthrope, but some paleoanthropologists maintain that shape-shifters, particularly men who transform into elands, are plentiful in early South African art. What is certain, though, is that shape-shifters appear in the earliest surviving fragment of literature, the Mesopotamian *Epic of Gilgamesh* dating from around 2000 BC. The ubiquity of the concept suggests an even earlier origin, for it appears in diverse cultures across several continents.

Transformation from one form to another was a prominent theme of classical mythology. Many transformation myths were given their canonical form in one of the most enduring works of Roman literature, Ovid's *Metamorphoses* (or "Transformations"), published in AD 8. In its first lines, Ovid makes clear his principal subject matter: "My mind leads me to speak now of forms changed into new bodies."[1] Ovid wrote of all sorts of transformations: from humans to animals, from ants and mushrooms to humans, and from humans to inanimate objects. The deep-rooted appeal of transformation is evidenced by the influence of Ovid's work on Dante, Boccaccio, Chaucer, Shakespeare, and many others.

One of the unusual transformations that Ovid recounts is based on the ancient Greek myth of the beautiful river nymph Daphne. The winged god of love, Eros (a favorite therianthrope) plays a key role in the story. Apollo, the Greek god of the arts, was a proud archer. When he mocked Eros for using a bow and arrow—a boy with a man's weapon, he called him—Eros shot Apollo with a golden arrow to create in him a passionate love for Daphne.

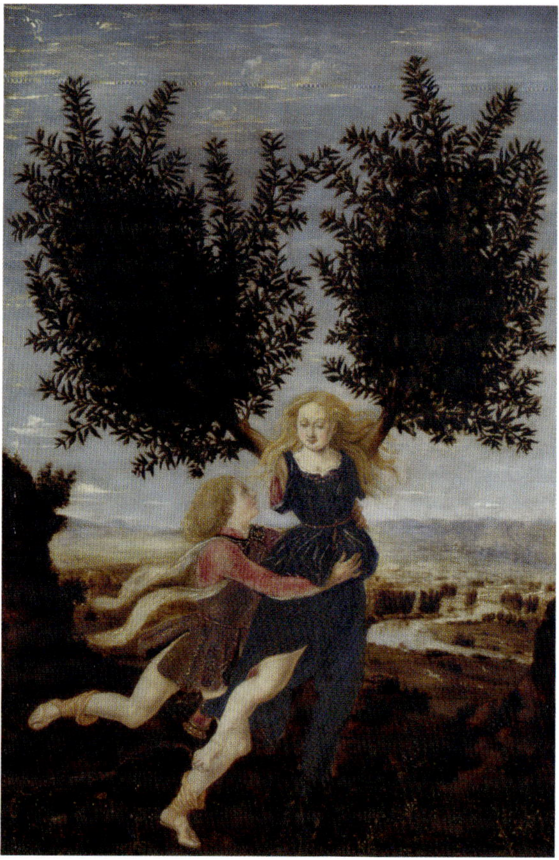

6.1. Piero Pollaiuolo (c. 1441–c. 1496). *Apollo and Daphne*, c. 1470–80. Oil on panel, 11⅝ × 7⅞ in. (29.5 × 20 cm). National Gallery, London.

He also shot Daphne with a love-repelling arrow. Daphne appealed to her father, the river god Peneus, to defend her from Apollo's passionate advances. She pleaded with him to "destroy this beauty by which I pleased o'er well." Peneus's solution was for Daphne to be transformed into a laurel tree, and soon "a down-dragging numbness seized her limbs, and her soft sides were begirt with thin bark. Her hair was changed to leaves, her arms to branches . . . and her head was now but a tree's top. Her gleaming beauty alone remained."[2] The unrepentant Apollo would later say that his favorite tree was the laurel and recommend its leaves for victory wreaths.

Through the ages, artists have been inspired by such tales of transformation, and have lent them a new reality by giving them visual form. In Piero Pollaiuolo's painting of Daphne's transformation, the landscape, based on the Arno River valley near Florence, adds to the credibility of the scene (plate 6.1). The sculptor Gian Lorenzo Bernini also portrayed the scene in one of his most animated and compelling works (plate 6.2).

6.2. OPPOSITE: Gian Lorenzo Bernini (1598–1680). *Apollo and Daphne*, 1625. Marble, 96 in. (243 cm) high. Galleria Borghese, Rome.

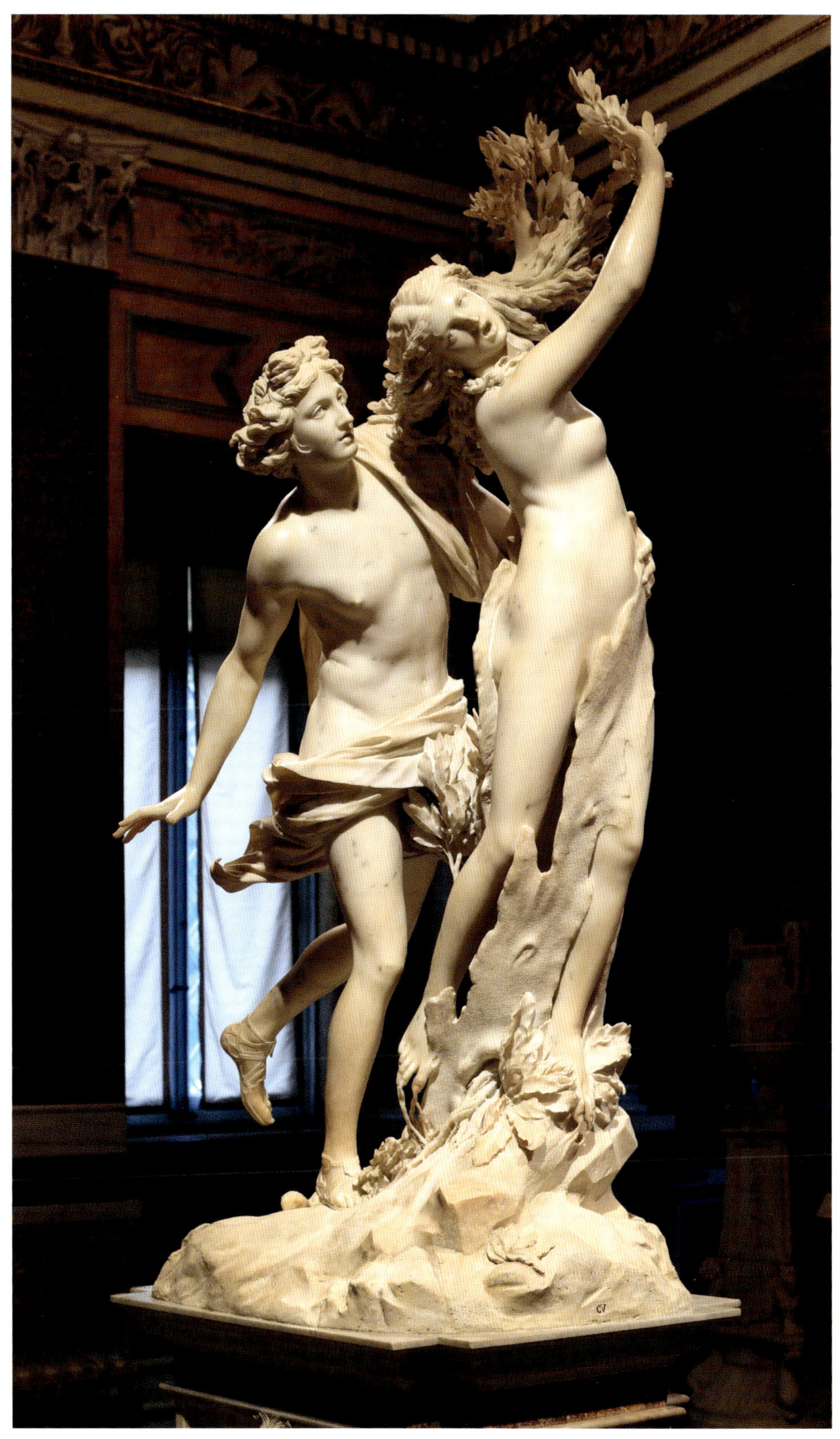

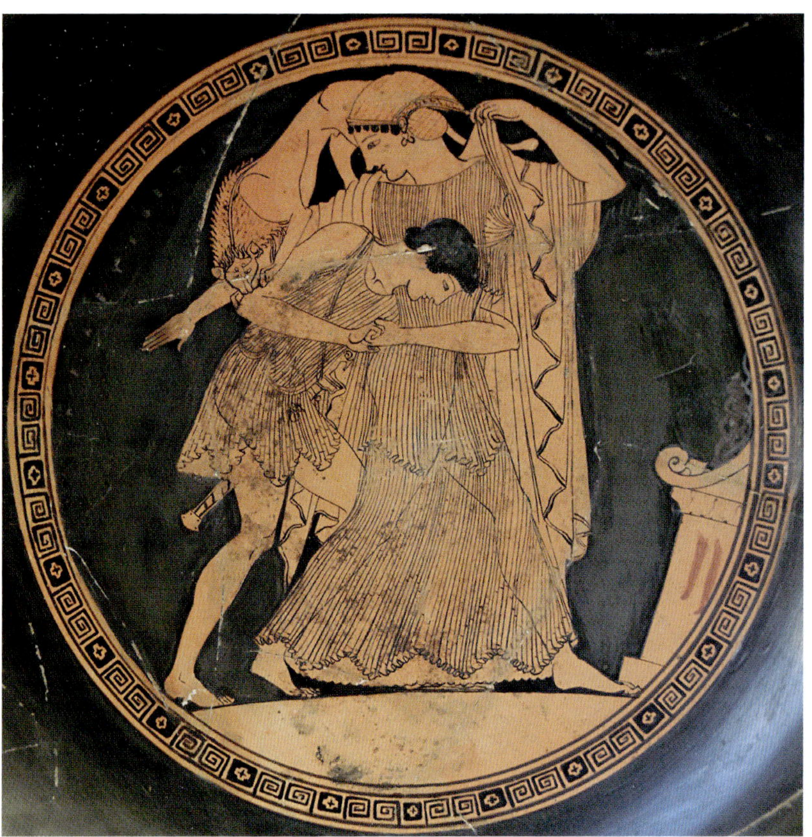

6.3. Thetis transforming into a lioness at Peleus's advance. Attic red-figure kylix, c. 490 BC. Found in Vulci, Etruria. Musée de la Bibliothèque Nationale de France, Paris.

A particularly versatile shape-shifter in Ovid's *Metamorphoses* is the beautiful sea goddess Thetis. The sea god Proteus is urgently attracted to Thetis but knows she is destined to produce a son mightier than his father. So, he instructs his mortal grandson Peleus to act for him. But when Peleus attempts to seduce Thetis, she transforms herself into a tigress. The wise centaur Chiron advises Peleus to catch Thetis sleeping and tie a rope around her before the act. After being bound, Thetis shifts into several shapes, including a serpent and an angry lioness (plate 6.3), but runs out of options and accedes to Peleus's advances. The product of their union is Achilles, who becomes the hero of the Trojan War.

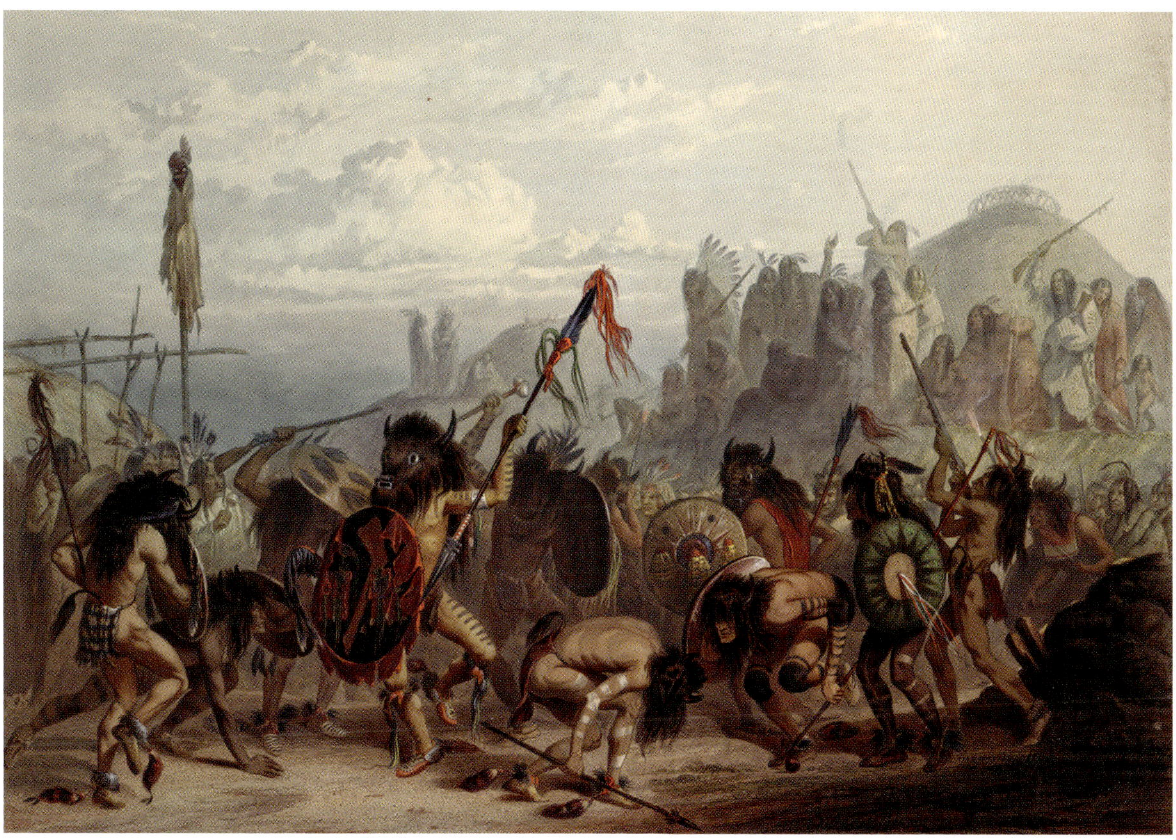

6.4. Karl Bodmer (1809–1893). *Bison-Dance of the Mandan Indians in Front of Their Medicine Lodge*, 1840–43. Aquatint from *Maximilian Prince of Wied's Travels in the Interior of North America*.

A human-to-animal transformation could happen in various ways. It could be at one's own volition, or it could be imposed by a witch or sorcerer. And there could be various incentives. Transformation, say into a wolf, could be the means to instill fear in an enemy. A partial transformation could allow one to take on the desirable attributes of another species. In recent times, some Cherokee people strove to take on the characteristics of wolves, foxes, and other animals that seemed impervious to the cold. Before starting on a winter journey, they would chant, "I become a real wolf, a real deer, a real fox, and a real opossum." Then they would give long howls or barks and scratch the ground. The process gave them confidence, and that confidence could improve their ability to survive the journey.[3]

6.5. Giuseppe Archimboldo (c. 1527–1593). *Vertumnus*, 1591. Oil on panel, 27½ × 22⅞ in. (70 × 58 cm). Skokloster Castle, Sweden.

Perhaps the earliest and most widespread means of transforming oneself into an animal was to don its skin. The practice could have originated simply as a means to keep warm; it could also have served as a hunting strategy, a rite to promote a hunt's success, or a step toward psychedelic transformation into an animal. Some would interpret the earliest artistic depictions of therianthropes, such as the Lion-Man, as a representation of that custom. The practice has survived to modern times, and wearing animal skins is a part of ritual dances in many cultures (plate 6.4).

An unusual shape-shifter appeared in Roman mythology in the form of the god of the seasons and plant growth, Vertumnus. Seasonal change is an interesting analogue of shape-shifting and may even have stimulated early ideas of human-animal transformation. In his *Metamorphoses*, Ovid tells how Vertumnus transformed himself into an old lady to persuade the lovely Pomona to let him into her orchard, where he managed to seduce her.

But, once again, it is a visual artist who has given us the defining image of Vertumnus—in this case, the Mannerist painter Archimboldo. His strangely fascinating canvas from 1591 represents multiple levels of transformation: it is an allegorical portrait of Rudolf II in the guise of Vertumnus, protector of the fruits and vegetables of all seasons (plate 6.5). One can't help wondering what Rudolf, King of Hungary and Croatia and Holy Roman Emperor, thought of his portrait.

One prominent shape-shifter is the werewolf, which appears in many cultures.[4] As just one example, Ovid and other ancient Greek writers recounted the tale of Lykaon, who tested Zeus's omniscience by serving him the roasted flesh of a human. Zeus understood the vile insult and retaliated by transforming Lykaon and his sons into wolves (plate 6.6). (The technical term for werewolf is *lycanthrope*, or "wolf-human" in Greek.)

Some purists maintain that, to be a true werewolf, you have to be able to transform back and forth between wolf and man. Thus, Lykaon wouldn't qualify. According to the werewolf expert Daniel Ogden, the best story of a true werewolf from the ancient world appears in the *Satyricon*, a Latin comic novel written by Petronius about AD 66.[5] In that tale, the slave Niceros is traveling by foot with a soldier friend. When they arrive among some tombs, his friend steps away, takes off his clothes, urinates a circle around them, and turns into a wolf. He then runs off into the woods, howling. The frightened Niceros goes to a friend's house and finds that a wolf has been there and slaughtered some sheep. But their slave sent a spear

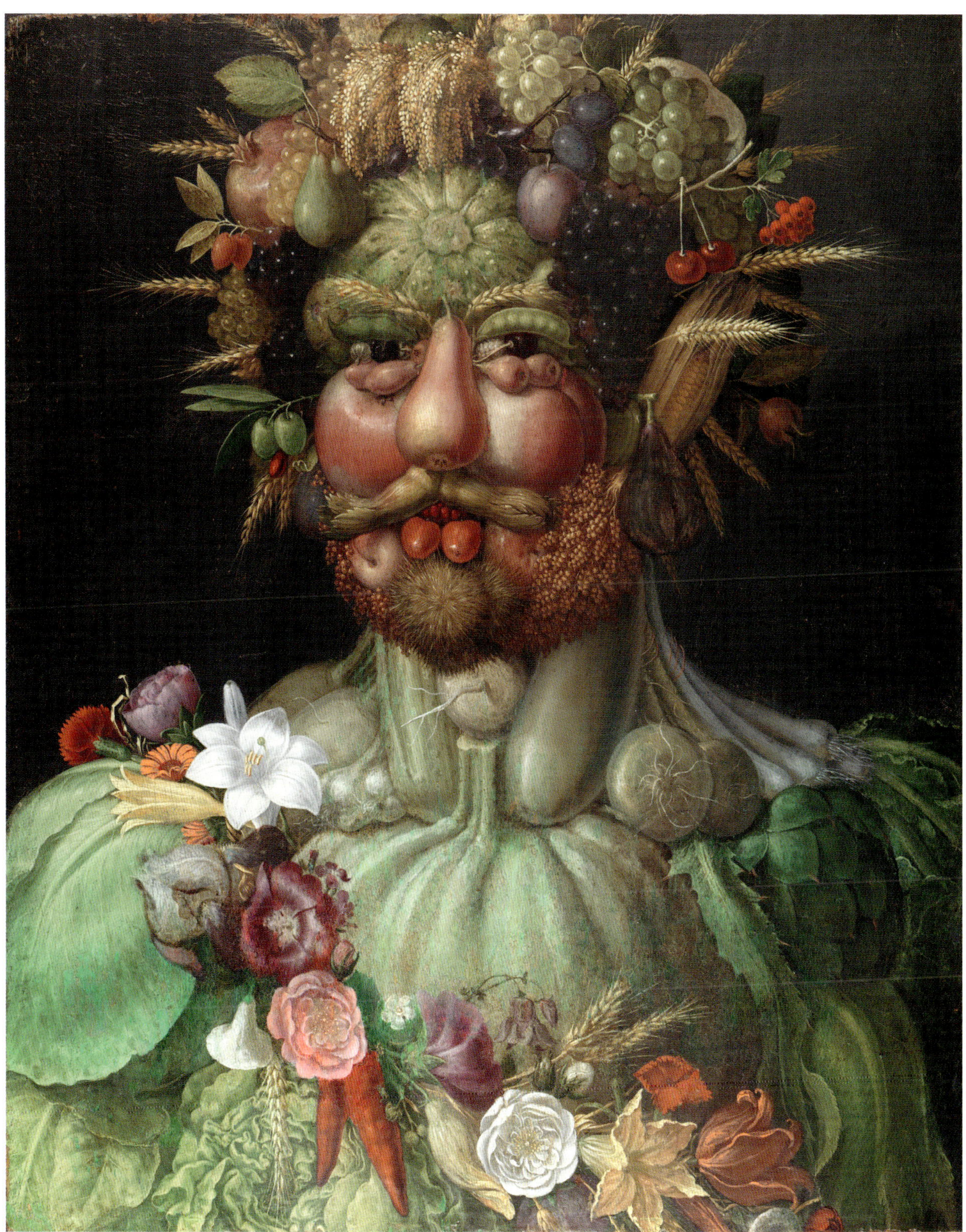

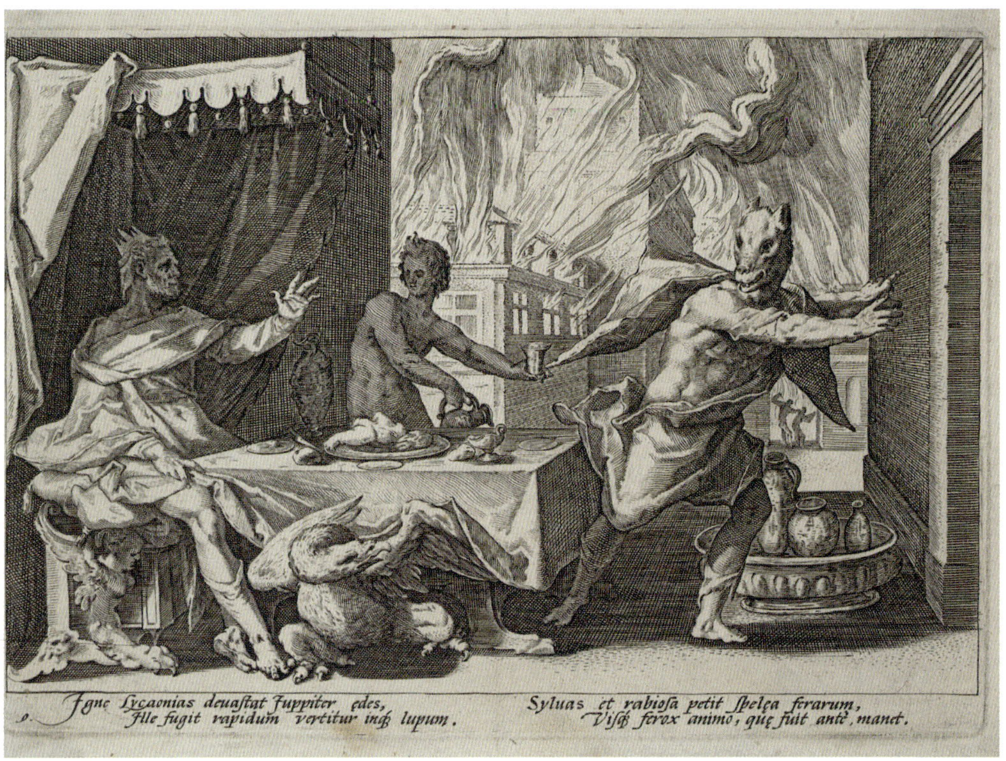

6.6. Workshop of Hendrick Goltzius (1558–1617). *Lykaon Changed into a Wolf*, 1589. Illustration to Ovid's *Metamorphoses*. Engraving, 8⅛ × 10⅝ in. (20.5 × 27.1 cm). National Gallery of Art, Washington, DC.

into the wolf's neck before he ran off. When Niceros returns home, he finds his soldier friend in his bed, with his wounded neck being treated by a doctor, and realizes he is a werewolf (plate 6.7).

In medieval Europe, there were many tales of men who could transform themselves into wolves. Those accounts were not seen as mere fictions, but regarded as true. Medieval codes of law even warned against "the madly audacious werewolf."

There are elements of a psychedelic or shamanistic phenomenon in the myths of werewolves. Virgil wrote about a man called Moeris who transformed himself into a wolf by consuming herbs and poisons. Turkish folklore makes a direct connection. The wolf was considered the totemic ancestor of the Turkish people, and through a long and arduous rite, a Turkish shaman could transform himself into a wolf-man.

Often it was the most feared animal in a particular region that became the focus of shape-shifting myths. In some places, that was the wolf; in others, it was another large predator. In India, it was believed that people's spirits could leave their bodies to possess and control tigers. In Africa there were were-lions and were-leopards. In many cultures, were-animals were tasked with carrying out nefarious deeds. Among Carib tribes, for example, the Kanaima was an evil spirit that could possesses people and transform them into deadly animals. Those seeking to kill someone in revenge could invite the Kanaima into themselves by taking psychoactive drugs or conducting a shamanistic ritual.

Shape-shifters could titillate as well as terrify. Zeus could transform not only others but himself when it served his purposes. It is not obvious why he had to transform himself into a swan when he wanted to make love to the beautiful Leda—after all, he was a god. But he did—to the delight of artists through the centuries. For some during the Renaissance, the image

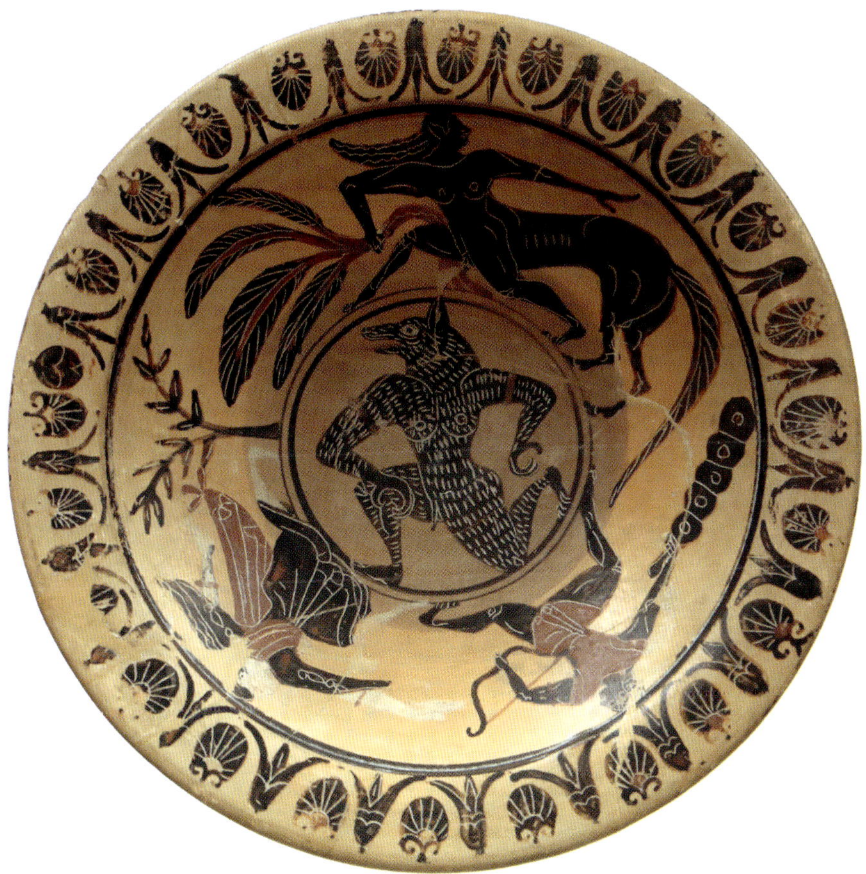

6.7. Tityos Painter. Black-figure plate with werewolf at center, c. 540–510 BC. Found at Vulci, Osteria Necropolis, Tomb 177. Museo Nazionale Etrusco di Villa Giula, Rome.

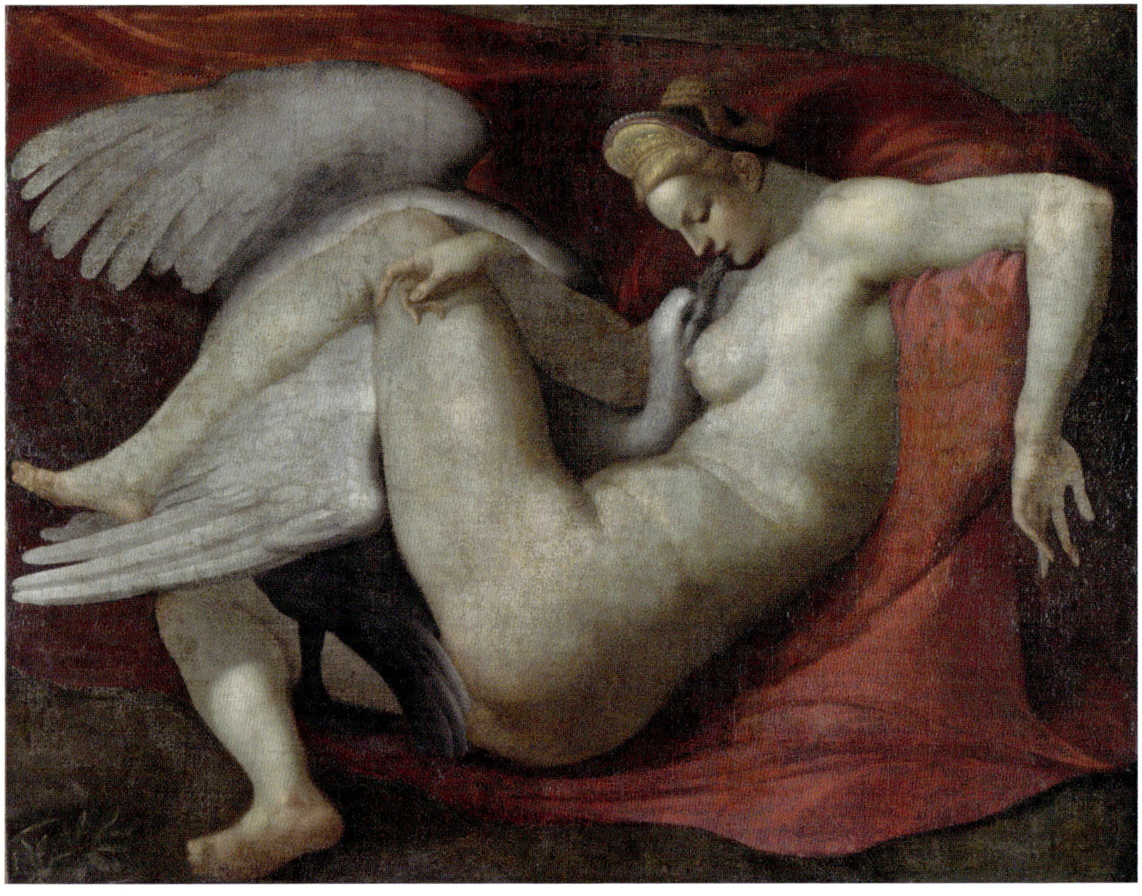

6.8. After Michelangelo Buonarroti (1475–1564). *Leda and the Swan*, after 1530. Oil on canvas, 41½ × 55½ in. (105.4 × 141 cm). National Gallery, London.

of Zeus in the form of a swan making love to, and in some cases raping, Leda was too risqué. Versions by many prominent artists, including Leonardo and Michelangelo, were destroyed. Fortunately, a sixteenth-century copy of Michelangelo's depiction of this bizarre erotic event survives (plate 6.8). Images of Leda and the swan have remained controversial to this day: in 2012, the London police demanded that photographer Derrick Santini's interpretation of the subject be removed from the window of a London art gallery, on the grounds that it was "violent pornography."

Many cultures also have tales of humans transforming into birds. The ancient Greeks were particularly fond of that phenomenon. Around 350 BC, the Greek writer Boios wrote what may have been the first poem devoted

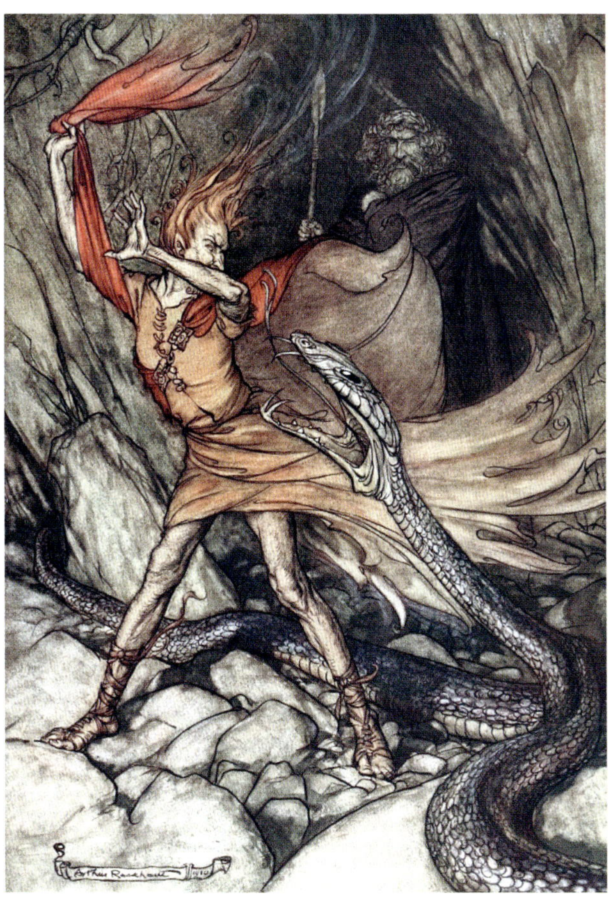

6.9. Arthur Rackham (1867–1939). Illustration to *The Rhinegold and the Valkyrie* by Richard Wagner, translated by Margaret Armour (London: William Heinemann, 1910), showing Alberich transformed into a snake.

to myths of metamorphosis. Known only in fragments, his *Ornithogonia* is concerned exclusively with human-to-bird transformations. The ubiquity of avian shape-shifters echoes that of other bird-human therianthropes, and may be similarly rooted in our envy of birds and our aspiration to gain their power of flight.

Just as snake-humans are surprisingly common, so is shape-shifting into a snake. An example is the dwarf Alberich, a character in Wagner's Ring cycle, who transforms himself into a dwarf—an episode memorably depicted by the English illustrator Arthur Rackham (plate 6.9). Once again, an artist's distinct style and vision determines our perception of a therianthrope, in this case the threatening nature of a shape-shifter.

The concept of the shape-shifter seems to reside so deep in the human subconscious that myth and ritual can give way to delusion. The word *lycanthropy* also refers to a psychological disorder in which a person believes that he or she has actually become a wolf. It started to be recognized as a mental affliction at a time when people in England still believed in werewolves. In 1597, James I of England identified lycanthropy as a form of depression in his treatise *Daemonologie*. Robert Burton expounded on that concept in his *Anatomy of Melancholy*, published in 1621. Similar psychological disorders are connected to the traditional shape-shifters of other cultures: sufferers in India and Asia may believe themselves to be were-tigers; those in Africa, were-lions and were-leopards. There is even a name for the disorder of believing one is a dog: *cynanthropy*. It is not clear why anyone would want to be an ox or cow, but that is termed *boanthropy*. According to the book of Daniel, Nebuchadnezzar II suffered from this disorder and "was driven from men, and did eat grass as oxen."

Most shape-shifters are humans who assume animal form, but there are also animals that transform into other species. The each-uisge is a water horse dwelling in the lakes and seas around the Scottish Highlands that can shape-shift into a normal horse, a handsome man, or an enormous bird. But woe unto the ordinary man who mounts the each-uisge when it appears as a horse. If they ride anywhere near water, the each-uisge will fix the rider to his seat, drown him, and devour him—except for his liver, which floats to the surface. In folktales, just as in paintings and sculptures, details like these increase the verisimilitude.

There is a type of character that appears in many mythologies called a trickster. Tricksters are clever, crafty creatures that play all sorts of tricks on humans and even on gods. They delight in breaking social and physical rules, and some are inventive shape-shifters. The San hunter-gatherers of southern Africa tell of a shape-shifting trickster called Kaggen. He usually takes the form of a praying mantis, but can also transform into an eland, a snake, or a caterpillar.

Loki is another shape-shifting trickster, one from Norse mythology. In some tales, Loki appears as a salmon; in others, as a mare or even a fly. His relationship to the gods varies: at times he is their loyal assistant, and at times he opposes them. Loki was responsible for the death of the god Baldr, and his punishment was to be bound to a tree in his human form, with a deadly serpent overhead (plate 6.9). Earthquakes resulted from Loki's agonies.

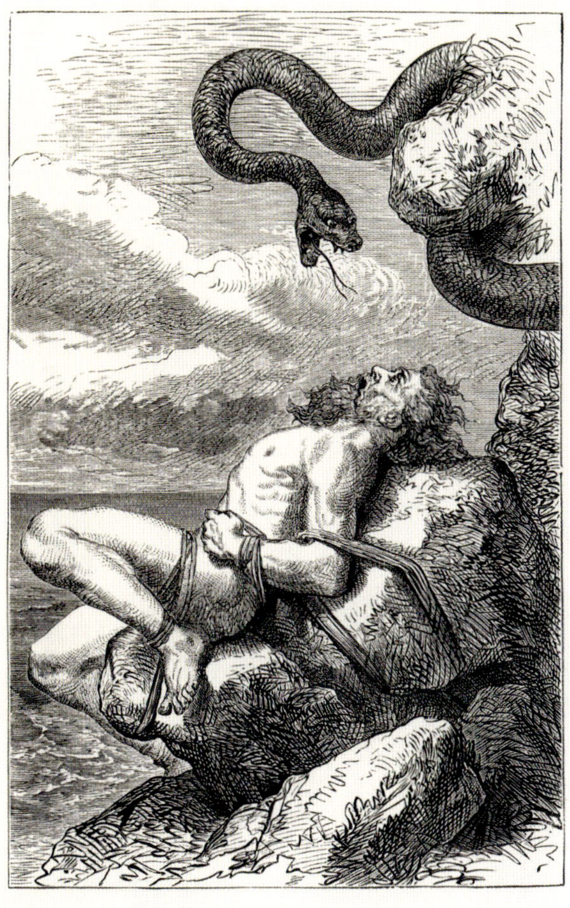

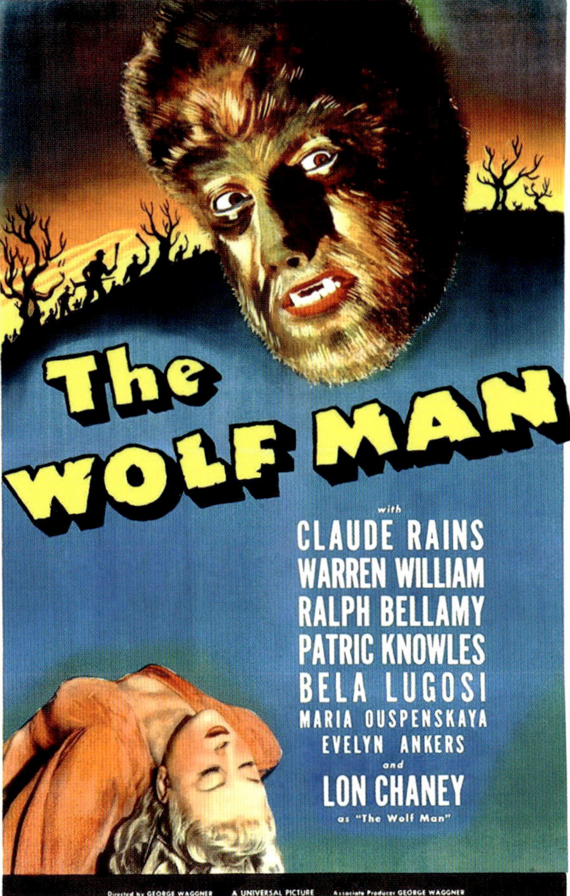

6.9. ABOVE LEFT: Charles Huard (1874–1965). *The Punishment of Loki*. Illustration from *The Heroes of Asgard: Tales from Scandinavian Mythology* by A. and E. Keary (New York: Macmillan, 1900).

6.10. ABOVE RIGHT: Poster for *The Wolf Man* (1941), starring Lon Chaney Jr. in the title role.

One of the central tenets of Hinduism, reincarnation, can be interpreted as a form of shape-shifting. After death, human souls can be reborn in one of several forms, depending on their karma. Those with poor karma may well find themselves reincarnated as animals. Buddhism has a related doctrine of rebirth.

Shape-shifters have continued to fascinate modern artists, including writers. One of the most famous examples is Franz Kafka's *Metamorphosis*. At the beginning of the novella, Gregor Samsa wakes from his unsettling dreams to find himself transformed into a monstrous insect with an "armorlike back," a "vaulted brown belly," and many "pathetically thin" legs.[6] But somehow he does not lose sight of his everyday concerns. As he struggles

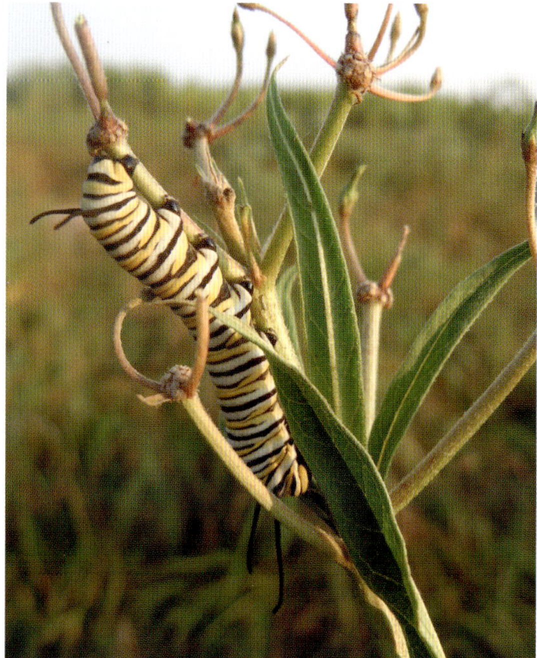

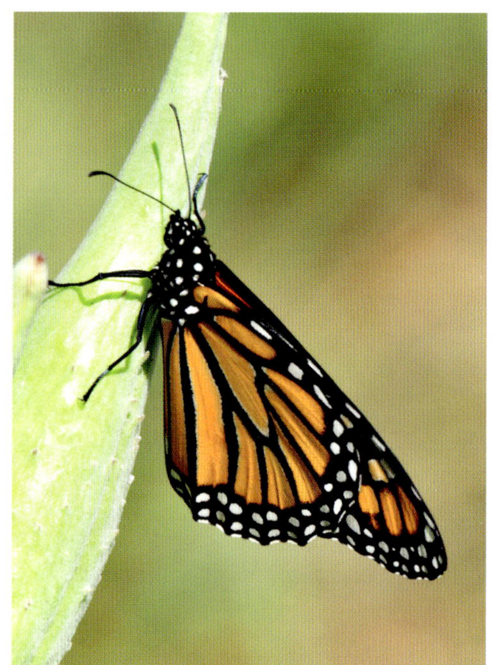

6.11. A monarch caterpillar and butterfly.

to move in his new body, his first concern is that when he gets to the office, his boss will berate him for being late. As the story progresses, Gregor observes passively as he becomes the cause of his family's deterioration. Kafka's use of shape-shifting to address the problems of modern life only underscores the enduring appeal of the phenomenon.

Other modern artists have drawn more directly from the traditional shape-shifting myths. The story of Daphne, for example, has been interpreted in multiple art forms. Edith Sitwell wrote a poem titled "Daphne" that William Walton transformed into an art song:

> She fled, and changed into a tree,
> That lovely fair-haired lady. . . .

Werewolf tales have lived on in a long series of movies, notably *The Wolf Man* (1941), in which Lon Cheney plays the title role (plate 6.10). Returning to his ancestral home in Wales, Cheney's character hears the local villagers recite a poem that portends his own fate:

> Even a man who is pure in heart, and says his prayers by night;
> May become a wolf when the wolfbane blooms and the autumn moon is bright.

Cheney went on to star in four sequels, and a new version of *The Wolf Man* was made in 2010 with Benicio del Toro as the werewolf.

Shape-shifting has a natural appeal to science fiction writers and filmmakers. One plotline in *Star Trek: Deep Space Nine* concerns the Dominion, an interstellar empire in the Gamma Quadrant of the galaxy. The founders and rulers of the Dominion are the Changelings, a race of liquid creatures capable of shape-shifting, not only into various other life-forms, including humans, but into objects like a key. A striking combination of mythological tradition and modern creativity.

It is conceivable that some shape-shifting myths could have been inspired by the remarkable transformations that actually take place in nature. One of the most beautiful is the metamorphosis of the lowly caterpillar into a monarch butterfly (plate 6.11).

Moreover, we know from the science of evolution that all species are, in a sense, shape-shifters: their form changes slowly over time due to genetic mutations and natural selection. In February 2021, concern arose about new variants of the Covid-19 virus caused by genetic mutations.[7] Scientists and the media termed this process "shape-shifting." A mythological concept took on a deeply troubling reality.

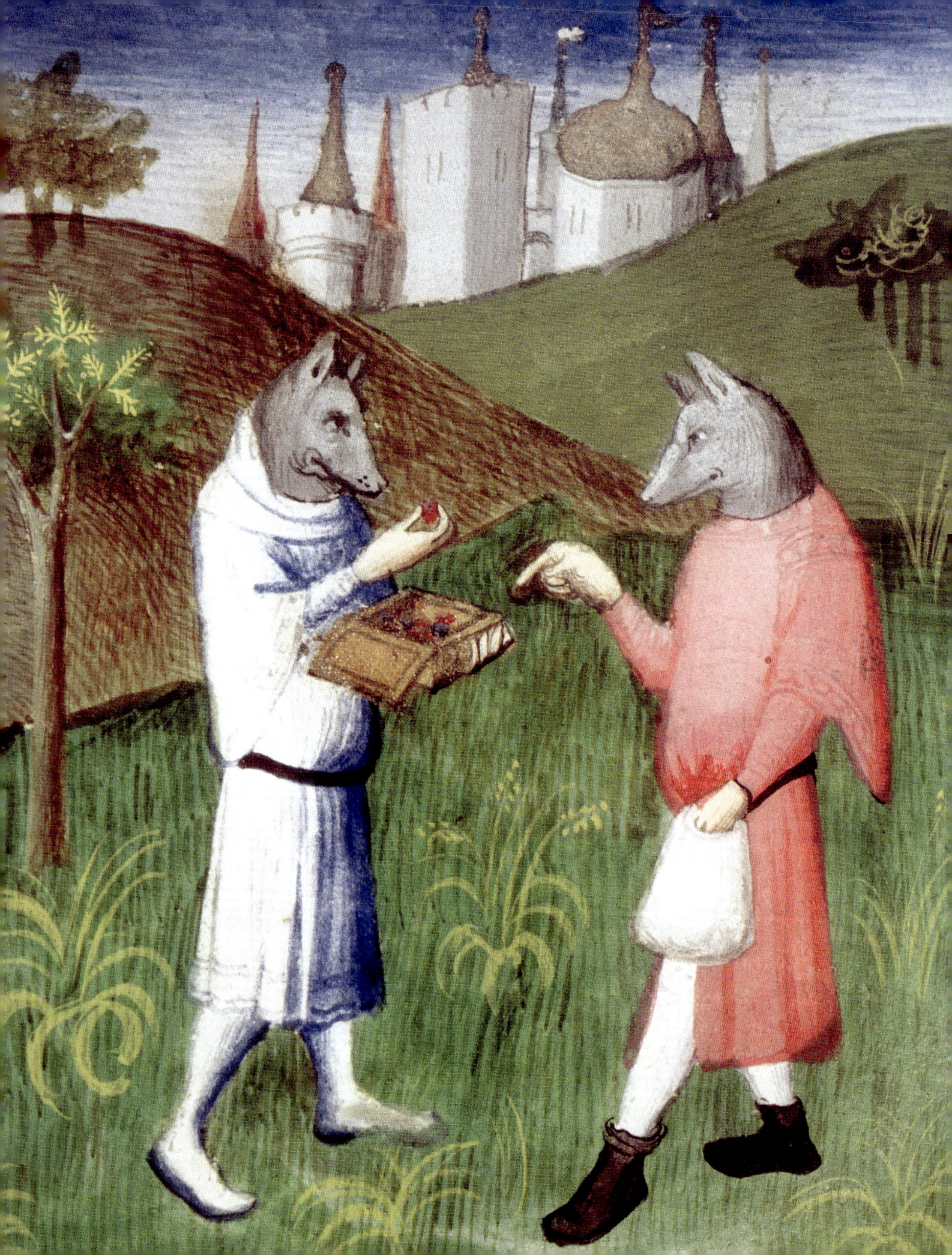

7
TALKING ANIMALS

There are many ways of combining humans and animals. Most therianthropes are physical combinations: some are hybrids—a lion's head on a human body, a woman with the lower body of a fish, or a small lovely woman with the wings of a butterfly—and some are shape-shifters who transform from human to animal. But there is another, highly popular kind of animal-human combination that appears in the myths and fables of many cultures: animals that think and talk like humans; animals that amuse us, teach us, and enlighten us. These are not usually considered therianthropes, but a duck called Donald with a human mind and vocal cords should qualify.

Detail of the dog-headed people of the Andaman Islands, from the Livre des merveilles du monde. See plate 7.1.

Many early animal-headed humans talked to their entirely human associates. The wolf-headed Egyptian deity Wepwawet conversed with the pharaoh, for whom he was a scout, and the horse-headed Hindu deity Hayagriva imparts pearls of wisdom to his followers. In his *Travels*, Marco Polo reported on dog-headed humans happily conversing with each other (plate 7.1). Later, the animal-headed beast of the fairy tale "Beauty and the Beast" talked his way from hated to beloved in many cultures and many languages.

But there are also a vast number of pure talking animals in early folktales. They populate two major historic collections of animal fables, one from India called the *Panchatantra*, and one from Greece identified with Aesop. These collections share some tales and both undoubtedly drew on even more ancient oral traditions.[1] The initial version of the *Panchatantra* is a Sanskrit text dating to around 200 BC. It consists of five volumes of interrelated tales. Early on it was translated into various Indian languages and then into many other languages around the world (plate 7.2). One version made its way to Europe in the eleventh century. One interpretation

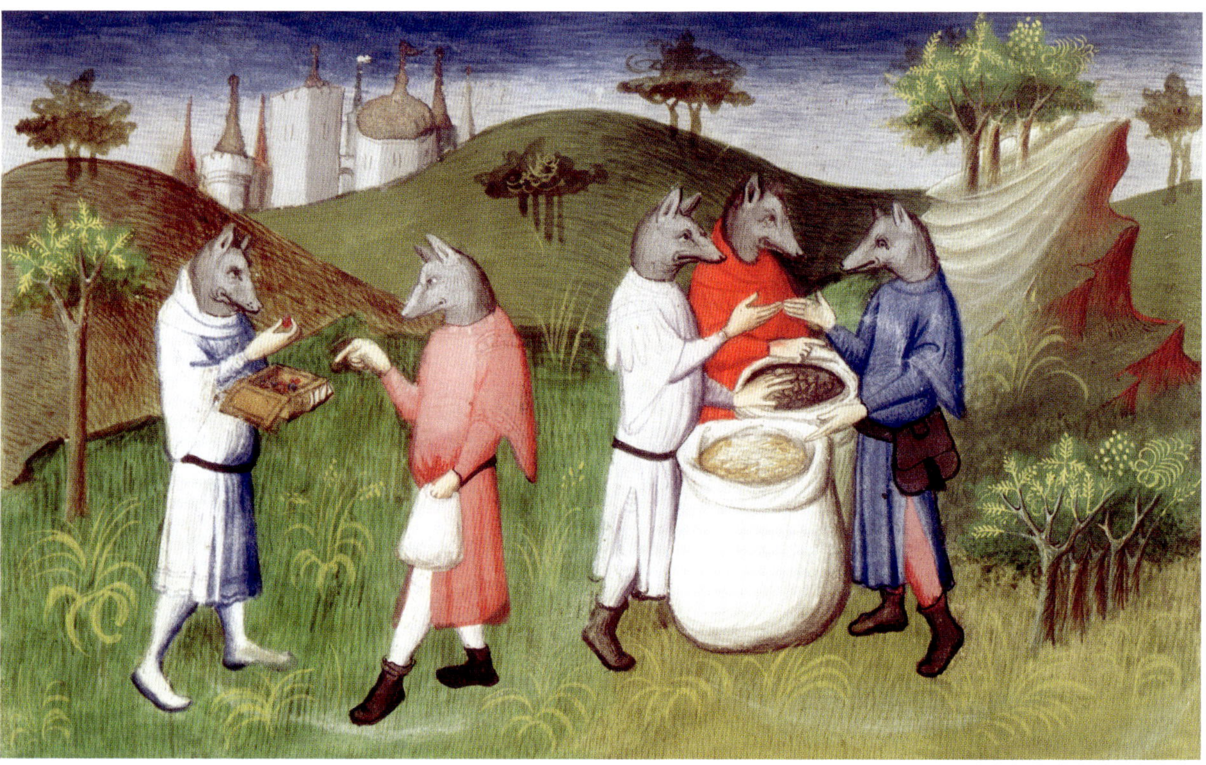

7.1. The dog-headed people of the Andaman Islands in the Indian Ocean, from a French translation of Marco Polo's travels included in the illuminated manuscript known as the Livre des merveilles du monde, c. 1410–12. Bibliothèque Nationale de France, Paris, MS Fr. 2810, fol. 76v.

of some of the stories is that the author used animals to safely teach a wayward ruling prince how to behave. One page from the *Panchatantra* depicts the jackal-vizier trying to persuade his lion-king that a bull-courtier is actually a traitor.

The semilegendary Greek slave-savant Aesop, who is supposed to have died in 564 BC, was one of the first creators and compilers of fables in the West. The first surviving written compilation of his fables dates to the first century AD, although it is known that there were earlier ones that have not survived. As in the *Panchatantra*, in Aesop's fables animals behave like humans and often communicate a moral or satiric message. An early favorite was "Belling the Cat," which tells the tale of a group of mice threatened by a marauding cat. They all get together to figure out how to protect themselves. They decide to put a bell around the cat's neck and thus be warned

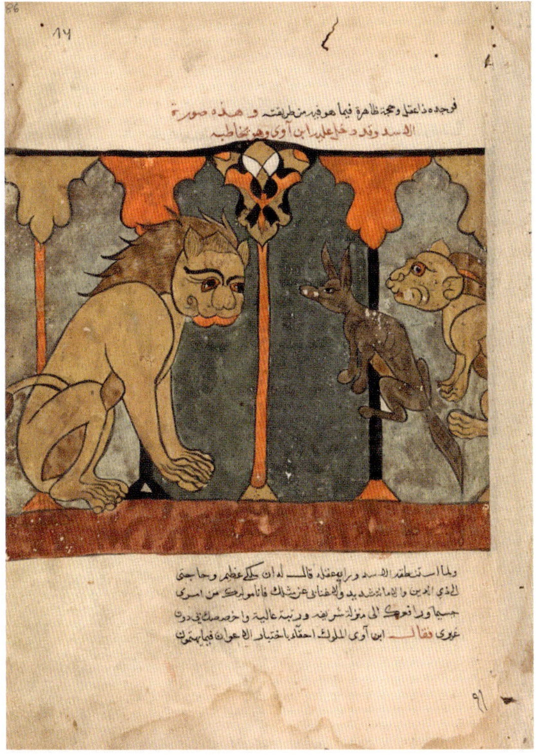

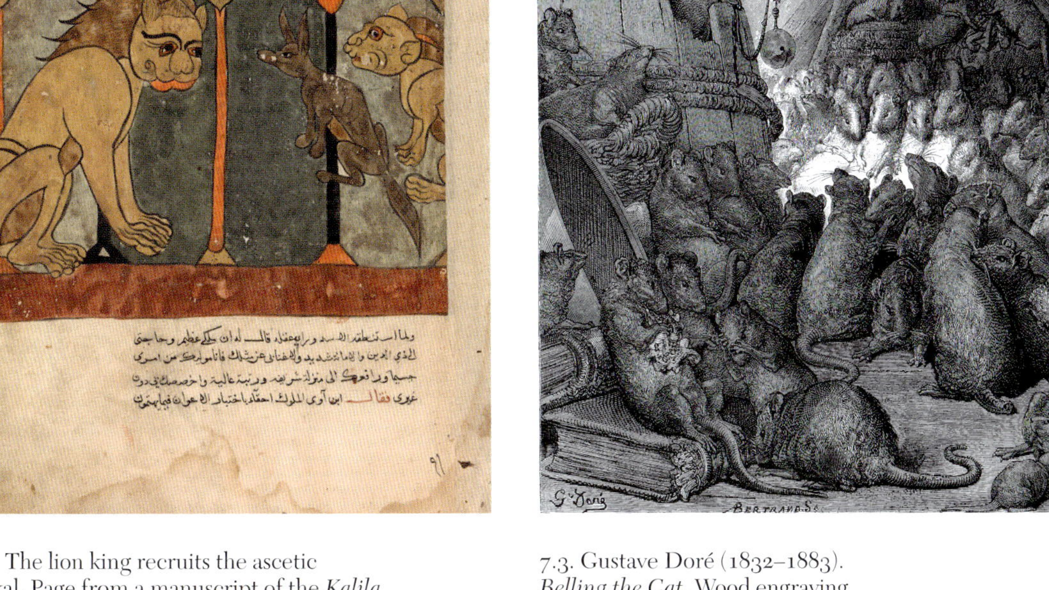

7.2. The lion king recruits the ascetic jackal. Page from a manuscript of the *Kalila wa Dimna*, an Arabic adaptation of the *Panchatantra*. Gujarati, after an Egyptian original, 1525–50. Metropolitan Museum of Art, New York.

7.3. Gustave Doré (1832–1883). *Belling the Cat*. Wood engraving from *Les Fables de Lafontaine* (Paris: Hachette, 1867).

of its approach (plate 7.3). A good idea. But then one mouse asks who will place the bell on the cat, and none of them volunteers. The moral of the story is the need to evaluate the practicality of a plan, not only its objective.

In all myth and fable there can be no more consequential talking animal than the serpent of the Garden of Eden (plate 7.4). Although in later depictions the serpent had a human head, the original was pure animal—with a human voice. The primary interpretation of the serpent was as an anti-God symbol, a Satan symbolizing the power of evil. The serpent was a talking creature that determined the future nature of humankind.

There is a continuous tradition of animal fables from prehistoric times to the present, and they remain a reliable means of amusing the reader and getting across a simple message at the same time. Take the time to build

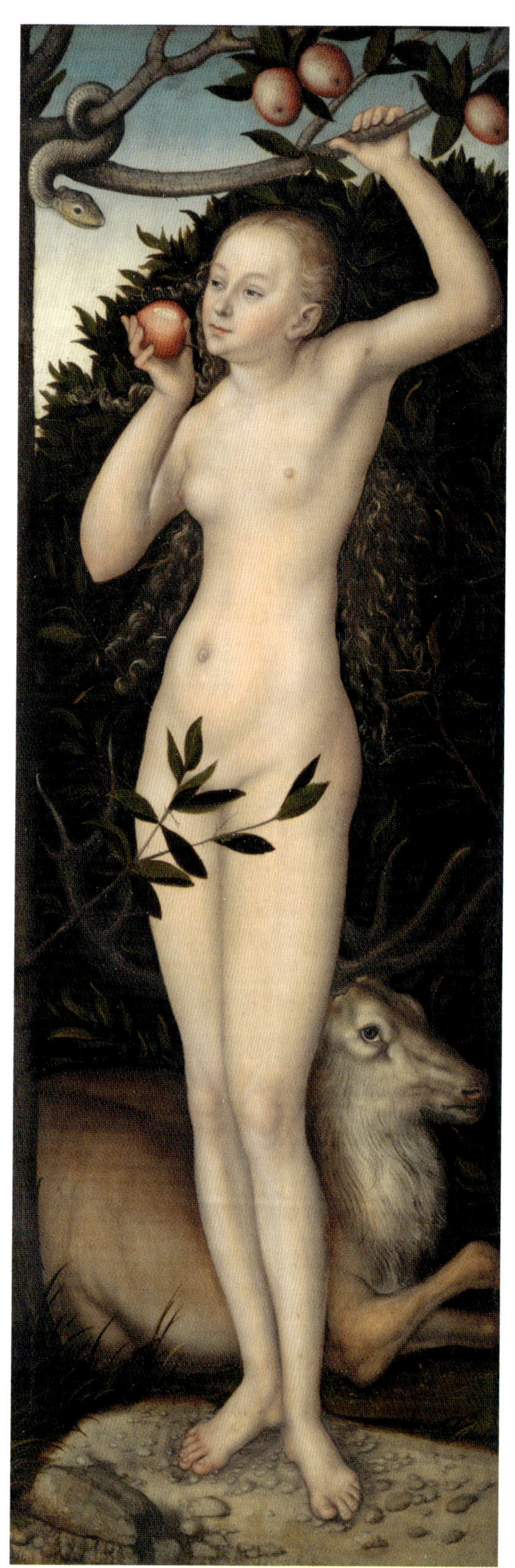

7.4. Lucas Cranach the Elder (1472–1553). *Eve*, 1533/37. Oil on panel, 41⅝ × 14⅜ in. (105.7 × 36.4 cm). Art Institute of Chicago.

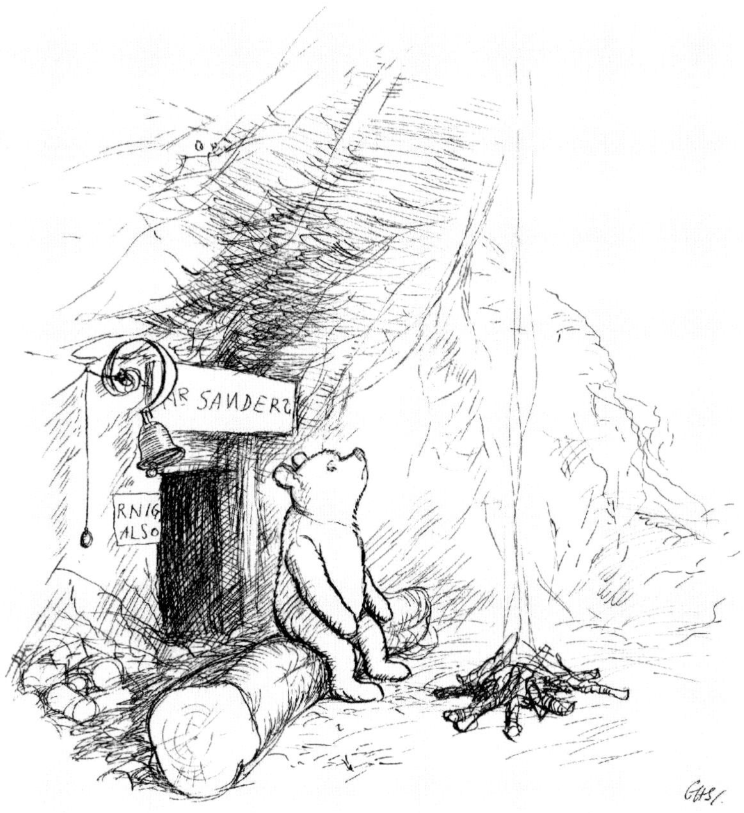

7.5. E. H. Shepard (1879–1976). Illustration from A. A. Milne's *Winnie-the-Pooh* (London: Methuen, 1926).

your house (or conduct any endeavor) properly, says the tale of the *Three Little Pigs*. How can you forget that big bad wolf blowing down the first two pigs' houses, made of straw and sticks, but failing to disturb the third pig's brick house? The tale is thought to long predate the first printed version in the 1840s. Much of children's literature carries on the tradition of animals talking.

In their spontaneous early actions, children often reflect deeply rooted human instincts. They feel close to animals and often communicate with them. That basic instinct in children is reflected in their love of Walt Disney's dozens of anthropomorphic characters, from Mickey Mouse to Donald Duck. Disney's animal characters have clear precedents not only in earlier children's literature—such as the appealing teddy bear, Winnie the Pooh, created by author A. A. Milne and illustrator E. H. Shepard in the 1920s (plate 7.5)—but also in the ancient fables of animals behaving like humans. Adults continue to use children's inherent connection to animals to communicate desired modes of behavior.

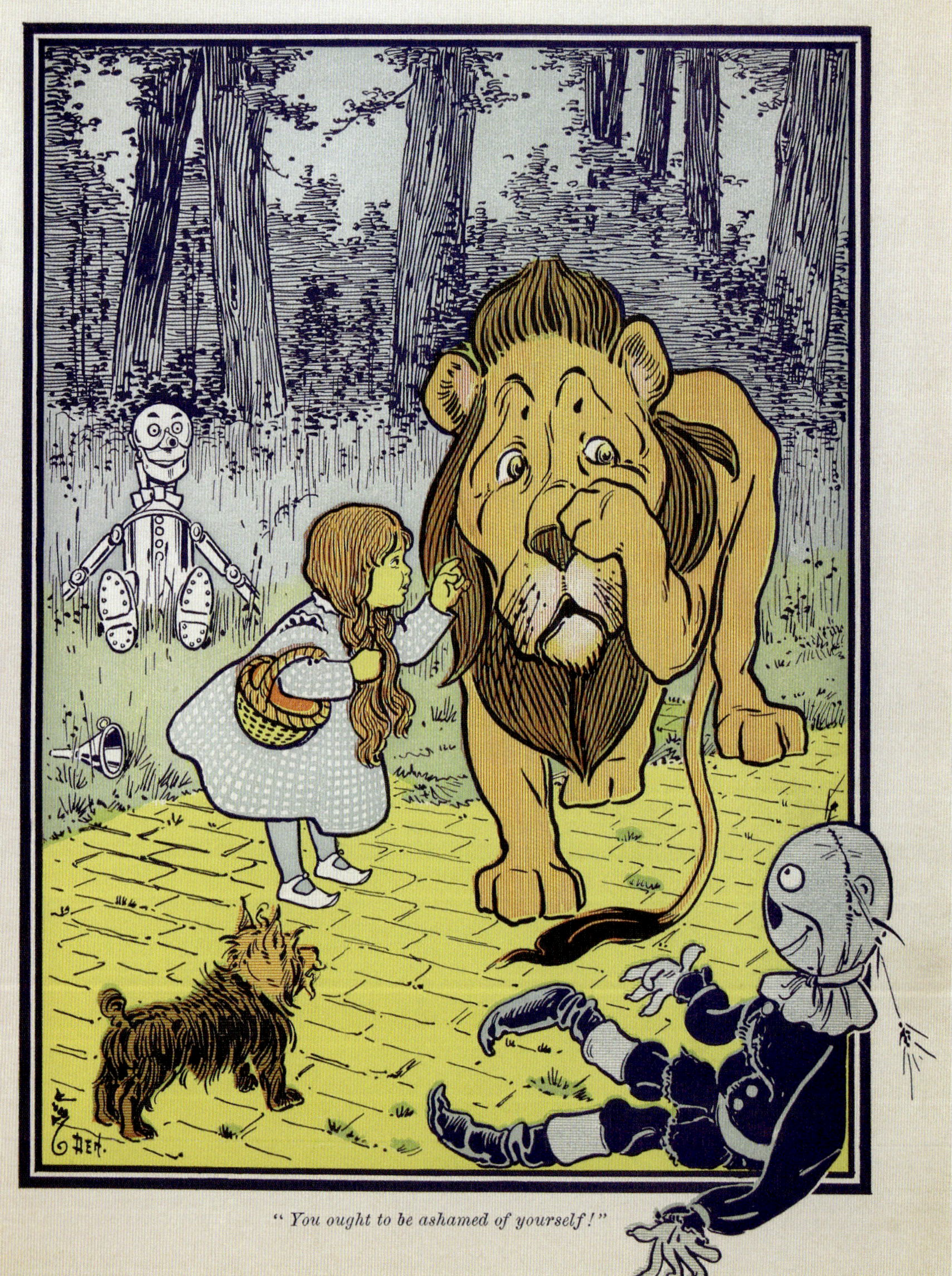

"You ought to be ashamed of yourself!"

The deep-rooted appeal of talking animals goes far beyond moralizing fables and cartoon characters. A talking animal is at the heart of one of the most popular films of all time. The Cowardly Lion was portrayed by Bert Lahr in the classic 1939 movie *The Wizard of Oz*. As in the early fables where the talking animals not only amuse but teach us, the Cowardly Lion has an important message. As soon as he is berated by Dorothy (played famously by the seventeen-year-old Judy Garland) for trying to bite her dog, he admits he is afraid of her, and is ashamed of it (plate 7.6). Lions, after all, are supposed to be brave "kings of the beasts." He believes that his fear makes him a failure. But later, when faced by danger to himself and his companions, he shows bravery. Courage is not the lack of fear, but acting bravely in the face of fear. As the lion declares near the end of the film, "What makes a king out of a slave? Courage!"

7.6. OPPOSITE: W. W. Denslow (1856–1915). Dorothy meets the Cowardly Lion, from L. Frank Baum's *The Wizard of Oz* (Chicago: George M. Hill Company, 1900).

Talking animals even found their way into a highly popular piece of classical music. Camille Saint-Saëns wrote *The Carnival of the Animals* in 1886, and in the late 1940s Ogden Nash was the first to write poetry to accompany Saint-Saëns's score. All sorts of animals join the carnival, including a lion, roosters, tortoises, an elephant, and kangaroos. At a prehistoric ball, even the fossils talk:

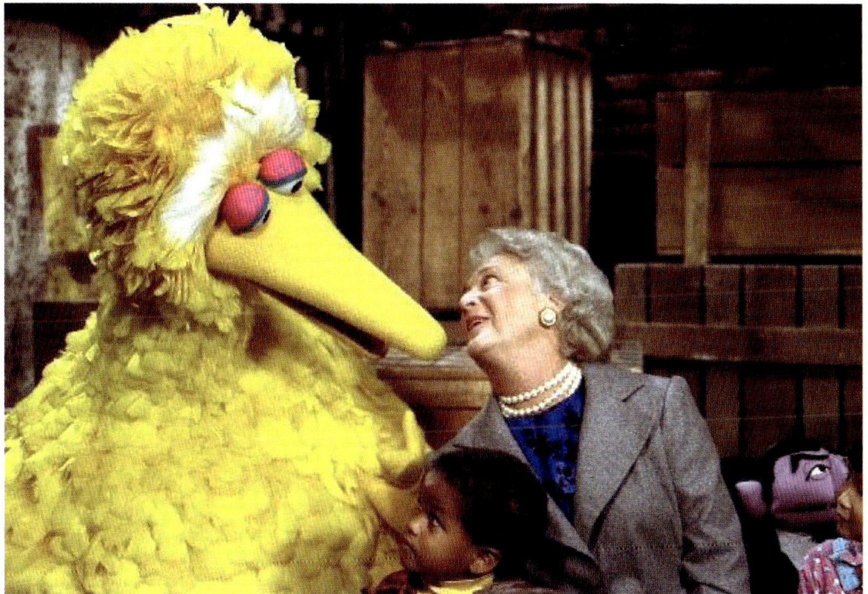

7.7. First Lady Barbara Bush meets Big Bird during a taping of *Sesame Street* in New York, October 19, 1989.

Amid the mastodonic wassail,
I caught the eye of one small fossil.
Cheer up, sad world, he said, and winked.
It's kind of fun to be extinct.

Talking animals continue to be used effectively to amuse, teach, and persuade. Since his first appearance in 1969, Big Bird has been teaching children and amusing all ages on the children's public television show *Sesame Street* (plate 7.7). In 2000, the eight foot two inch tall, bright yellow anthropomorphic bird was named a Living Legend by the United States Library of Congress. A legend, but very real to many.

The appeal of talking animals has also been recognized by companies trying to sell products and services to the public. One very effective animal spokesman is a gecko named Martin who speaks with a cockney accent on behalf of the insurance company GEICO (plate 7.8).[2] Who hasn't heard Martin's advice that "fifteen minutes could save you fifteen percent or more on your car insurance"? Martin helped GEICO grow from being a minor player in the field to the second-largest auto insurer in the United States.

Animal tales existed in early cultures well before writing, at a time when humans had a necessarily close relationship with nature and the animals on which they depended. Our closeness to animals appears in a human inclination to talk to animals, and not only our pet dogs and cats. We see nothing strange when John Keats addresses his thoughts to a bird in a poem titled *Song*:

Stay, ruby-breasted warbler, stay,
　　And let me see thy sparkling eye,
Oh brush not yet the pearl-strung spray
　　Nor bow thy pretty head to fly.

Stay while I tell thee, fluttering thing,
　　That thou of love an emblem art,
Yes! patient plume thy little wing,
　　Whilst I my thoughts to thee impart.[3]

Many, young and old, have found talking to animals to be enjoyable, therapeutic, and useful in other ways. Saint Francis preached to the birds and asked them to appreciate God's "greatest of gifts, the freedom of the air," a phrase that harkens back to early humans' envy of flight. When the eminent U.S. representative and civil rights leader John Lewis was a boy growing up in rural Alabama, he aspired to be a preacher. At the age of five he practiced preaching to the chickens on his family's farm. It's unclear whether this changed the chickens' lives, but Lewis went on to be a powerful and persuasive speaker.

We have a deeply rooted inclination to believe that animals communicate with us in some way and understand us when we talk to them. Animals that talk back to us have a long history and are important members of the family Therianthrope.

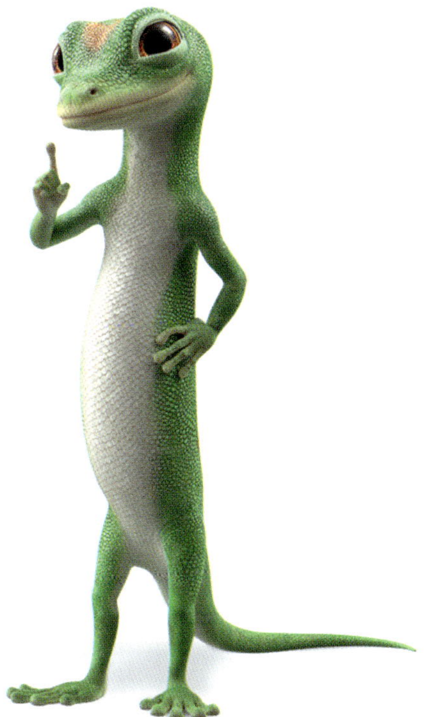

7.8. Martin, the GEICO gecko.

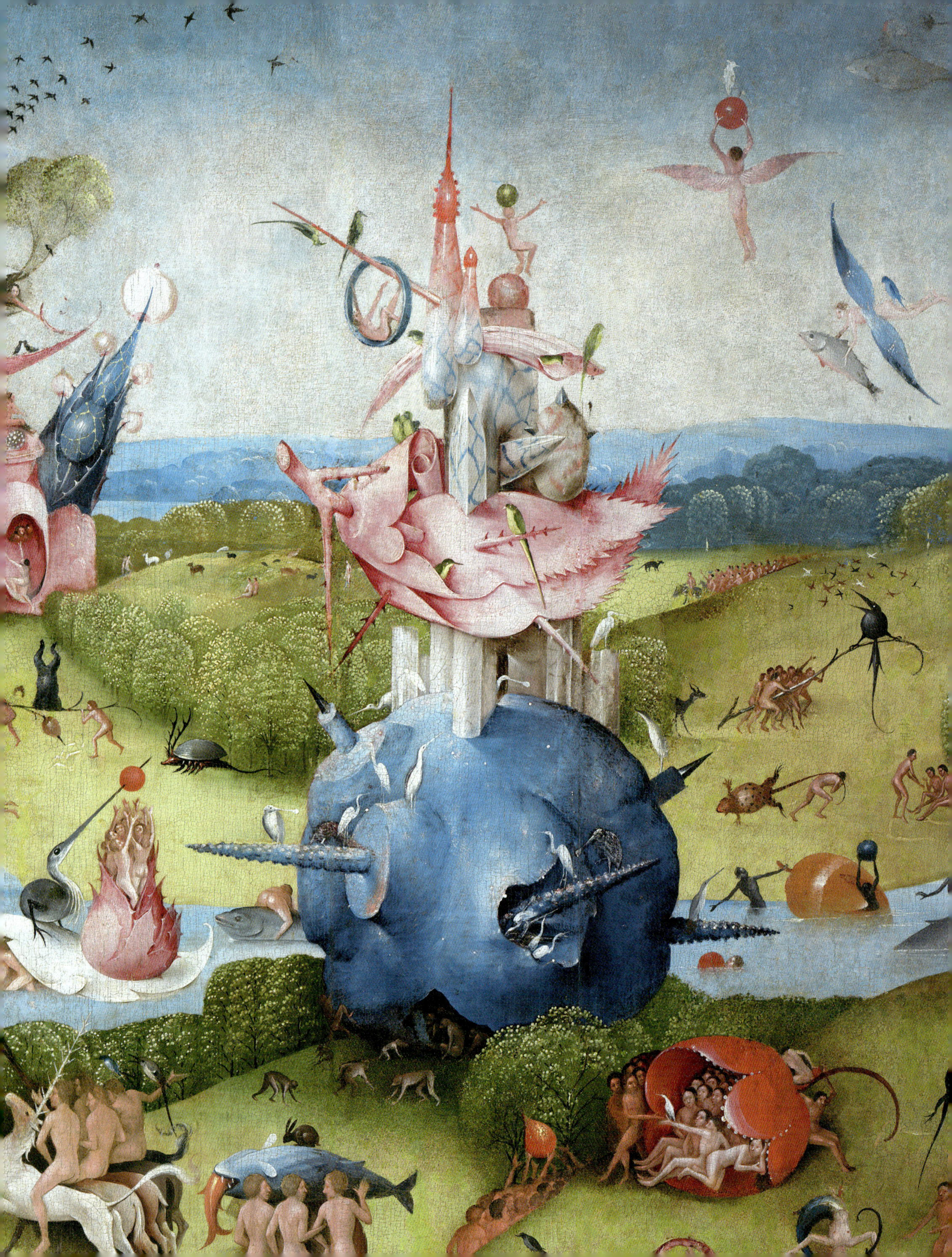

8
ORIGINS AND MEANINGS

Detail of Hieronymus Bosch's *Garden of Earthly Delights*. See plate 8.9.

As we have seen, an immense variety of animal-human creatures have flourished in many cultures through the ages. The ubiquity of these fantastical creatures indicates that they are in some way integral to human nature. Why is that? To find an answer, we must seek their origins. Where and when did the idea of therianthropes originate?

The representation of combined animal-human figures dates back to the earliest days of figurative art. During the Upper Paleolithic era, or late Stone Age, around 40,000 years ago, early humans started painting captivating images on the walls of caves from Africa and Asia to Europe and even Australia and Indonesia.

Cave paintings had been discovered over the centuries, but their significance was not recognized until 1879, when an amateur archaeologist, Don Marcelino Sanz de Sautuola, explored a cave on his property in northern Spain. Sautuola had seen prehistoric objects from caves in southern France at an exhibition in Paris, and wanted to see whether he could find any in his meandering cave called Altamira.

Sautuola brought along his eight-year-old daughter, María, and while the father scraped and dug the floor of the cave for ancient objects, the daughter wandered around the cave. And while he was looking down, she was looking up. When María saw images of animals floating on the ceiling of the cave, she cried, "Look, Papa, oxen!" Sautuola's first reaction was to laugh, and then—seeing the amazing scene above them—he was overwhelmed to silence. The ceiling was resplendently alive with images of reindeer, horses, and bison (plate 8.1). When he looked more closely, he observed that the artists had used slight humps on the ceiling to give a three-dimensional effect to some of their creations.

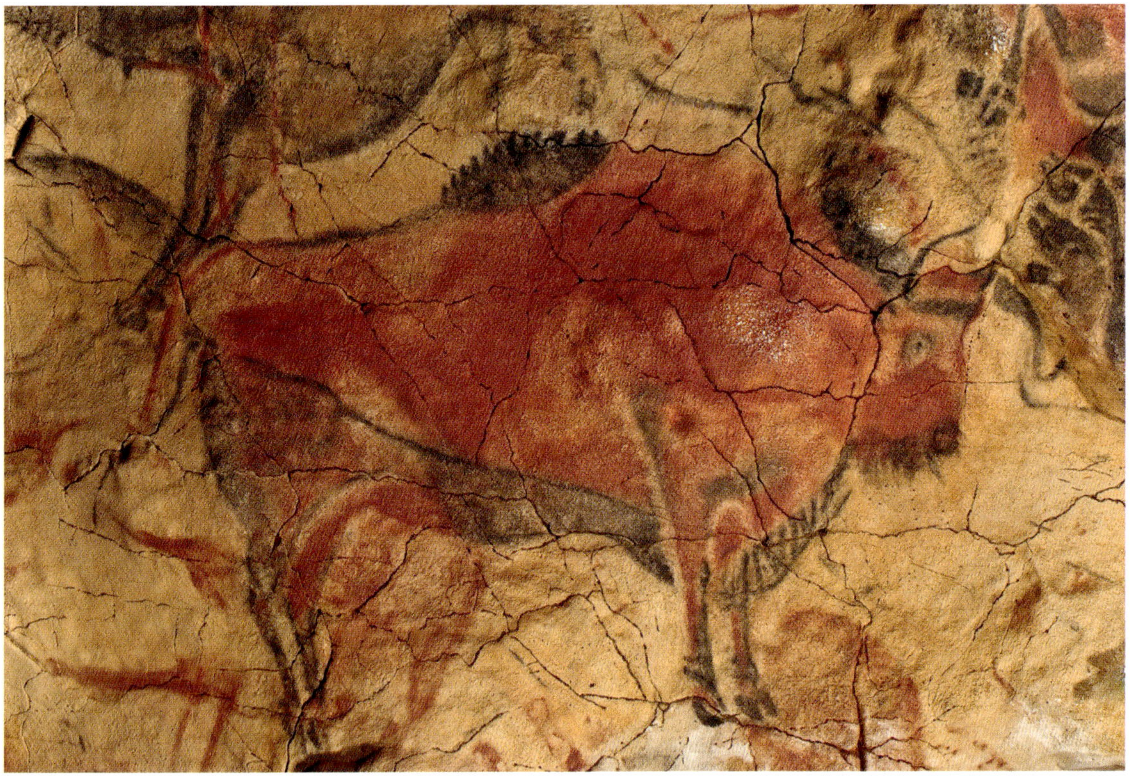

8.1. Copy of a painting of a bison from the ceiling of the cave of Altamira, c. 12,000 BC. Museo Nacional y Centro de Investigación de Altamira, Santillana del Mar, Spain.

The Sautuolas' discovery on that November day in 1879 initiated a period of controversy. At first, the paintings of Altamira were acclaimed and elevated by a visit from the king of Spain. Then, after Sautuola published a cautious pamphlet on his findings in 1880, suggesting that the paintings were Paleolithic, and presented it at professional meetings, the experts ganged up against him. The paintings were just too fine to have been created by "primitive man." Sautuola must have created them himself or hired someone to do so. It wasn't until other cave paintings were discovered in the south of France, with proof of their age (for example, being covered with a thick layer of calcite) that the antiquity of the Altamira art was acknowledged. But that was not until 1902, fourteen years after Sautuola's death.[1] Modern dating methods now place the date of Altamira's ceiling paintings at around 12,000 BC.

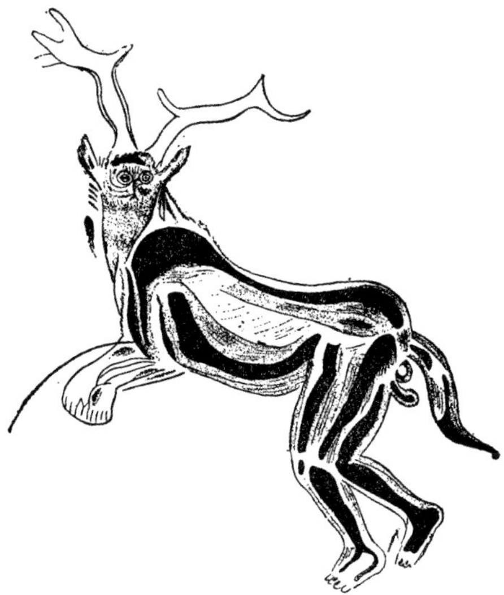

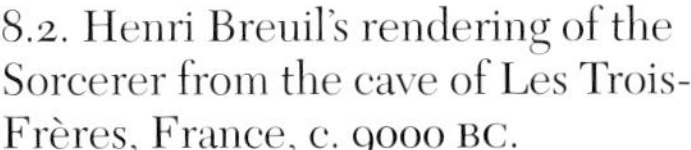

8.2. Henri Breuil's rendering of the Sorcerer from the cave of Les Trois-Frères, France, c. 9000 BC.

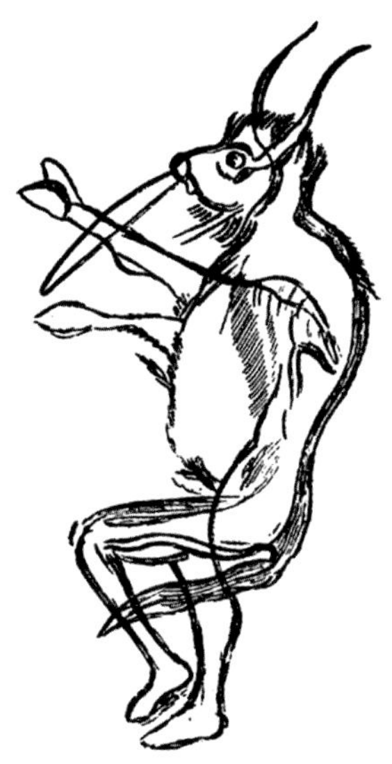

8.3. Henri Breuil's rendering of the Small Sorcerer with a Musical Bow from the cave of Les Trois-Frères, France, c. 13,000 BC.

Particularly relevant for our inquiry are the French caves of Les Trois-Frères and Lascaux, and Henri-Édouard-Prosper Breuil, a highly influential early paleoanthropologist. Born in 1877 in Mortain, France, Breuil was ordained a Catholic priest in 1900. Although he was a passionate believer throughout his life, by the time he was ordained he had become deeply fascinated by Stone Age art and had decided to devote his life to its study. He was known as Abbé Breuil and then, to his pleasure, as the Pope of Prehistory.

The cave of Les Trois-Frères in southwest France was discovered by Count Henri Bégouën in 1912 and explored by him and Breuil during the 1920s. Deep in the cave, seemingly inaccessibly high on a wall, they discovered an extraordinary image—of a creature with the body and tail of a horse, the antlers and ears of a stag, and the head, legs, and penis of a man (plate 8.2). His long beard covers his chest. While the creature is sideways to us, he has seen us and has turned his head to look at us. His two black, circular eyes stare at us. He is a remarkable example of a therianthrope created from an artist's imagination. Breuil made a drawing of the creature and named him the Sorcerer. Dating to around 9000 BC, the Sorcerer is engraved into the stone, but, unlike all the other figures in that part of the cave, his basic form is also painted boldly in black.

There are a few other, if less dramatic, therianthropic figures in the Trois-Frères Cave. One bison-human dating to about 13,000 BC is known as the Small Sorcerer with a Musical Bow (plate 8.3)—although it's impossible that those two lines extending from the creature's nose are a bow for a stringed musical instrument and also unlikely that they are a hunting bow.[2]

Oddly, there are very few human figures among the multitude of horses and bison and reindeer on the walls of Paleolithic caves. A notable exception was found in the cave of Lascaux in the Périgord region of France. Discovered in 1940, Lascaux has the most abundant and varied array of wall paintings and engravings of any cave explored thus far. Deep into this complex cave is a space called the Apse, in whose floor is a hole leading into a vertical space termed the Shaft that descends some sixteen feet. On the wall of the Shaft is one of the rare narrative scenes in Paleolithic art, and one of the rare depictions of a human, or at least a part-human.[3] Its location is such that only one person can view it at a time.

This scene, known as the Hunting Accident, shows a bison enraged, with the hair on its back standing straight up and its horns lowered for a charge (plate 8.4). He has been wounded by a spear, and his entrails are pouring out of his belly. Next to the bison is a sparsely outlined figure, lying or in the midst of falling. This figure has the body of a man but the head of a bird. His left hand, which looks like the claw of a bird, his erect penis, and his narrow, pointed feet all point toward the bison. A bird on a stick lies next to him. This and the creature's head are the only birds portrayed in the entire cave.

The bison, horses, and other animals represented in Lascaux, Les Trois-Frères, and many other caves are notable because of their realism. Even motion is communicated in a sophisticated way. So why aren't humans depicted with comparable realism? That is one of the mysteries of Upper Paleolithic art. The bird-man in the Hunting Accident and his ilk are quite different in style and essence from the bison and horses on cave walls. They show another level of artistic creativity, akin to modernism's efficiency in revealing the essence of a figure. Their source is elsewhere than the observed world.

It was not only on the walls of caves that early humans depicted therianthropes. One of the earliest—and most striking—representations is a small sculpture of a man with the head of a lion. (As described in the preface, this figure inspired this book; see plates 0.1 and 0.2.) Dating from

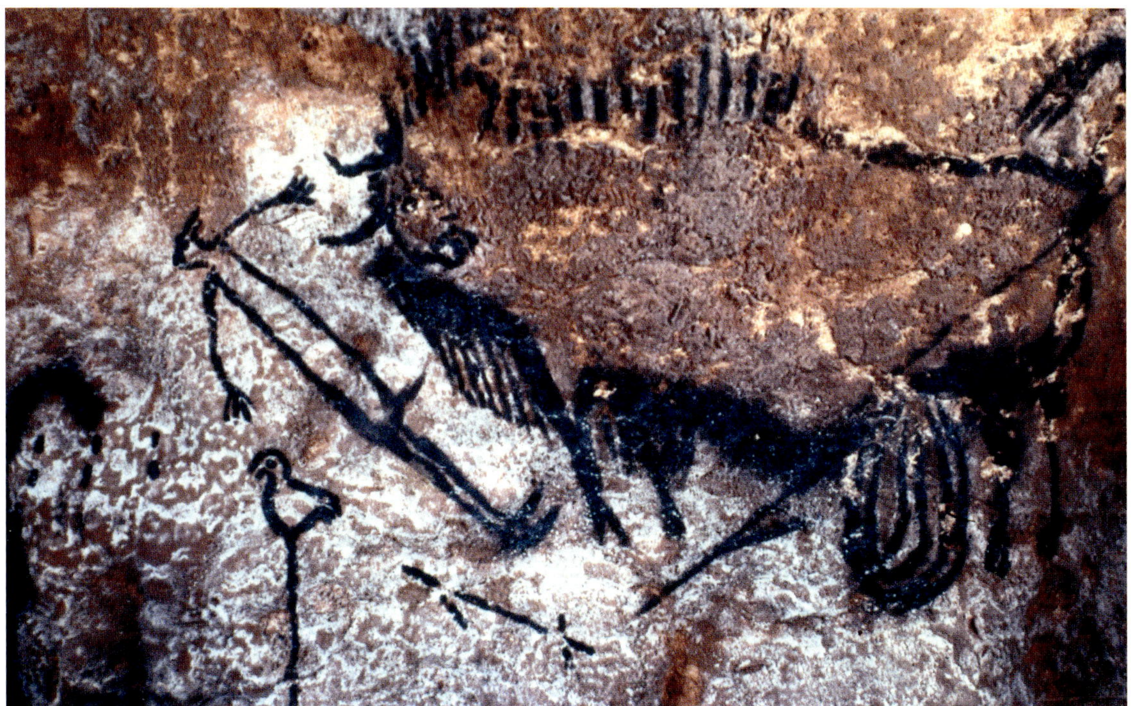

8.4. The Hunting Accident, cave of Lascaux, France, c. 15,000 BC.

38,000 to 33,000 BC, the Löwenmensch, or Lion-Man, was discovered in the Hohlenstein-Stadel Cave in Baden-Württemberg, Germany. It was carved out of woolly mammoth ivory using a flint knife and is about 12 inches (31 cm) tall. Either it represents a man, perhaps a shaman, wearing a lion's-head mask, or it is one of the first examples of a true animal-human hybrid. The medium of sculpture discourages the kind of sketchy abstraction shown in the wall paintings. It is estimated that the Lion-Man took four hundred hours to carve, and its wear marks suggest that it was an object of veneration, perhaps a totem of some kind.

Paleolithic depictions of therianthropes are not confined to Europe. Indeed, some of the earliest cave paintings, dating to at least 41,000 BC, before the oldest known European cave art, were recently discovered on the Indonesian island of Sulawesi. And they may contain the earliest depictions of therianthropes. Their discoverers write: "Humans seem to have an adaptive predisposition for inventing, telling and consuming stories. Prehistoric cave art provides the most direct insight that we have into the earliest storytelling in the form of narrative compositions or 'scenes' . . . from

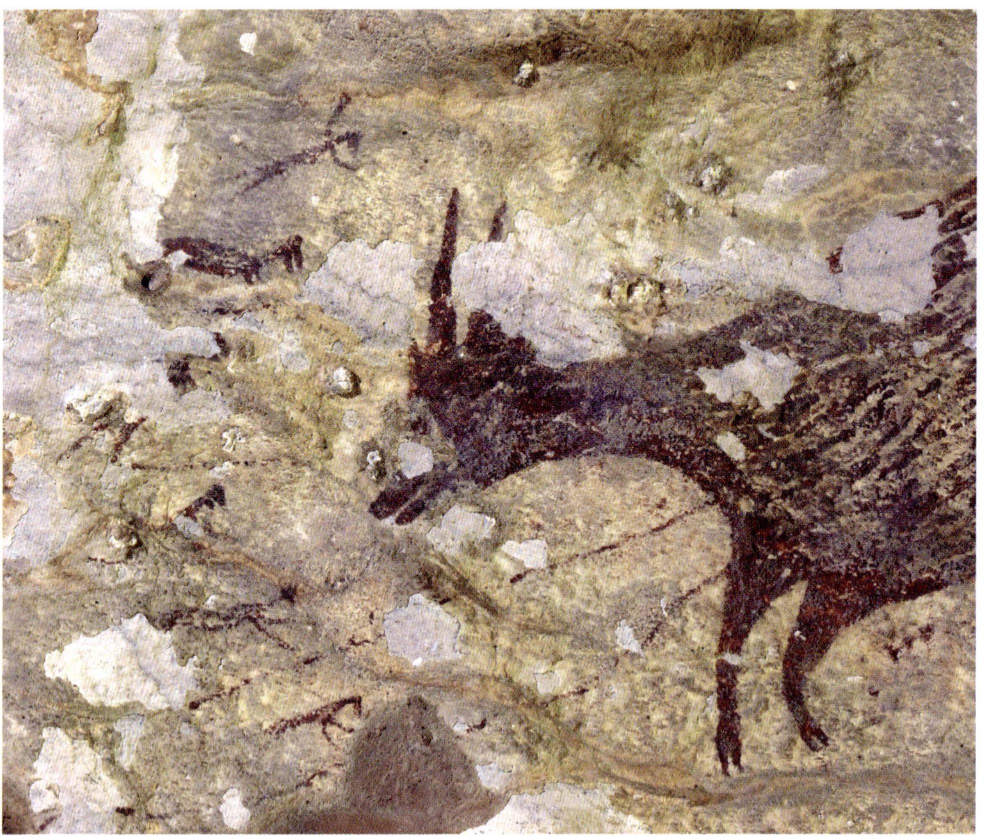

8.5. Anoa (dwarf buffalo) with possibly therianthropic hunters surrounding its head. Leang Bulu' Sipong 4 cave, Sulawesi, Indonesia, c. 41,000 BC.

which one can infer actions taking place among the figures." They describe a panel from the limestone cave of Leang Bulu' Sipong 4 that "portrays several figures that appear to represent therianthropes hunting wild pigs and dwarf bovids." The figures are not easy to make out, but some "look like they have snouts or muzzles, and one even has a beak and another a tail" (plate 8.5).[4]

Ever since Don Marcelino Sanz de Sautuola published his paper on the Altamira Cave, explanations of cave art have been abundant—and contentious. But there is little evidence aside from the paintings themselves to confirm or deny these theories. That paucity of surrounding fact opens the field for speculation, and there has been a lot. Some assert that the paintings are a display of totemic clan animals, or hunting magic. Others suggest that they could have been intended as a test of observational skills. Others believe they facilitated visionary experiences or played a role in initiation rites. Others present a quite different idea, based on a more modern conception of art: that cave paintings provided a "refuge from the flux of living at nature's mercy."[5]

Abbé Breuil believed that the meaning of cave art resided in early humans' dependence on hunting, and their desire to influence animal behavior. He considered the animal-human figures to be humans wearing masks. While the masks had a practical purpose in the field, of allowing hunters to approach closer to their prey, they also took on a mystical meaning. As Breuil wrote, the effectiveness of the strategy "convinced man that the mask or disguise itself possessed a ghostly magical power over game."[6]

But for every theory there have been skeptics. For example, critics of the seemingly logical view that the art represents hunting magic point out that most of the animals represented are not those that were hunted. Of all the hundreds of animals represented in Lascaux, for example, there is not one image of a reindeer, the inhabitants' principal source of meat. More broadly, some experts discount any theory that claims to understand what stimulated the art and what it means. Only noninterpretive, "objective" descriptions are allowed. But in a field where definite conclusions cannot be reached, plausible theories can be informative, even if not verifiably true.

Because of its age and the lack of any associated records, Upper Paleolithic cave art is inevitably mysterious. But there still exists a living culture that is descended from Paleolithic hunter-gatherers, and whose own art can be seen as analogous in some ways to prehistoric cave painting: the San of Southern Africa. One of the oldest continuous cultures on earth, the San comprise various hunter-gatherer groups living in southern Africa, including Botswana, Namibia, and South Africa. Recent DNA studies have concluded that the ancestors of today's San began to diverge from other human populations in Africa about 200,000 years ago and were fully isolated by 100,000 years ago.[7] The San were prolific painters, adorning the walls of rock shelters as long ago as 5500 BC.[8]

Although the San stopped painting at the end of the seventeenth century, some eighteenth-century anthropologists who learned the San languages were able to speak to San people who were contemporaries of those last painters. Unlike the European cave painters, the San often represented human figures in their art, and about 5 percent of those are therianthropes, often combining the body of a human with the head of an eland, the species of antelope they revered (plates 8.6 and 8.7).

A leading interpreter of San rock shelter paintings is David Lewis-Williams, who first developed his theories in his doctoral dissertation in anthropology at the University of Natal in 1979.[9] There and in subsequent publications, Lewis-Williams combined his analysis of the content of the rock art with recorded accounts of San healing practices. His scholarship places shamans at the creative heart of San art. It was the shaman's role in facilitating entry into altered states of consciousness that inspired many of the figures on the walls, and in particular the therianthropic figures. This theory had been anticipated by earlier anthropologists and was amplified by followers such as Pieter Jolly, who interpreted the animal-humans as shamans who, "in altered states associated with dream or trance, were in the process of fusing with, or have already fused with, animals and birds."[10]

There are many early written accounts of shamans in diverse cultures. The term *shaman* originated with the Tungus tribe in Siberia, with the root of the word meaning "to know." Early explorers in Central Asia, including Marco Polo in the thirteenth century, observed group leaders who led dances wearing animal hides and antlers (plate 8.8). They gradually appeared to enter another world. But the concept of shamanism also lived on in many early religions, including in Greek paganism. Tibetan Buddhism is prominent among the present-day religions that reflect shamanistic ritual.

There are striking similarities between the approaches that shamans in different cultures use to take their followers into that other world of altered states of consciousness. A common technique is to use some kind of psychoactive substance. Among the Aztecs and Maya of Central America it has been mushrooms and psychoactive water lilies. Across the Amazon basin it has been various herbal combinations to drink or smoke. For Native Americans it has been peyote. Forms of physical stress are also used in many cultures: dehydration, sleep deprivation, constant drumming, or repetitive dancing. A prominent San ritual was—and remains—the healing or trance dance led by a shaman. Women start the dance at night, clapping and singing a traditional song, and are later joined by men. The dancers stomp in a circle around a campfire for hours. Some of them start to have out-of-body experiences.

Transformation into an animal is an integral part of shamanism. Thomas Dowson and Martin Port point out a possible reason for that: The sha-

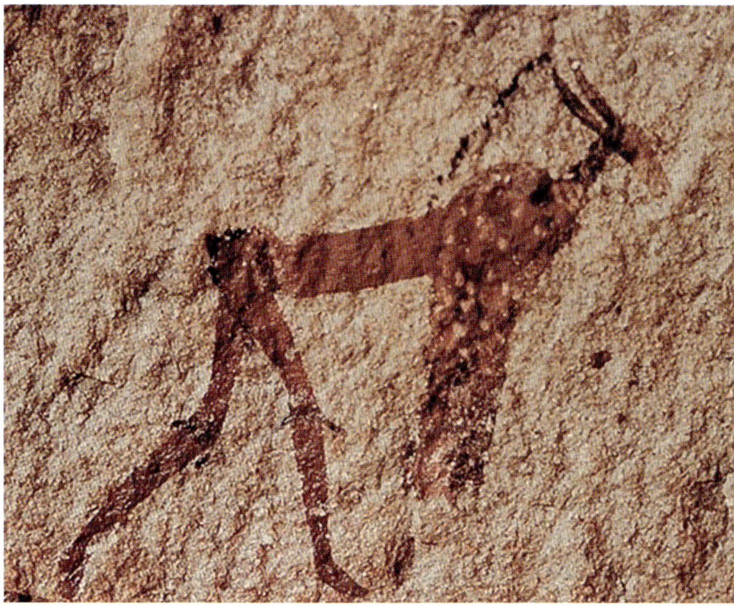

8.6. Therianthropic figure in San rock art from the Drakensberg, South Africa.

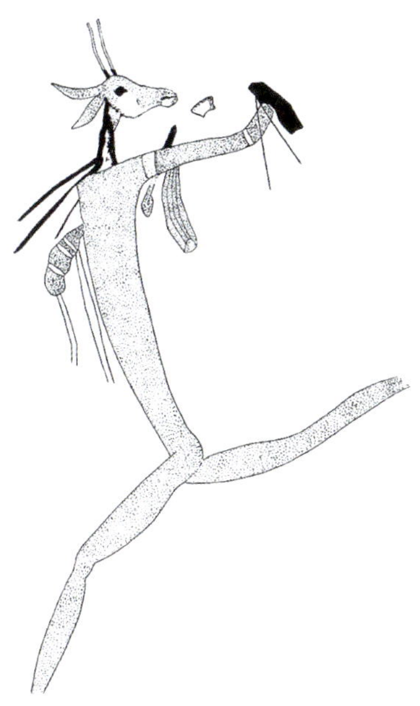

8.7. Drawing of a therianthropic figure in San rock art from the Eastern Cape, South Africa.

manistic journey into the other world is arduous at best, and nonhuman strength is required.[11] Taking on the strength of a lion makes the journey possible. It is very common for shamans in various cultures to dress in a powerful animal's fur, and some place antlers on their heads. In their journey to the other world, they become part animal.

The clear connection between shamanism and San rock art led Lewis-Williams and his collaborators to reexamine Upper Paleolithic art in the context of his "neuropsychological" model. In an important 1988 publication, Lewis-Williams collaborated with Thomas A. Dowson to elaborate this theory.[12] The French expert on cave art Jean Clottes later joined Lewis-Williams in creating the beautifully illustrated *Shamans of Prehistory*, in which they present a strong case that shamanism played a determinative role in creating European cave art. They write that "in that time and in that region people began to use their shared continuum of altered states of consciousness as a resource."[13]

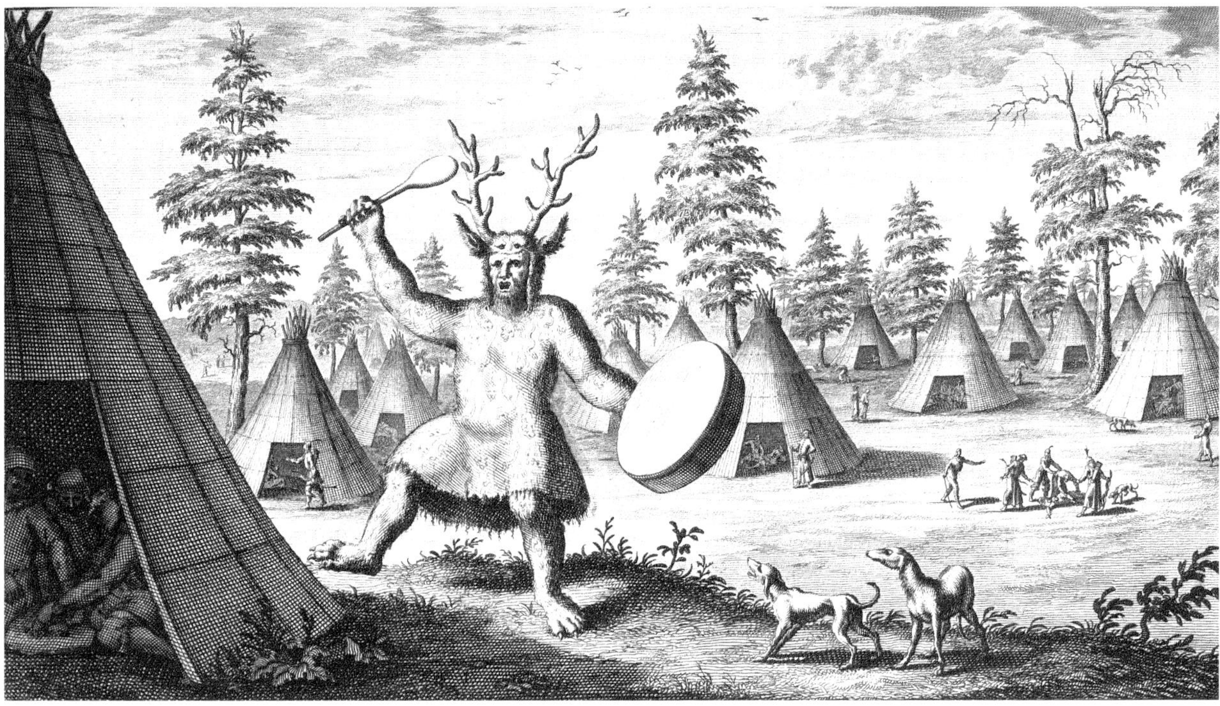

8.8. The earliest known depiction of a Siberian shaman by a European artist, from Nicolaes Witsen's *Noord en Oost Tartarye* (Amsterdam, 1692).

It is quite plausible that images such as the Sorcerers and the Hunting Accident originated in the human mind in altered states of consciousness. It's quite possible that protoshamans had a role in accessing those states. And quite possible that the shamans themselves were the artists who created the images. That theory is supported by the way the animals seem to float on the walls, as in a dream, with no indication of the horizon or vegetation.

Shamans lead their followers deep into their subconscious, to that place where there is a spontaneous level of imagination, a creativity unhampered by logic. It is there that, driven by strong positive or negative feelings about animals, therianthropes appear. That subconscious, spontaneous level of creativity is then complemented by a conscious level of creativity when artists create images of these therianthropes. And here is the second role of the shaman. To imagine a novel creature is one thing, but to believe that it actually exists out there, in a realm reached by the shaman and his followers, is another. An image at a hallowed place within a cave is a generator and sustainer of belief. As a recognized spiritual leader, the shaman can sanction and reinforce this belief. The fanciful being represented in art is accepted by the group and becomes part of its belief system. Sun gods, animal-headed humans, and angels descend and multiply.

Whether the details of this shamanic theory are accurate or not, it is certain that Upper Paleolithic art, including the therianthropes, was created in a time when early humans were confronted with a mysterious and complex natural world on which they completely depended. Those early hunter-gatherers must have—consciously or unconsciously—sought an understanding that could be the basis for prediction. Those who better understood animals, who could relate to the instincts of a saber-toothed tiger or the movements of a reindeer, had a better chance of survival. It was natural to aspire to the freedom of an eagle. That identification with animals could give birth to visions, in dreams or in states of trance, of therianthropes. There would be an inclination to believe in supernatural explanations, for example the notion of a sun god. Shared beliefs might even produce a form of social cohesion that could have competitive survival value for the group. So human imagination came to the service of human needs. Explanations, wherever they originated, would be embraced.

An example of an explanatory belief held by many early cultures was the notion of two other worlds besides the one in which we live: something above the real world and something below. Their existence could help explain the mystery of death. They are the worlds of myth, and it is there that many animal-human creatures have their origins and being. Some cultures have taken the concept of other worlds further than others. The Puranas, a body of Hindu texts, describe fourteen other worlds: seven upper and seven lower. The concept resides deep in the human subconscious, and some notion of heaven and hell became fundamental to most religions.

Any explanation of cave art is more plausible if it can be applied across multiple hunter-gatherer cultures. Its plausibility is also enhanced if it would have contributed to group coherence and thus group survival. Lewis-Williams's neuropsychological theory has both attributes.

The therianthropes of the Upper Paleolithic and their descendants through the ages demonstrate another important principle: the ability of art to produce belief. The scenes of horses and stags on the walls of caves showed viewers that art could represent reality convincingly. And that credibility extended to the image of a human with a bird's head or a stag-horse-human deep inside a revered cave. Art has been playing that role ever since.[14] Artists tap into their subconscious. They exist and work in a world of imagination and creativity, and their angels are real beings in that world. That aura of reality is communicated to the viewer. The Assyrian winged guardian spirits and the Egyptian sphinx may have descended directly from prehistoric therianthropes, or not. But they are products of the same inherent and deep-seated human creative imagination. As Jean Clottes put it, the belief in therianthropic beings must constitute "part of the universals of the human mind."[15]

Art retains its power to create an alternative, and credible, world. Sigmund Freud, in his *Totem and Taboo*, described early humans before religion and before science as having to rely on creative imagination, on "thought." And he noted that "in only a single field of our civilization has the omnipotence of thoughts been retained, and that is the field of art."[16] The magic of art persists.

It is hard to conceive of that long period in human history when humans believed deeply in therianthropic gods and demigods. As science developed and the world eventually experienced the first Industrial Revolution and became "modern," myths began to be considered "just myths." Some regretted the loss. In his sonnet "The World Is Too Much with Us," the Romantic poet William Wordsworth wrote:

> Great God! I'd rather be
> A Pagan suckled in a creed outworn;
> So might I, standing on this pleasant lea,
> Have glimpses that would make me less forlorn;
> Have sight of Proteus rising from the sea;
> Or hear old Triton blow his wreathèd horn.[17]

It was too late to go back, but Wordsworth felt that the world that had believed in myth was preferable in some ways to the modern world with its "objective" relationship with nature. It was better to believe in a powerful sea god than simply to view the sea as H_2O. We have retained some remnant of that sentiment to the present. There is still a desire to believe in angels and mermaids and dogs that talk and communicate wisdom, or simply amuse. There is a sense in which myths and therianthropes are still real.

That reality is a product of the creative power of the subconscious. For our ancient ancestors, the depths of the mind, the subconscious, was the source of guidance through their mysterious world. It was the locus of creativity, and it remains so today in science as well as art. The eminent mathematician Richard W. Hamming taught his students how to solve a scientific problem requiring a creative solution. He advised them to "saturate the subconscious with the problem," to think of nothing else for days or weeks. And then, "one day we have the solution."[18] The modern-day subconscious finds solutions, just as it found solutions for our earliest ancestors.

The journey into the other world can be initiated by many different means. In many cultures, shamans lead people to the place in the deep subconscious where myths are born and therianthropes exist. But dreams can lead us there as well. As Joseph Campbell writes in *The Mythic Image*, "Through dreams a door is opened to mythology, since myths are of the nature of dream, and that, as dreams arise from an inward world unknown to waking consciousness, so do myths: so, indeed, does life."[19] There is also a striking similarity between the experiences induced by LSD or psilocybin and those experienced by the mystics of early Judaism and Christianity and, in more recent times, by poets like Alfred Lord Tennyson, Ralph Waldo Emerson, and Walt Whitman.[20] They left egocentrism and the ordinary behind to find in nature "peace and joy and knowledge that pass all the argument of the earth."[21] That sense, that felt significance has become part of many religions, including Hinduism, Buddhism, and Christianity. Yoga, in its many religious and nonreligious forms, represents a manifestation of that process. It has been called "the experimental union of the individual with the divine,"[22] and uses practices close to those of the shaman: practices intended to take the spirit beyond the realm of the everyday.

What is common to many of these mystical experiences is a sense of inexplicable significance, or sacredness. As William James expressed it, "Mystical states seem to those who experience them to be also states of knowledge. They are states of insight into depths of truth unplumbed by the discursive intellect . . . and as a rule they carry with them a curious sense of authority."[23] They draw on the primordial sense of the reality of other worlds, what some would call heaven and hell, the heaven where they have found God.

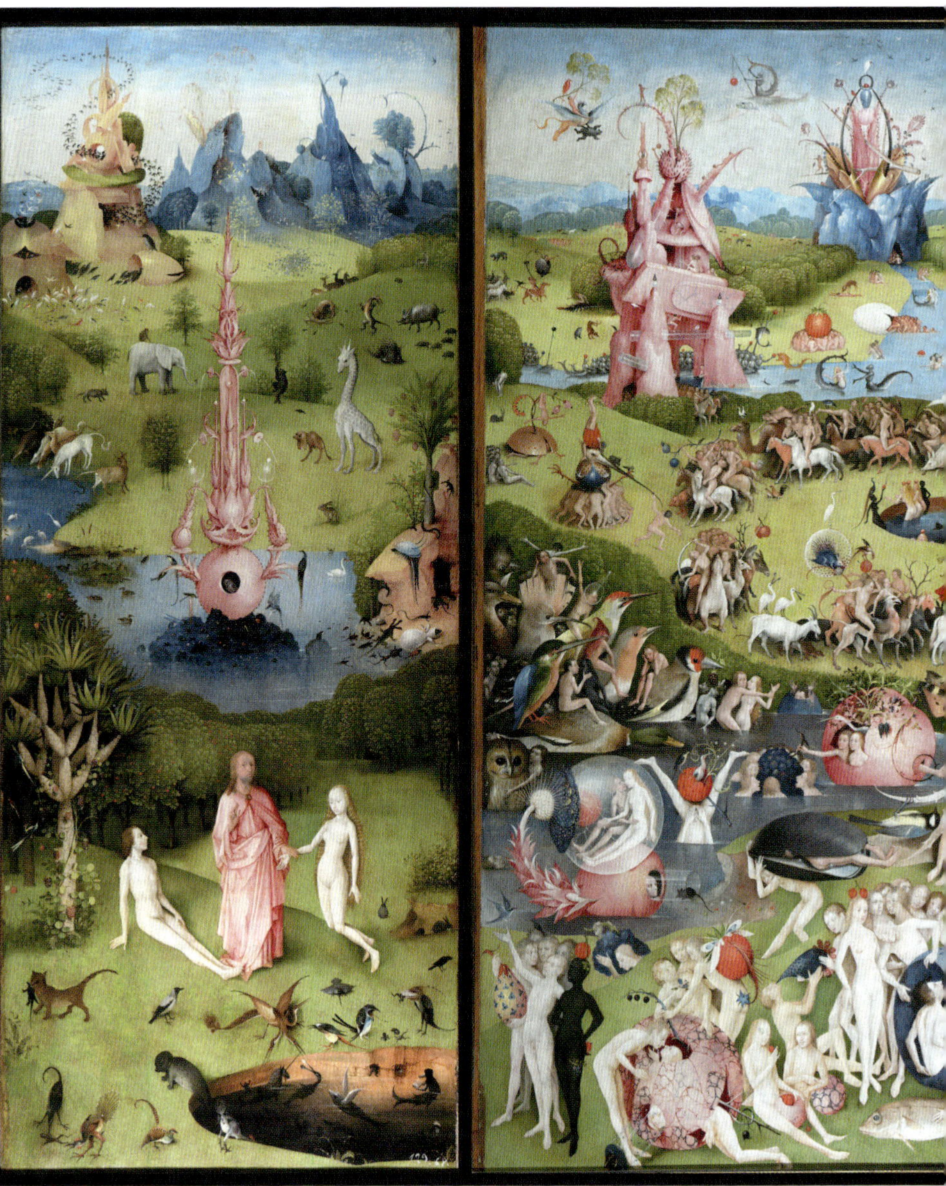

8.9. Hieronymus Bosch (c. 1450–1516). *The Garden of Earthly Delights*, 1490–1500. Oil on panel; central panel, 73⅛ × 67⅞ in. (185.8 × 172.5 cm); wings, 73⅛ × 30⅛ in. (185.8 × 76.5 cm). Museo del Prado, Madrid.

The artists who created images of animal-humans during the Upper Paleolithic era believed in the reality of what they represented. Their outlook reappeared some 40,000 years later with Surrealism, a cultural and artistic movement that asserted the validity, indeed the "superior value," of the products of the subconscious, as expressed in dreams: exactly the concept embodied in the Sorcerer of Trois Frères and the Hunting Accident of Lascaux.

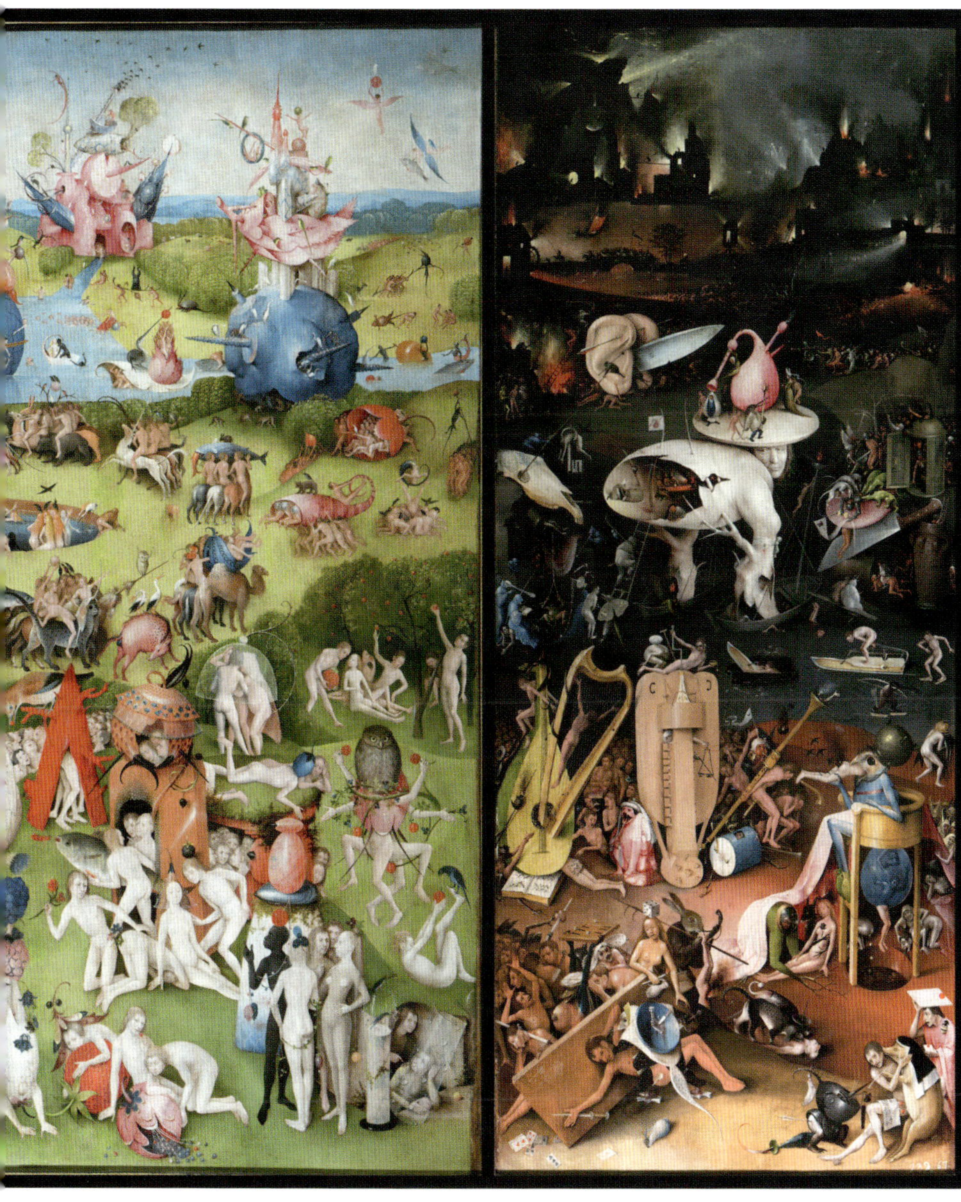

Modern Surrealist painting was more directly anticipated by the Netherlandish master Hieronymus Bosch. Around 1500, Bosch populated his dreamlike paintings with fantastical creatures, including merpeople and winged humans (plate 8.9). It was some four centuries later that Surrealism reemerged.

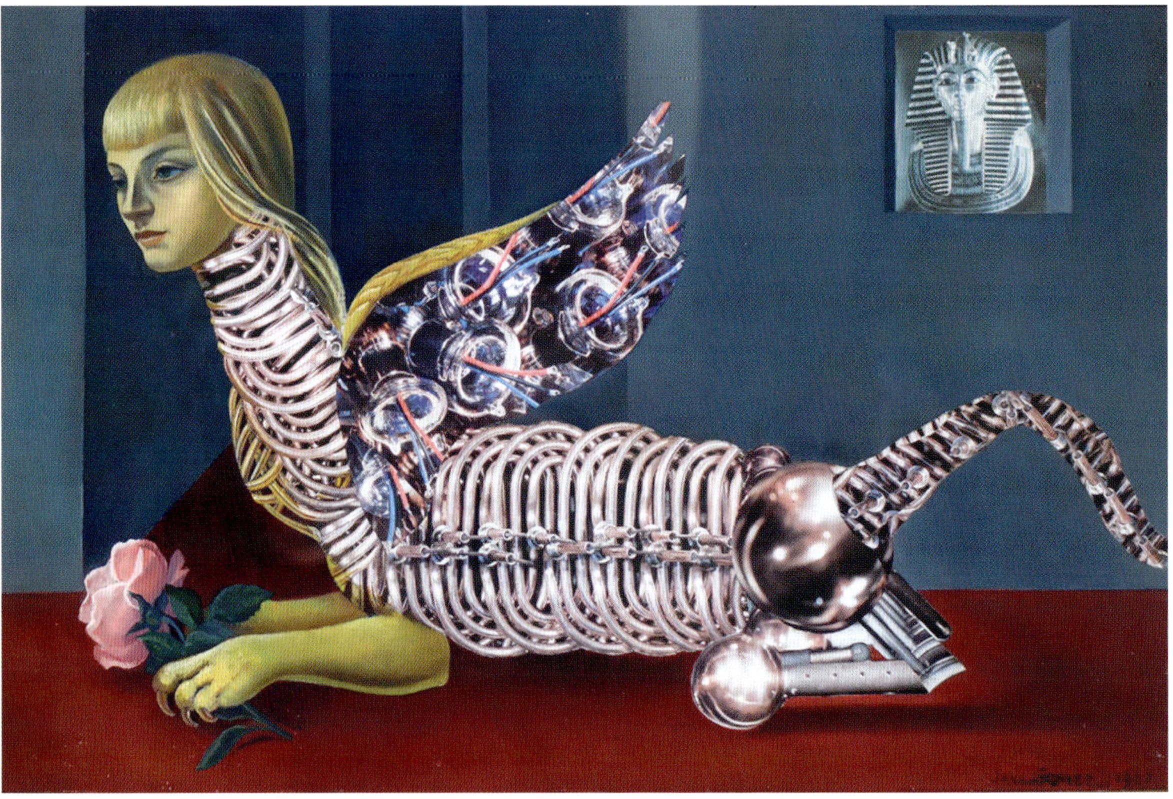

8.10. Jane Graverol (1905–1984). *The School of Vanity*, 1967. Oil and collage on cardboard, 27 3/4 × 41 7/8 in. (70 × 106 cm). Private collection.

In his *Surrealist Manifesto* of 1924, the French poet André Breton expressed his belief in the "transmutation of those two seemingly contradictory states, dream and reality, into a sort of absolute reality, of surreality, so to speak." Breton defined Surrealism as "pure psychic automatism, by which one proposes to express, either verbally, in writing, or by any other manner, the real functioning of thought. Dictation of thought in the absence of all control exercised by reason, outside of all aesthetic and moral preoccupation."[24]

Revealing the images residing in the subconscious was central to Surrealism, just as it was to shamanism in prehistoric times. Surrealism became a major force in freeing painting from a limiting dependency on either observable reality or purely abstract forms. The fundamental appeal of Surrealism is reflected in its international spread, to Eastern Europe, the Caribbean, Asia, North Africa, Australia, and Latin America.[25]

The Belgian Surrealist painter Jane Graverol considered her canvases to be "waking, conscious dreams." In her 1967 painting *The School of Vanity*, she created a modern therianthrope: an animal-human creature with mechanical elements (plate 8.10). One of her inspirations is shown in the background: the funeral mask of the Egyptian pharaoh Tutankhamun.

Joseph Campbell described myth as "the secret opening through which the inexhaustible energies of the cosmos pour into human cultural manifestation."[26] I would add a related definition, that myths—and therianthropes—are the secret opening through which the inexhaustible energies of human creativity become manifested in culture.

Therianthropes appear in the earliest art created by humans and presumably existed in the human imagination before that. They have peopled—or animal-peopled—the mythology of many cultures through the ages. And they continue to embody meaning for artists, and the viewers of their works, to this day. We saw how Paul Klee converted his vision of an angel into his *Angelus Novus*, which in turn had a deeply important mystical meaning for the German philosopher Walter Benjamin. And we saw how the Minotaur, born in ancient Greece, was redolent with meaning for Picasso, and animated his grand *Minotauromachy*. The human mind of the present has the same structure as that of early *Homo sapiens sapiens*, and contains, in its depths, the same fundamental forms.

Some of the elements in the subconscious that are revealed in dreams are unique to the individual. But, as we have seen multiple times in our inquiry, there are also elements held in common between diverse cultures. Many of them go back to the earliest days of human development. Carl Jung referred to these shared elements as the "collective unconscious." He described

> a second psychic system of a collective, universal, and impersonal nature which is identical in all individuals. This collective unconscious does not develop individually but is inherited. It consists of pre-existent forms, the archetypes, which can only become conscious secondarily and which give definite form to certain psychic contents.[27]

The animal-human beings envisioned by our early human ancestors arose from this collective unconscious, which persists to this day. Before they are inundated with experiences and facts and concepts, children have access to the inherited collective unconscious. A major component of the collective unconscious relates to the instincts that had survival value during the early stages of human evolution. One such instinct was an understanding closeness to animals, which is reflected in children's natural interest in all creatures, from tiny insects to horses to talking ducks. Steven D. Nash expressed it well when he described children's relationship with animals: "Our own innocence at that stage of our lives finds obvious resonance in other beings who are similarly uncomplicated by the sophistication of adulthood."[28]

It is not only in children that echoes of the collective unconscious can be discovered. They are evident in certain inclinations shared by people of all ages, including an appreciation of angels and other winged humans, of talking animals, of therianthropes generally. That appreciation, very much alive today, connects us with humanity's earliest days.

Our natural affinity for animals is strikingly prominent in Eastern religions. The Vedic people, early hunter-gatherers who lived in remote areas of India, provide a link between early humans' respect for animals and the attitudes toward animals involved in the Jain, Hindu, and Buddhist religions. Both the Hindu doctrine of reincarnation and the Buddhist doctrine of rebirth dictate a highly respectful attitude towards animals (plate 8.11). Indeed, many Hindu gods are represented by animals or therianthropes. Recall the elephant-headed Ganesha discussed in chapter 1.

In a curious way, the sympathetic attitude toward animals that originated in the prescientific mind has actually been intensified by modern science: today we have an increased understanding of similarities between humans and animals, and an increased concern with the extinction of species.[29]

From prehistory, with the Sorcerer and the Lion-Man, through Mesopotamian sculptures of animal-headed gods, to the *Winged Victory*, Picasso's *Minotauromachy*, and modern-day cartoons, art has been the means of giving visible form to the therianthropes conceived by the human imagination. Through art, private visions become collective realities. Myths, and the therianthropes that inhabit them, become real. Our appreciation of art also reflects the connection with nature that was crucial to survival in our earliest days. Paul Cézanne asked that painting "give us the flavour of nature's eternity," and indeed it has.[30]

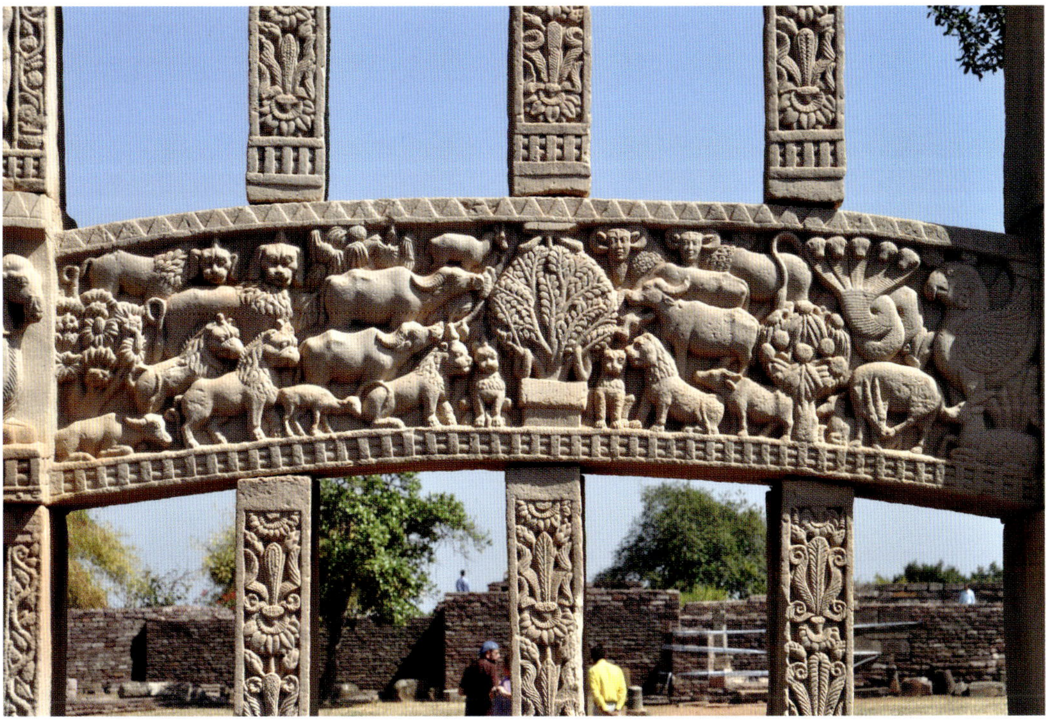

8.11. The Buddha, represented by the Bodhi Tree, worshipped by animals. Gateway of the Sanchi complex, Madhya Pradesh, India.

A final note: Throughout this book we have emphasized that, despite their deep cultural importance, therianthropes are real only insofar as people believe in them. However, modern science may be able to create actual therianthropes. Research on cross-species organisms has been carried out for some time. It was found, for example, that mice injected with human fetal brain cells were smarter than their peers. Recently, human stem cells have been introduced into monkey embryos. The goal is to produce organs and tissues for transplantation, but the researchers envision further possibilities, writing, "These results may help to better understand early human development and primate evolution and develop strategies to improve human chimerism in evolutionarily distant species."[31]

I doubt, however, that those future chimeras will be able to hold a candle to the Minotaur or Ganesha. I doubt they will be as threatening as a werewolf, or as enchanting as the angels and mermaids we have encountered in these pages.

ACKNOWLEDGMENTS

In the preface, I mention the World Wide Web as the invention that allowed me to research this book during the Covid-19 crisis. So, first of all, I want to thank Tim Berners-Lee, who is often credited with the creation of the web. But I benefited from more than a connected internet. There are now abundant information resources on the web, but the one that was central to my research was Wikipedia: its articles and references to supporting academic papers. I also found many of the illustrations, happily in the public domain, on Wikipedia. So I express my gratitude to Wikipedia founders Jimmy Wales and Larry Sanger, their colleagues, and their predecessors, Richard Stallman and Rick Gates. (I'll resist going back to Denis Diderot and the eighteenth-century French encyclopedists, but you can find them, of course, on Wikipedia.).

I was lucky to have as a friend an expert on fairy tales, Ruth Bottigheimer, whom I know as Sue. Sue generously reviewed early sections of the manuscript. I also benefited from suggestions from my son Christopher and granddaughter Sage, and from Maria Reuge Kelly. Once again, my son Lawrence was my most thoughtful and severe, and thus my most helpful, adviser.

I was also fortunate to attract the interest of John Shea, professor of anthropology at Stony Brook University. His suggestions and encouragement at a critical time in the development of the manuscript were highly valuable. I also benefited from stimulating conversations with Steven Nash and access to his remarkable library.

I was pleased when David Fabricant, publisher at Abbeville Press, agreed to publish this book and am grateful for his meticulous and thoughtful editing. My sincere thanks also go to the entire team at Abbeville: to Misha Beletsky for his design, Julia Sedykh for her layout, Lauren Orthey for her photo research, Peter Rooney for his index, Louise Kurtz for her production expertise, and Colette Laroya for her marketing acumen.

Finally, as usual, I want to thank my wife, Betsy, for her advice and unwavering support during my intemperate preoccupation with therianthropes.

NOTES

Preface

1. An extensive list of therianthropes is given in Wikipedia: "List of Hybrid Creatures in Folklore," https://en.wikipedia.org/wiki/List_of_hybrid_creatures_in_folklore. Another compendium, which includes the mythological context, is Frank Hamel's (nonillustrated) *Werewolves, Bird-Women, Tiger-Men, and Other Human Animals* (1915; repr. Mineola, NY: Dover, 2007).

1. Animal-Headed Humans

1. Terry Pratchett, quoted in Dusty Rainbolt, *Ghost Cats: Human Encounters with Feline Spirits* (Guilford, CT: Lyons Press, 2007), p. 7.
2. Joseph Campbell, *The Masks of God* (New York: Viking, 1962), p. 94.
3. Henry Glassie, "Mud and Mythic Vision: Hindu Sculpture in Modern Bangladesh," in *Myth: A New Symposium*, ed. Gregory Schrempp and William Hansen (Bloomington: Indiana University Press, 1984), p. 216.
4. Daedalus is a highly developed figure in Greek mythology, representing the combination of art, practical science, and wisdom. He is mentioned in Homer's *Odyssey*, and his name seems to occur in Linear B tablets dating to 1400 BC. When he attracted Minos's ire and was imprisoned in the labyrinth with his son, Icarus, he attempted to escape by crafting wings: an idea reflective of the instinct that created winged human therianthropes. During their flight, however, Icarus ignored his father's advice and flew too close to the sun, which melted the wax holding his wings to his body and caused him to fall to his death.
5. Quoted in the exhibition brochure *Picasso's Greatest Print: The Minotauromachy in All its States* (Los Angeles County Museum of Art, 2006).
6. The seven states of the *Minotauromachy* are reproduced in *Picasso's Greatest Print*. They are also shown at https://www.lacma.org/picasso-index.

2. Winged Beings

1. This chapter draws on a variety of sources, including Richard Ebbs, "Angels: A History of Angels in Western Thought," https://www.bibliotecapleyades.net/vida_alien/alien_watchers14.htm.
2. Joseph Campbell with Bill Moyers, *The Power of Myth* (New York: Anchor, 1991), p. 23.
3. "Over the Rainbow" was composed by Harold Arlen with lyrics by Yip Harburg.
4. "Cylinder Seals in Ancient Mesopotamia: Their History and Significance," *World History Encyclopedia*, https://www.worldhistory.org/article/846/cylinder-seals-in-ancient-mesopotamia---their-hist/.
5. Charles L. Barstow, "Famous Pictures: Fifth Paper—Sacred and Religious Subjects," *St. Nicholas: An Illustrated Magazine for Young Folks* 39 (1912), p. 335.
6. Walter Benjamin, "Theses on the Philosophy of History," in *Illuminations: Essays and Reflections*, trans. Harry Zohn (New York: Schocken, 1969), p. 249.
7. Sapna Maheshwari and Vanessa Friedman, "Victoria's Secret Swaps Angels for 'What Women Want.' Will They Buy It?" *New York Times*, June 16, 2021.
8. Ibid.

4. Merpeople

1. There is a remarkable lack of literature on therianthropes written for a broad audience. A notable exception is Vaughn Scribner's *Merpeople: A Human History* (London: Reaktion, 2020), a detailed, richly illustrated, deeply researched, and delightfully readable book on mermaids and mermen. This chapter gratefully draws on Scribner's book.
2. Although writing was once thought to have had a single origin, in ancient Sumer, it is now believed to have emerged independently in several other places, including Egypt, China, and Mesoamerica.
3. Scribner, *Merpeople*, p. 98.
4. *Encyclopaedia Britannica*, 11th ed., s.v. "Burne-Jones, Sir Edward."
5. Strictly, Scribner gives that accolade to merpeople rather than mermaids. Scribner, *Merpeople*, p. 26.

5. Centaurs and Satyrs

1. Philostratus the Elder, *Imagines*, 2.3.
2. J. K. Rowling, "The Forbidden Forest," chap. 15 in *Harry Potter and the Philosopher's Stone* (London: Bloomsbury, 1997). The Harry Potter fantasies became the best-selling book series in history, selling more than 500 million copies.

6. Shape-Shifters

1. Ovid, *Metamorphoses: A New Translation*, trans. Charles Martin (New York: W. W. Norton, 2005), p. 15.
2. Ovid, *Metamorphoses*, trans. Frank Justus Miller, rev. G. P. Goold (Cambridge, MA: Harvard University Press, Loeb Classical Library, 1984), vol. 1, p. 553.
3. See Frank Hamel, *Werewolves, Bird-Women, Tiger-Men, and Other Human Animals* (1915, repr. Mineola, NY: Dover, 2007), who cites James Frazer's *The Golden Bough*, third ed. (London: Macmillan, 1906), vol. 1, p. 155.
4. Daniel Ogden has written a detailed and authoritative study of werewolves (with 814 footnotes and 975 bibliographic references): *The Werewolf in the Ancient World* (Oxford: Oxford University Press, 2021).
5. Ogden, *Werewolf*, p. 4.
6. Franz Kafka, *The Metamorphosis and Other Stories*, trans. Donna Freed (New York: Barnes and Noble, 2003), p. 7. (*The Metamorphosis* was first published in 1915.)
7. An article in the *New York Times* of February 5, 2021, by Roxanne Khamsi was titled, "The Coronavirus Is a Master of Mixing Its Genome, Worrying Scientists."

7. Talking Animals

1. Some of the early folktales have even been traced back to oral traditions in the Bronze Age. See, for example, Sara Graça da Silva and Jamshid J. Tehrani, "Comparative Phylogenetic

Analyses Uncover the Ancient Roots of Indo-European Folktales," *Royal Society Open Science* 3, no. 1 (January 2016), https://doi.org/10.1098/rsos.150645.
2. The GEICO gecko was created by the Martin Agency and first appeared on August 26, 1999, during a Screen Actors Guild strike that prevented the use of live actors. Human ingenuity combined with ancient traditions can make strikes more costly than imagined.
3. "Song," in John Keats, *The Complete Poems* (Middlesex, UK: Penguin, 1983), p. 48.

8. Origins and Meanings

1. The sad tale of Sautuola is recounted by Paul G. Bahn and Jean Vertut in *Journey through the Ice Age* (Berkeley: University of California Press, 1997), pp. 17–22.
2. See, for example, Jonathan L. Friedmann, "Whence Came the Musical Bow?" https://thinkingonmusic.wordpress.com/2016/05/19/whence-came-the-musical-bow/.
3. The literature on the cave of Lascaux is vast, but an engaging account of the cave and the Shaft scene is in Gregory Curtis, *The Cave Painters: Probing the Mysteries of the World's First Artists* (New York: Anchor, 2007), pp. 92–120. Curtis notes that the Shaft, now difficult to access, may originally have been accessible from the outside.
4. Maxime Aubert et al., "Earliest Hunting Scene in Prehistoric Art," *Nature* 576 (December 11, 2019): p. 442, https://www.jstor.org/stable/3888859?seq=1.
5. Judith Thurman, "Letter from Southern France: First Impressions; What Does the World's Oldest Art Say about Us?" *New Yorker*, June 23, 2008, https://www.newyorker.com/magazine/2008/06/23/first-impressions.
6. Henri Breuil, *Four Hundred Centuries of Cave Art*, trans. Mary E. Boyle (Montignac, Dordogne: Centre d'Études et de Documentation Préhistorique, 1952), quoted in Curtis, *Cave Painters*, p. 76.
7. Karl Zimmer, "A Single Migration from Africa Populated the World, Studies Find," *New York Times*, September 21, 2016.
8. Adelphine Bonneau, "The Earliest Directly Dated Rock Paintings from Southern Africa: New AMS Radiocarbon Dates," *Access* 91, no. 356 (April 2017): pp. 322–33.
9. David Lewis-Williams, *Believing and Seeing: Symbolic Meanings in Southern San Rock Painting* (London: Academic Press, 1981).
10. Pieter Jolly, "Therianthropes in San Rock Art," *The South African Archaeological Bulletin* 57, no. 176 (December 2002): pp. 85–103.
11. Thomas A. Dowson and Martin Port, "Special Objects—Special Creatures: Shamanistic Imagery and the Aurignacian Art of South-west Germany," in *The Archaeology of Shamanism*, ed. Neil Price (London: Routledge, 2001), pp. 165–77.
12. David Lewis-Williams and Thomas A. Dowson, "The Signs of All Times: Entoptic Phenomena in Upper Paleolithic Art," *Current Anthropology* 29, no. 2 (1988): pp. 201–45.
13. Jean Clottes and David Lewis-Williams, *The Shamans of Prehistory: Trance and Magic in the Painted Caves* (New York: Abrams, 1988), p. 114.
14. This concept of art's role in "realization," particularly as put forward by Henri Bergson, is discussed by T. E. Hume in "Bergson's Theory of Art," reprinted in *The Problems of Aesthetics: A Book of Readings*, ed. Eliseo Vivas and Murray Krieger (New York: Rinehart, 1953), pp. 125–38.
15. Jean Clottes,"Thematic Changes in Upper Paleolithic Art," *Antiquity* 70 (1996), p. 287.
16. Sigmund Freud, *Totem and Taboo* (New York: W. W. Norton, 1950), p. 90.
17. Composed circa 1802, the poem was first published in Henry Wordsworth, *Poems, in Two Volumes*, 1807.
18. Richard W. Hamming, *The Art of Doing Science and Engineering: Learning to Learn* (San Francisco: Stripe, 2020), p. 328.
19. Joseph Campbell, *The Mythic Image* (Princeton, NJ: Princeton University Press, 1974), p. xi.
20. Psychedelic experiences and the history of research related to them are well described in Michael Pollan, *How to Change Your Mind: What the New Science of Psychedelics Teaches Us about Consciousness, Dying, Addiction, Depression, and Transcendence* (New York: Penguin Press, 2018).
21. Walt Whitman, *Leaves of Grass: The First (1855) Edition* (New York: Penguin, 1986), p. 29.
22. William James, *The Varieties of Religious Experience: A Study in Human Nature* (1902; repr. New York: Modern Library, 1936), p. 391.
23. James, *Varieties of Religious Experience*, p. 371.
24. André Breton, *Manifestoes of Surrealism*, trans. Richard Seaver and Helen R. Lane (Ann Arbor: University of Michigan Press, 1972), p. 26.
25. The international character of Surrealism was persuasively displayed in a show at the Metropolitan Museum of Art in 2021 titled *Surrealism beyond Borders*.
26. Joseph Campbell, *The Hero with a Thousand Faces* (New York: Pantheon/Bollingen, 1949), p. 3.
27. C. G. Jung, *The Archetypes and the Collective Unconscious* (London: Routledge, 1996), p. 43.
28. Steven D. Nash, "Some Thoughts and Reflections on the Use of Illustration in Biodiversity Education Campaigns," *Journal of Threatened Taxa* 1, no. 2 (2009), p. 119.
29. One engaging book on animal culture, from sperm whales to macaws to chimpanzees, is Carl Safina's *Becoming Wild: How Animal Cultures Raise Families, Create Beauty, and Achieve Peace* (New York: Picador, 2020).
30. Joachim Gasquet, *Joachim Gasquet's Cézanne: A Memoir with Conversations*, trans. Christopher Pemberton (London: Thames & Hudson, 1991), p. 148.
31. Tao Tan et al., "Chimeric Contribution of Human Extended Pluripotent Stem Cells to Monkey Embryos ex vivo," *Cell* 184, no. 8 (April 15, 2021): pp. 2020–32, https://doi.org/10.1016/j.cell.2021.03.020.

GLOSSARY

Anthropomorphism. (From the Greek *anthropos*, "human," and *morphe*, "form.") The attribution of human qualities to nonhuman entities.

Aigikampos. A fish-tailed goat.

Boanthropy. A psychological disorder in which the sufferer believes he or she is a cow or ox.

Centauride. A female centaur.

Cynanthropy. A psychological disorder in which the sufferer believes he or she is a dog.

Cynocephaly. The condition of having a human body and the head of a dog.

Ichthyocentaur. A sea creature with the upper body of a human, the lower front half and forelegs of a horse, and the tail of a fish.

Leokampos. A fish-tailed lion.

Lycanthrope. (From the Greek *lukanthropos*, "wolf man.") A werewolf.

Lycanthropy. The magical transformation of a person into a wolf. Also, a psychological disorder in which the sufferer believes he or she turns into a wolf.

Naga. A race of half-human, half-serpent beings in Hindu and Buddhist mythology.

Pardalokampos. A fish-tailed leopard.

Taurokampos. A fish-tailed bull.

Tetramorph. A symbolic arrangement of four differing elements. In Christian art, the tetramorph is often a combination of the symbols of the four Evangelists: a man (Matthew), a lion (Mark), an ox (Luke), and an eagle (John).

Therianthrope. (From the Greek *therion*, "beast," and *anthropos*, "man.") Any mythical being that is part human and part animal. Also used to refer to a person who identifies with or as an animal.

Therianthropy. The condition of being a therianthrope. Also, the ability to shape-shift between human and animal form.

Theriocephaly. (From the Greek *therion*, "beast," and *kefali*, "head.") The condition of having the body of a human and the head of an animal.

BIBLIOGRAPHY

The most important sources are shown in **bold** type.

Armstrong, Karen. *A Short History of Myth*. New York: Canongate, 2006.

Bahn, Paul G., and Jean Vertut. *Journey Through the Ice Age*. Berkeley: University of California Press, 1997.

Borges, Jorge Luis. *The Book of Imaginary Beings*. Translated by Andrew Hurley. New York: Penguin Classics, 2006. First published 1957.

Boyer, Pascal. *The Naturalness of Religious Ideas: A Cognitive Theory of Religion*. Berkeley: University of California Press, 1994.

Briggs, Katharine. *British Folk Tales and Legends: A Sampler*. London: Routledge Classics, 2002. First published 1977.

Briggs, Katharine. *An Encyclopedia of Fairies: Hobgoblins, Brownies, Bogies, and Other Supernatural Creatures*. Harmondsworth, UK: Penguin, 1976.

Brown, Donald. *Human Universals*. New York: McGraw-Hill, 1991.

Campbell, Joseph. *The Hero with a Thousand Faces*. Princeton, NJ: Princeton University Press, 1948.

Campbell, Joseph. *The Masks of God: Oriental Mythology*. New York: Viking, 1962.

Campbell, Joseph. *The Mythic Image*. Princeton, NJ: Princeton University Press, 1974.

Campbell, Joseph, with Bill Moyers. *The Power of Myth*. New York: Anchor, 1991.

Cassirer, Ernst. *Language and Myth*. Translated by Susanne K. Langer. New York: Dover, 1953.

Clottes, Jean, ed. *Chauvet Cave: The Art of Earliest Times*. Translated by Paul G. Bahn. Salt Lake City: University of Utah Press, 2003.

Clottes, Jean, and David Lewis-Williams. *The Shamans of Prehistory: Trance and Magic in the Painted Caves*. New York: Abrams, 1998.

Cohen, Simona. *Animals as Disguised Symbols in Renaissance Art*. Leiden, Netherlands: Brill, 2008.

Curtis, Gregory. *The Cave Painters: Probing the Mysteries of the World's First Artists*. New York: Anchor, 2007.

Dissanayake, Ellen. *Homo Aestheticus: Where Art Comes from and Why*. New York: The Free Press, 1992.

Dundes, Alan, ed. *Sacred Narrative: Readings in the Theory of Myth*. Berkeley: University of California Press, 1984.

Dutton, Denis. *The Art Instinct: Beauty, Pleasure, and Human Evolution*. New York: Bloomsbury, 2009.

Eason, Cassandra. *Fabulous Creatures, Mythical Monsters, and Animal Power Symbols: A Handbook*. Westport, CT: Greenwood Press, 2008.

Francfort, Henri-Paul, and Robert N. Hamayon. *The Concept of Shamanism: Uses and Abuses*. Budapest: Academiai Kaido, 2001.

Gombrich, E. H. *Art and Illusion: A Study in the Psychology of Pictorial Representation*. Princeton, NJ: Princeton University Press, 1969. First published 1960.

Guenther, Mathias. *Tricksters and Trancers: Bushman Religion and Society*. Bloomington, IN: Indiana University Press, 1999.

Guthrie, R. Dale. *The Nature of Paleolithic Art*. Chicago: University of Chicago Press, 2005.

Hamel, Frank. *Werewolves, Birdwomen, Tiger-men, and Other Human Animals*. Mineola, NY: Dover, 2007. First published in 1915 as *Human Animals*.

Hammer, Carl. *Freak Show: Sideshow Banner Art*. San Francisco: Chronicle, 1996.

Hancock, Graham. *Supernatural: Meetings with the Ancient Teachers of Mankind*. London: Arrow Books, 2006.

Heck, Christian, and Rémy Cordonnier. *The Grand Medieval Bestiary: Animals in Illuminated Manuscripts*. New York: Abbeville Press, 2012.

Hodgson, Derek. *The Roots of Visual Depiction in Art*. Newcastle upon Tyne, UK: Cambridge Scholars Publishing, 2021.

James, William. *The Varieties of Religious Experience: A Study in Human Nature*. New York: The Modern Library, 1936. First published 1902.

Kipling, John Lockwood. *Beast and Man in India: A Popular Sketch of Indian Animals in Their Relations with the People*. New York: Macmillan, 1904. Available as a Project Gutenberg e-book.

Kowalski, Jesse, ed. *Enchanted: A History of Fantasy Illustration*. New York: Abbeville Press, 2020. Catalog of an exhibition organized by the Norman Rockwell Museum, Stockbridge, MA.

Lao, Meri. *Sirens: Symbols of Seduction*. Translated by John Oliphant. Rochester, VT: Park Street Press, 1998.

Lévi-Strauss, Claude. *Myth and Meaning: Cracking the Code of Culture*. New York: Schocken, 1995. First published 1979.

Lévi-Strauss, Claude. *The Savage Mind*. Chicago: University of Chicago Press, 1966. First published 1962.

Lévi-Strauss, Claude. *Totemism*. Translated by Rodney Needham. Boston: Beacon Press, 1963.

Lewis-Williams, David. *The Mind in the Cave*. New York: Thames and Hudson, 2002.

Lewis-Williams, David, and David Pearce. *Inside the Neolithic Mind*. New York: Thames and Hudson, 2005.

Lorblanchet, Michel, and Paul Bahn. *The First Artists: In Search of the World's Oldest Art*. London: Thames and Hudson, 2017.

Matthews, John, and Caitlin Matthews. *The Element Encyclopedia of Magical Creatures: The Ultimate A–Z of Fantastical Beings from Myth and Magic*. New York: Barnes and Noble, 2005.

Mithen, Steven. *The Prehistory of the Mind: The Cognitive Origins of Art and Science*. London: Thames and Hudson, 1996.

Ogden, Daniel. *Dragons, Serpents, and Slayers in the Classical and Early Christian Worlds*. New York: Oxford University Press, 2013.

Ogden, Daniel. *The Werewolf in the Ancient World*. Oxford: Oxford University Press, 2021.

Ovid. *Metamorphoses: A New Translation*. Translated by Charles Martin. New York: W. W. Norton, 2005. Originally published AD 8.

Palmedo, Philip F. *Deep Affinities: Art and Science*. New York: Abbeville Press, 2020.
Pollan, Michael. *How to Change Your Mind: What the New Science of Psychedelics Teaches Us about Consciousness, Dying, Addiction, Depression, and Transcendence*. New York: Penguin Press, 2018.
Ritvo, Harriet. *The Platypus and the Mermaid: And Other Figments of the Classifying Imagination.* Cambridge, MA: Harvard University Press, 1997.
Rowland, Beryl. *Animals with Human Faces: A Guide to Animal Symbolism.* Knoxville, TN: University of Tennessee Press, 1973.
Schrempp, Gregory, and William Hansen, eds. *Myth: A New Symposium*. Bloomington: Indiana University Press, 1984.
Scribner, Vaughn. *Merpeople: A Human History*. London: Reaktion, 2020.
Solomon, Anne. "Rock Arts, Shamans, and Grand Theories." In *The Oxford Handbook of the Archaeology and Anthropology of Rock Art*, ed. Bruno David and Ian J. McNiven, 565–85. New York: Oxford University Press, 2018.
Tucker, Michael. *Dreaming with Open Eyes: The Shamanic Spirit in Contemporary Art and Culture.* London: HarperCollins, 1992.
Wittkower, Rudolf. *Allegory and the Migration of Symbols*. New York: Thames and Hudson, 1987.

INDEX

Page numbers in *italics* refer to plates.